MATH SMART!

Over 220 Ready-to-Use Activities to Motivate & Challenge Students, Grades 6-12

JUDITH A. MUSCHLA ◆ GARY R. MUSCHLA

JOSSEY-BASS
A Wiley Imprint
www.josseybass.com

Published by Jossey-Bass
A Wiley Imprint
989 Market Street, San Francisco, CA 94103-1741   www.josseybass.com

Jossey-Bass books and products are available through most bookstores. To contact Jossey-Bass directly
call our Customer Care Department within the U.S. at 800-956-7739, outside the U.S. at 317-572-3986
or fax 317-572-4002.

Jossey-Bass also publishes its books in a variety of electronic formats. Some content that appears in
print may not be available in electronic books.

Library of Congress Cataloging-in-Publication Data
Muschla, Gary Robert.
     Math smart! over 220 ready-to-use activities to motivate and challenge students, grades
  6-12 / Gary Robert Muschla and Judith A. Muschla
     p. cm.
    ISBN 0-13-060049-0
    ISBN 0-7879-6642-8 (layflat)
    1. Mathematics—Study and teaching (Middle school)   2. Mathematics—Study and
  teaching (Secondary)   I. Muschla, Judith A.   II. Title.

QA11.M765 2001
510'.71'2—dc21   2001042119

FIRST EDITION
HB Printing 10 9 8 7 6 5

For Erin

About the Authors

Gary Robert Muschla received his B.A. and M.A.T. from Trenton State College and taught at Appleby School in Spotswood, New Jersey for more than 25 years. He spent many of his years in the classroom teaching mathematics at the elementary level. He has also taught reading and writing and has been a successful freelance writer, editor, and ghostwriter. He is a member of the Authors Guild and the National Writers Association.

Mr. Muschla has authored other resources for teachers, including: *Writing Resource Activities Kit* (The Center for Applied Research in Education, 1989), *The Writing Teacher's Book of Lists* (Prentice Hall, 1991), *Writing Workshop Survival Kit* (The Center, 1993), *English Teacher's Great Books Activities Kit* (The Center, 1994), and *Reading Workshop Survival Kit* (The Center, 1997). He currently writes and conducts workshops for teachers, students, and parents.

Judith A. Muschla received her B.A. in Mathematics from Douglass College at Rutgers University and is certified to teach K–12. She has taught mathematics in South River, New Jersey for over 25 years. She has taught math at various levels at South River High School, ranging from basic skills through Algebra II. She has also taught at South River Middle School where, in her capacity as a Team Leader, she helped revise the mathematics curriculum to reflect the standards of the NCTM, coordinated interdisciplinary units, and conducted mathematics workshops for teachers and parents. She was the recipient of the 1990–91 Governor's Teacher Recognition Program in New Jersey. Along with teaching, she is currently a member of the Standards Review Panel for the Mathematics Core Curriculum Content Standards in New Jersey.

Math Smart! Over 220 Ready-to-Use Activities to Motivate and Challenge Students, Grades 6–12 is the fifth book Gary and Judith Muschla have co-authored. They have also written *The Math Teacher's Book of Lists* (Prentice Hall, 1995), *Hands-on Math Projects with Real-Life Applications* (The Center, 1996), *Math Starters! 5- to 10-Minute Activities to Make Kids Think, Grades 6–12* (The Center, 1999), and *The Geometry Teacher's Activities Kit* (The Center, 2000).

Acknowledgments

We would like to thank Michael Pfister, Principal of South River High School; James Quinn, Jr., Principal of Appleby School; and our colleagues for their support of our efforts in writing this book.

Most special thanks to Michelle Philpott, whose meticulous review and insightful suggestions helped us to polish and finalize this book.

We also would like to thank Susan Kolwicz, our editor, for her encouragement and support in yet another book. Without her recommendations and guidance, the writing of this resource would have been a far more difficult task.

We also appreciate the efforts of Diane Turso, our development editor, who helped us to put the manuscript in its final form, and Tom Curtin, our production editor, whose efforts brought the overall project to completion.

Thanks, too, to Eileen Ciavarella, whose artwork enhances the diagrams and figures of our activities.

Finally, we'd like to thank our students, who make teaching an exciting and satisfying career.

About Mathematics Instruction

Math curriculums across the country are being updated and revised to prepare students for the challenges of the twenty-first century. While giving proper emphasis to the basics, the New Standards concentrate on problem-solving, critical thinking, and the use of technology.

The need for effective mathematics instruction clearly has never been more important. While a comprehensive curriculum can be the foundation of successful teaching, the best math instruction goes beyond the curriculum to excite and stimulate students. It encourages students to learn how to think with numbers, recognize relationships, and make connections between mathematical concepts. The best math instruction inspires students to explore math and helps to make them "math smart."

This book will aid you in providing your students with activities that will broaden their understanding and increase their appreciation of math. We'd like to offer our best wishes to you in your teaching.

Gary and Judith Muschla

How to Use This Resource

The purpose of *Math Smart! Over 220 Ready-to-Use Activities to Motivate and Challenge Students, Grades 6–12* is to present students with math activities that will help them to:

- Develop an intuitive sense of numbers.
- Think critically and creatively about math.
- Have fun with math.

This resource is divided into seven sections, containing a total of 222 activities. Answer Keys are included at the end of the book. Following is a brief description of each section.

- Section 1, "Whole Numbers: Theory and Operations," has 40 activities. This section includes a variety of activities on basic operations, factors, multiples, writing and solving word problems, divisibility rules, patterns, and sequences.
- Section 2, "Fractions, Decimals, and Percents," contains 45 activities. This section includes activities on operations with fractions, decimals, and percents, place value, ratio and proportion, comparing, ordering, discounts, and sales tax.
- Section 3, "Measurement," has 20 activities. The activities include both English and Metric measures, conversions of length, weight, and capacity, time, and temperature.
- Section 4, "Geometry," contains 45 activities. Among the activities of this section are activities on angles, polygons, the Pythagorean Theorem, congruent and similar triangles, circles, properties of geometric figures, area, perimeter, and volume.
- Section 5, "Algebra," contains 40 activities. Some of the activities of this section include the order of operations, integers, expressions, linear equations and inequalities, binomials, trinomials, and graphing.
- Section 6, "Data Analysis," contains 12 activities. The activities of this section cover bar graphs, pictograms, histograms, line graphs, circle graphs, and measures of central tendencies.

- Section 7, "Potpourri," has 20 activities. Some of the activities here include mystery numbers, following math directions, deciphering codes and dates, symmetry, and mathematical palindromes.

Each activity stands alone and is numbered according to the section. For example, Activity 2-10, "Fractions and Magic Squares," is the tenth activity of Section 2. Activity 4-39, "Finding Measures Associated with Circles," is the thirty-ninth activity of Section 4, while Activity 7-11, "Scrambled Math," is the eleventh activity of Section 7.

The title of each activity focuses on the skills or concepts the activity addresses. The table of contents, therefore, also acts as a skills/concepts/topics list. If you are teaching polygons, for example, you would turn to Section 4, "Geometry," and find Activity 4-9, "Naming Polygons," and Activity 4-10, "Finding the Number of Sides and Angle Measures of Regular Polygons," both of which could reinforce the skills and concepts you are teaching.

The activities are designed for efficient and practical implementation. Each has easy-to-follow student directions, and most require no materials other than the activity itself. Moreover, the activities can be used for various purposes: to supplement your math program, for reinforcement, for challenges, or for substitute plans.

The activities in each section generally progress from basic to complex and follow the sequence of the typical math curriculum. You should select the activities that best meet the needs of your students and program.

To ease your workload, as well as help to motivate students, many of the activities are designed with self-checks. As students work through the activity, their answers will result in their being able to decipher a message, uncover an important or unusual math fact, or discover interesting information.

Many of the activities are appropriate for the use of calculators. Whether to use calculators, however, is a decision you should make, depending upon your specific program and the needs and abilities of your students.

The "Answer Key" contains the answers to the problems. Each key is organized according to section. Most problems of the activities have one answer; however, some have multiple answers. Some answers are based on the reasoning of students, and in such cases you should accept answers that students can justify.

We suggest that you select the activities of this resource that best bolster your program. Choosing activities that expand students' mathematical horizons will help them to better understand and appreciate math.

Contents

About Mathematics Instruction   ix

How to Use This Resource   xi

Section 1
WHOLE NUMBERS: THEORY AND OPERATIONS   1

1-1   Finding Mistakes in Addition and Subtraction   3

1-2   The Basics of Multiplication   4

1-3   Multiplying Whole Numbers   6

1-4   Multiplying Whole Numbers Using Digits 1 Through 9   8

1-5   Dividing Whole Numbers with Remainders   9

1-6   Finding Missing Numbers in Long Division   10

1-7   Correcting Multiplication and Division Problems   12

1-8   Multiplication and Division Crossnumber Puzzle   14

1-9   Whole Number Operations Crossnumber Puzzle   16

1-10   Finding the Largest and Smallest Numbers   18

1-11   Writing Word Problems   19

1-12   Writing Word Problems with Specific Phrases   20

1-13   Using the Order of Operations to Form Calculator Words   21

1-14   Equations and Order of Operations, I   22

1-15   Equations and Order of Operations, II   23

1-16   Finding Patterns and Missing Numbers   24

1-17   Finding Place Value: Ones to Billions   26

1-18   A Place Value Crossnumber Puzzle   27

1-19   Rounding Whole Numbers   28

1-20   Identifying Names of *Very* Large Numbers   29

1-21   Using Rules for Divisibility   31

1-22   Rules for Determining Divisibility by 7 and 11   33

1-23   Finding Factors of Numbers   35

1-24 Finding the Greatest Common Factor   36

1-25 Euclid's Method for Finding the Greatest Common Factor   37

1-26 Perfect, Abundant, and Deficient Numbers   38

1-27 Classifying Numbers as Prime or Composite   39

1-28 Expressing Composite Numbers as the Product of Primes   40

1-29 Identifying Emirps   41

1-30 Examples of Goldbach's Conjecture   42

1-31 Finding the Least Common Multiple   43

1-32 Finding the Squares and Cubes of Numbers   44

1-33 Simplifying Expressions with Exponents   45

1-34 Using Scientific Notation   46

1-35 Converting Scientific Notation to Standard Form   47

1-36 Finding Missing Numbers in Patterns and Sequences   48

1-37 Writing About Numbers   49

1-38 Solving Tricky Math Problems   50

1-39 Scrambled Math Words   51

1-40 Matching Signs and Symbols   52

Section 2
FRACTIONS, DECIMALS, AND PERCENTS   53

2-1   Finding Equivalent Fractions   55

2-2   Simplifying Fractions   57

2-3   Improper Fractions and Mixed Numbers   58

2-4   Comparing Fractions and Mixed Numbers   60

2-5   Ordering Fractions   61

2-6   Writing Word Names for Fractions   62

2-7   Fractions in Everyday Use   64

2-8   Adding and Subtracting Fractions and Mixed Numbers
      Crossnumber Puzzle   65

2-9   Subtracting Mixed Numbers, with Regrouping   67

2-10 Fractions and Magic Squares   69

2-11 Multiplying Simple Fractions, I   70

2-12 Multiplying Simple Fractions, II   71

2-13 Multiplying Fractions and Mixed Numbers   72

2-14 Dividing Simple Fractions   74

2-15 Dividing Fractions and Mixed Numbers   75

2-16 Dividing Mixed Numbers   76

2-17 Fraction Crossnumber Puzzle—All Operations   77

Contents

2-18 Using Decimal Word Names   79

2-19 Decimal Place Value   80

2-20 Comparing Decimals   81

2-21 Ordering Decimals   82

2-22 Rounding Decimals   83

2-23 Expressing Fractions as Decimals   84

2-24 Expressing Decimals as Fractions   86

2-25 Adding and Subtracting Decimals   87

2-26 Adding and Subtracting Decimals—A Magic Square   88

2-27 Making Change   89

2-28 Multiplying Decimals   90

2-29 Dividing Decimals by Whole Numbers and Decimals   91

2-30 Finding the Largest and Smallest Sums, Differences, Products, and Quotients—Decimals   92

2-31 Decimals—All Operations   93

2-32 Writing Decimal Word Problems   94

2-33 Fractions and Decimals Crossword Puzzle   95

2-34 Fractions and Decimals—Finding Patterns   97

2-35 Ratio and Proportion   98

2-36 Matching Fraction, Decimal, and Percent Equivalencies   100

2-37 Ordering Fractions, Decimals, and Percents   101

2-38 Finding Percents of Numbers   102

2-39 Finding What Percent a Number Is of Another Number   103

2-40 Finding the Number When a Percent of It Is Known   104

2-41 Solving the Three Types of Percentage Problems   105

2-42 Percent of Increase and Decrease   106

2-43 Percents and Discounts   108

2-44 Percents and Sales Tax   109

2-45 Fractions, Decimals, and Percents—Word Problems   110

Section 3
MEASUREMENT   111

3-1 Measuring Line Segments with Rulers (Inches)   113

3-2 Units of Length in the English System   114

3-3 Units of Weight in the English System   116

3-4 Units of Liquid Measure in the English System   118

3-5 Using the English System of Measurement   120

3-6 Converting Units in the Metric System, I   121

3-7   Converting Units in the Metric System, II   123

3-8   Using Metric Units of Weight   124

3-9   Computing Units of Measure (English and Metric)   125

3-10   Making Sense of Measurement   126

3-11   Converting Units of Time   128

3-12   Using Time Cards   129

3-13   Converting Fahrenheit to Celsius   131

3-14   Converting Celsius to Fahrenheit   132

3-15   Measurement and Language   134

3-16   A Measurement Crossword Puzzle   135

3-17   Measurement Puzzlers   137

3-18   Measurements Used in Outer Space   138

3-19   Tools of Measurement   140

3-20   Measurement Trivia   142

Section 4
GEOMETRY   143

4-1   Geometry Crossword Puzzle   145

4-2   Identifying Types of Angles   147

4-3   Measuring Angles with a Protractor, I   148

4-4   Measuring Angles with a Protractor, II   149

4-5   Calculating the Measures of Angles in a Diagram   150

4-6   Identifying Parallel and Perpendicular Lines   152

4-7   Parallel Lines, Perpendicular Lines, and Angles   153

4-8   Identifying Angles Formed by Parallel Lines and Transversals   154

4-9   Naming Polygons   156

4-10   Finding the Number of Sides and Angle Measures
        of Regular Polygons   157

4-11   Words and Numbers of Triangles Crossword Puzzle   158

4-12   Identifying Acute, Obtuse, and Right Triangles   160

4-13   Classifying Triangles   161

4-14   Drawing Triangles   163

4-15   Finding the Sum of the Measures of Angles in a Triangle   164

4-16   Finding the Measures of Angles in Triangles, I   165

4-17   Finding the Measures of Angles in Triangles, II   166

4-18   Identifying Segments, Angles, and Types of Triangles   168

4-19   Using the Pythagorean Theorem   169

4-20   Testing for Acute, Obtuse, and Right Triangles   170

Contents   xvii

4-21   Finding the Missing Lengths of the Sides of 45°–45°–90°
       and 30°–60°–90° Triangles   171

4-22   Identifying Congruent Triangles   173

4-23   Using SSS, SAS, ASA, AAS, and HL to Verify Congruent Triangles   174

4-24   Proving Two Triangles Are Congruent   176

4-25   Properties of Special Quadrilaterals, I   178

4-26   Properties of Special Quadrilaterals, II   179

4-27   Identifying Quadrilaterals   180

4-28   Properties of Parallel Lines and Quadrilaterals   181

4-29   Finding the Measures of Angles in a Quadrilateral   182

4-30   Dividing a Square into Pentomino Pieces   183

4-31   Identifying Geometric Figures in Circles   184

4-32   Finding the Measures of Missing Angles and Arcs in a Circle   186

4-33   Measures of Segments, Angles, and Arcs   188

4-34   Determining Which Figures Form Cubes   190

4-35   Finding Perimeters and Areas of Squares and Rectangles   191

4-36   Finding Perimeters and Areas of Rectangles   192

4-37   Finding Perimeters and Areas of Quadrilaterals   193

4-38   Finding Perimeters and Areas of Triangles   195

4-39   Finding Measures Associated with Circles   197

4-40   Finding the Circumference and Area of Circles   199

4-41   Finding the Areas of Plane Figures   200

4-42   Finding the Volume of Rectangular Prisms   201

4-43   Finding Volume and Surface Area   203

4-44   Geometry Puzzlers   205

4-45   Geometry Word Scramble   206

Section 5
ALGEBRA   209

5-1   Using the Order of Operations (Whole Numbers)   211

5-2   Using the Order of Operations (Whole Numbers and Exponents)   212

5-3   Evaluating Expressions (Whole Numbers)   213

5-4   Using the Number Line   214

5-5   Using Vectors and the Number Line   215

5-6   Adding Integers   217

5-7   Subtracting Integers   218

5-8   Multiplying and Dividing Integers   219

5-9   Integer Operations   220

5-10 Writing and Simplifying Expressions   221

5-11 Evaluating Expressions (Integers and Exponents)   222

5-12 Simplifying Absolute Value Expressions   223

5-13 Simplifying Expressions (Combining Similar Terms)   224

5-14 Matching and Evaluating Expressions   225

5-15 Solving One-step Equations   227

5-16 Solving Linear Equations with Variables on One Side   228

5-17 Solving Multi-step Equations with Variables on One Side   229

5-18 Solving Equations with Variables on Both Sides   230

5-19 Evaluating Formulas   231

5-20 Solving Inequalities   233

5-21 Graphing Inequalities and Combined Inequalities   234

5-22 Multiplying and Dividing Monomials   236

5-23 Adding and Subtracting Polynomials   237

5-24 Multiplying Polynomials by Monomials and Polynomials   238

5-25 Factoring Binomials and Trinomials   240

5-26 Factoring Trinomials   243

5-27 Solving Equations by Using the Zero Product Property   244

5-28 Simplifying Rational Expressions   245

5-29 Multiplying and Dividing Rational Expressions   247

5-30 Adding and Subtracting Rational Expressions   249

5-31 Dividing Polynomials   251

5-32 Solving Rational Equations   252

5-33 Finding the Slope and Y-intercept of a Line   253

5-34 Identifying Points and Lines   255

5-35 Evaluating Functions   257

5-36 Solving Systems of Equations   258

5-37 Simplifying Radical Expressions   259

5-38 Adding, Subtracting, Multiplying, and Dividing Radical Expressions   260

5-39 Solving Radical Equations   261

5-40 Solving Quadratic Equations   262

Section 6
DATA ANALYSIS   263

6-1 Constructing a Bar Graph   265

6-2 Constructing a Pictogram   267

Contents

6-3 Constructing a Histogram 269
6-4 Constructing a Line Graph 271
6-5 Constructing a Conversion Chart 272
6-6 Creating Multiple Line Graphs 274
6-7 Understanding Circle Graphs, I 275
6-8 Understanding Circle Graphs, II 276
6-9 Creating a Stem-and-Leaf Plot 278
6-10 Creating a Box-and-Whisker Plot 279
6-11 Finding the Mean, Median, Mode, and Range 281
6-12 Using the Mean, Median, Mode, and Range 282

Section 7
POTPOURRI 283

7-1 Knowing Your Math Facts 285
7-2 Equivalent Values 286
7-3 Identifying Math Words 288
7-4 Facts and Mystery Numbers 289
7-5 Mathematicians and Their Achievements 291
7-6 Math and Interesting Facts 293
7-7 Following Math Directions 295
7-8 Math Is Everywhere 296
7-9 Math and Me 297
7-10 Find the Pattern 298
7-11 Scrambled Math 299
7-12 Working with Variables 300
7-13 Deciphering Dates in Roman Numerals 301
7-14 Using a Number-box Cipher 303
7-15 Lines of Symmetry and Braille 304
7-16 A Puzzle of Numbers and Languages 305
7-17 Math Words Used Every Day 307
7-18 Mathematical Palindromes 308
7-19 Codebreaking 309
7-20 A Personal Statement About Mathematics 310

Answer Key 311

Section 1

WHOLE NUMBERS: THEORY AND OPERATIONS

1-1   Finding Mistakes in Addition and Subtraction

Many, *but not all*, of the following problems have a mistake in computation. Correct the problems, then write the letter of each problem above its answer to complete the phrase below. **Note:** Not all letters will be used.

R.	67	G.	438	P.	784	T.	829	I.	387
	+23		+297		+596		+457		+684
	80		735		1,390		1,287		1,171

I.	2,384	R.	2,845	A.	4,695	E.	2,937	O.	9,421
	+7,392		+9,383		+5,384		+3,698		+8,693
	9,676		11,127		9,079		7,535		17,114

O.	87	N.	539	E.	608	H.	721	V.	863
	-69		-327		-539		-308		-544
	28		252		79		413		1,407

S.	4,609	S.	6,007	C.	7,840	E.	5,634	N.	8,973
	-2,748		-5,388		-6,367		-2,182		-4,619
	2,861		719		1,473		3,552		4,252

Addition and subtraction are

9,776	212	319	69	90	619	6,635

18,114	1,380	3,452	12,228	10,079	1,286	1,071	18	4,354	1,861

1-2   The Basics of Multiplication

Fill in the boxes with the correct number to complete the multiplication problems.

1.
```
    8 4
×  □ 9
  7 □ 6
2 □ 2
3,□ □ 6
```

2.
```
   7 □
×  8 2
  □ 5 2
6 □ 8
6,□ 3 2
```

3.
```
   □ 7
× 6 □
  3 7 6
2 □ 2
3,1 9 6
```

4.
```
    5 6
×  □ 5
  2 □ 0
3 9 2
4,□ □ 0
```

5.
```
    6 3
×  □ □
  3 1 5
2 5 2
2,8 3 5
```

6.
```
   4 □ 6
×    5 7
  3 □ 7 2
□ 4 8 0
2 8,2 7 2
```

7.
```
   □ 0 □
×    3 8
  4 8 5 6
1 □ □ 1
2 □,□ 6 6
```

8.
```
   □ 7 8
×    □ 4
  1 1 □ 2
1 3 9 0
1 5,0 □ 2
```

9.
```
   4 3 □
×    7 6
  2 □ 8 0
3 0 □ 0
3 2,6 8 0
```

10.
```
   9 4 □
×    6 4
  3 7 8 8
5 6 □ 2
6 □,□ 0 8
```

11.
```
   □ 8 7
×    8 □
  5 4,9 6 0
```

12.
```
   4 3 □
×    □ 9
  3 9 5 1
4 □ 9
8,3 4 1
```

1-2 The Basics of Multiplication
(Continued)

13.
```
    □ □ 4
  ×   6 8
  ─────────
    6 3 5 2
  4 7 6 □
  ─────────
  5 3, □ □ 2
```

14.
```
    8 □ 6
  × □ 6 3
  ─────────
    2 4 7 8
  4 □ 5 6
  ─────────
  5 7 8 2
  6 □ 0, □ 3 8
```

15.
```
      □ 3 8
  ×   6 0 □
  ───────────
      2 9 5 2
    □ □ □
  ───────────
    4 4 2 8
  4 □ 5, □ 5 2
```

16.
```
    6 7 □ 2
  ×     5 4
  ───────────
    2 □ 9 2 8
  3 □ 6 6 0
  ───────────
  3 □ □, 5 2 8
```

17.
```
    □ 0 7 8
  ×     8 □
  ───────────
    2 4 4 6 8
  3 2 6 2 4
  ───────────
  3 5 0, □ 0 8
```

18.
```
    9 6 7 □
  ×     4 7
  ───────────
    6 □ 7 4 6
  3 □ 7 1 2
  ───────────
  4 □ 4, □ 6 6
```

19.
```
      7 0 □ 9
  ×     3 6 2
  ─────────────
      1 4 0 1 8
    4 □ 0 □ 4
  2 1 0 2 7
  ─────────────
  2, 5 3 □, □ 5 8
```

20.
```
      6 □ 7 4
  ×     5 □ 6
  ─────────────
      3 8 2 □ 4
    □ 0 9 9 2
  3 1 8 7 0
  ─────────────
  3, 7 3 5, □ □ 4
```

1-3   Multiplying Whole Numbers

Solve each problem below. Find the products on the *Matho* board and cross out the products. **Note:** Some of the products are not on the board. After crossing out as many products as you can, answer the question.

1. $57 \times 76 =$ _____

2. $38 \times 68 =$ _____

3. $62 \times 84 =$ _____

4. $92 \times 18 =$ _____

5. $41 \times 59 =$ _____

6. $728 \times 45 =$ _____

7. $649 \times 75 =$ _____

8. $760 \times 83 =$ _____

9. $409 \times 34 =$ _____

10. $867 \times 29 =$ _____

11. $876 \times 10 =$ _____

12. $934 \times 91 =$ _____

13. $236 \times 52 =$ _____

14. $628 \times 367 =$ _____

15. $837 \times 406 =$ _____

16. $2,736 \times 45 =$ _____

17. $8,679 \times 74 =$ _____

18. $8,407 \times 68 =$ _____

19. $9,004 \times 263 =$ _____

20. $5,734 \times 367 =$ _____

1-3   Multiplying Whole Numbers
(Continued)

M	A	T	H	O
576,176	48,675	2,419	214,378	5,628
642,246	4,332	1,566	8,760	2,719
2,368,052	84,994	**Free Space**	230,476	876
84,894	339,822	2,548	63,080	123,120
32,760	2,104,378	2,917	652,246	25,143

Be sure you have crossed out as many products as you can. Have you crossed out five in order along a row, column, or diagonal? If yes, which one?

_____

_____

1-4   Multiplying Whole Numbers Using Digits 1 Through 9

In the multiplication problem $138 \times 42 = 5{,}796$, each digit from 1 to 9 occurs once. Many other multiplication problems follow the same pattern, although the digits are in a different order. Place the digits 1 through 9 (using each digit only once) in the spaces below to complete the equations. Some numbers have been supplied for you.

1. _ 8 _ × 1 2 = _ 7 _ 6

2. 2 _ 7 × _ 8 = _ 3 _ _

3. 1 7 _ _ × 4 = _ _ _ 2

4. 1 _ 6 3 × 4 = 7 _ _ _

5. _ _ 8 × 2 _ = 5 3 _ _

6. _ 5 _ × 2 8 = 4 _ _ 6

7. 1 _ 6 × 3 _ = _ 2 _ 4

8. 1 5 9 × 4 _ = _ _ _ 2

Now here is a real challenge! Complete the next problem in the same manner, using the digits 1 through 9. **Hint:** The digits 1 through 9 appear on each side of the equal sign.

_ 2 _ 4 _ 8 _ _ × 6 = _ _ _ 2 8 _ _ 4 6

Name _____   Date _____

1-5 Dividing Whole Numbers with Remainders

Find the quotient and remainder of each division problem. Then answer the question at the bottom of the page.

1. $25\overline{)410}$ **2.** $31\overline{)2,334}$ **3.** $12\overline{)1,076}$ **4.** $130\overline{)2,347}$

5. $92\overline{)3,318}$ **6.** $86\overline{)1,983}$ **7.** $68\overline{)2,792}$

8. $54\overline{)3,729}$ **9.** $74\overline{)3,850}$ **10.** $46\overline{)4,509}$

Look at your remainders. What is the pattern?_____

_____

_____

1-6 Finding Missing Numbers in Long Division

Fill in the boxes with the correct number to complete the division problems.

1.
```
      3 □ R 2
   ┌─────────
2 □)8 7 6
     6 9
    □8 6
    1 8 4
        2
```

2.
```
       1 □ R 28
    ┌─────────
7 5)□2 8
    7 □
    1 7 8
    1 □0
      2 8
```

3.
```
      2 □ R 33
   ┌─────────
4 8)9 □3
    □6
    3 3
```

4.
```
        7 R 13
   ┌─────────
6 □)4 □2
    4 6 9
      1 3
```

5.
```
      □9 R 20
   ┌─────────
6 4)3 □9 6
    3 2 0
      5 9 6
      □□6
        2 0
```

6.
```
        7 □ R 56
    ┌─────────
□7)6 8 4 2
    6 0 9
      7 5 2
      6 9 6
        5 6
```

7.
```
      4 □9 R 5
   ┌─────────
□9)8 3 4 6
   □6
    7 4
    □7
    1 7 6
    □□1
        5
```

8.
```
       1 7 □ R 17
    ┌─────────
3 4)□1 0 3
    3 4
    2 □0
    2 3 8
      3 □3
      3 0 6
          1 7
```

9.
```
       1 3 □ R □□
    ┌─────────
5 6)7 □7 3
    5 6
    □87
    1 □8
    1 9 3
    1 6 8
        □□
```

Name _____   Date _____

1-6   Finding Missing Numbers in Long Division (Continued)

10.
```
            1 □ 6 R 14
      46 ) 9 □ 3 0
           4 6
           4 4 3
           4 1 4
             2 □ 0
             □ 7 6
               1 4
```

11.
```
              4 □ R 74
      8 □ ) 3 □ 4 6
            3 5 2
              4 2 6
              □ □ 2
                7 4
```

12.
```
             3 □ R 8
      □ 3 ) 2 □ □ 8
            2 1 9
                  8
```

13.
```
             4 □ 1 R 15
      □ 7 ) 2 6 8 8 2
            2 6 8
                8 2
                6 7
                1 5
```

14.
```
              8 □ □ R 40
      9 □ ) 7 □ 8 4 0
            7 □ □
            1 8 4
            1 8 0
                4 0
```

15.
```
               7 □ R 3 □ 0
      6 □ 5 ) 4 8 3 □ 0
             4 3 0 5
             5 2 7 0
             4 9 2 0
                 3 □ 0
```

16.
```
                 1 □ 8 5 R 188
      □ □ □ ) 9 □ 6 3 0 8
              8 7 2
              7 4 3 0
              6 □ 7 6
              4 □ 4 8
              4 3 6 0
                1 8 8
```

© 2002 by John Wiley & Sons, Inc.

Name _____ **Date** _____

1-7   Correcting Multiplication and Division Problems

Many, *but not all,* of the following problems have a mistake in computation. Correct the problems, then write the letter of each problem above its answer to complete the phrase on the next page. **Note:** Not all letters will be used.

Q.
```
    48
  × 76
  -----
   278
   336
  -----
 3,638
```

C.
```
    90
  × 47
  -----
   630
   360
  -----
 3,230
```

P.
```
    86
  × 54
  -----
   344
   400
  -----
 4,344
```

O.
```
    63
  × 70
  -----
   441
   400
  -----
 4,473
```

A.
```
    39
  × 84
  -----
   156
   312
  -----
 3,276
```

E.
```
   638
  ×  68
  ------
  5004
  3798
 ------
 42,984
```

B.
```
   409
  ×  74
  ------
  1636
  2863
 ------
 30,636
```

I.
```
   962
  ×  45
  ------
  4810
  3848
 ------
 43,290
```

F.
```
   746
  ×  87
  ------
  5122
  5876
 ------
 63,882
```

P.
```
    489
  × 706
  ------
   2734
   3423
 -------
 344,034
```

A.
```
        27 R 8
    34 ) 8 2 6
         6 8
         ---
         2 4 6
         2 3 8
         -----
             8
```

S.
```
        1 2
    62 ) 7 4 4
         6 2
         ---
         1 2 4
         1 2 4
         -----
```

Name _____   **Date** _____

1-7   Correcting Multiplication and Division Problems (Continued)

S.
```
        54 R 8
75 ) 4058
     375
     308
     300
       8
```

N.
```
        93 R 25
86 ) 7923
     774
     283
     258
      25
```

M.
```
        104 R 20
57 ) 5928
     57
     228
     208
      20
```

T.
```
        81 R 92
96 ) 7768
     768
     188
      96
      92
```

O.
```
        1584 R 36
43 ) 67,248
     43
     242
     215
      374
      354
       208
       172
        36
```

R.
```
        818 R 31
69 ) 56,473
     552
     127
      69
      583
      552
       31
```

I.
```
        75 R 4
84 ) 63,004
     588
     420
     420
       4
```

Along with addition and subtraction, multiplication and division are

30,266	3,276	12	750r4	4,230

4,410	345,234	43,384	818r31	24r10	80r88	43,290	1,563r39	92r11	54r8

in mathematics.

13

1-8 Multiplication and Division Crossnumber Puzzle

Solve each problem and complete the puzzle.

Across	**Down**

Across

1. 338 ÷ 26 = _____

3. 19 × 5 = _____

5. 1,260 ÷ 30 = _____

6. 1,596 ÷ 38 = _____

8. 16 × 36 = _____

10. 1,292 ÷ 4 = _____

12. 8 × 12 = _____

14. 1,520 ÷ 20 = _____

16. 426 ÷ 6 = _____

17. 5,916 ÷ 102 = _____

18. 49 × 2 = _____

Down

2. 27 × 12 = _____

3. 6,882 ÷ 74 = _____

4. 15 × 35 = _____

5. 27 × 18 = _____

7. 38 × 54 = _____

9. 87 × 87 = _____

10. 3,732 ÷ 12 = _____

11. 15 × 25 = _____

13. 2,037 ÷ 3 = _____

15. 8,432 ÷ 124 = _____

1-8 Multiplication and Division Crossnumber Puzzle (Continued)

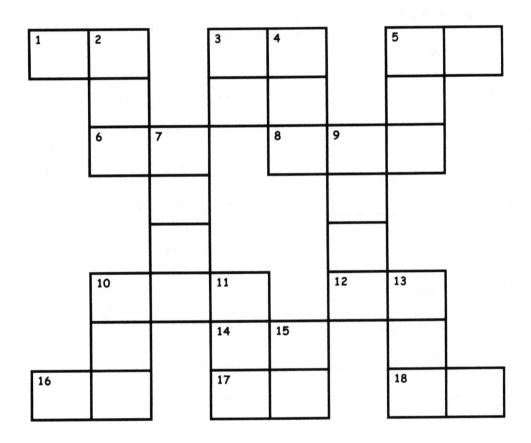

1-9   Whole Number Operations Crossnumber Puzzle

Solve each problem and complete the puzzle.

Across

1. $926 \times 11 =$ _____

3. $681 - 393 =$ _____

6. $19{,}053 \div 87 =$ _____

8. $8{,}159 - 2{,}847 =$ _____

9. $837 + 56 =$ _____

11. $14 \times 27 =$ _____

12. $9{,}693 \div 3 =$ _____

14. $9{,}879 - 3{,}124 =$ _____

15. $172 + 619 =$ _____

17. $1{,}187 - 549 =$ _____

18. $210 \times 19 =$ _____

20. $12{,}065 \div 19 =$ _____

21. $2{,}235 \div 15 =$ _____

23. $141 \times 437 =$ _____

Down

1. $76 + 28 + 34 =$ _____

2. $2{,}288 \div 26 =$ _____

4. $602 \div 7 =$ _____

5. $2{,}473 \times 95 =$ _____

7. $1{,}469 + 258 =$ _____

10. $3{,}806 - 45 =$ _____

11. $3{,}525 - 419 =$ _____

13. $329 \times 786 =$ _____

16. $5{,}672 + 3{,}491 =$ _____

19. $2{,}052 \div 38 =$ _____

21. $1{,}067 - 960 =$ _____

22. $5{,}177 \div 167$ _____

1-9 Whole Number Operations
Crossnumber Puzzle (Continued)

Name _____   **Date** _____

1-10   Finding the Largest and Smallest Numbers

Using the digits 1, 2, 5, and 7, place one digit in each square to find the *largest* sum, difference, product, and quotient. Each digit must be used in each problem. The quotient must be a whole number.

1.   2.   3. 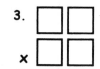   4.

Using the digits 3, 4, 6, 8, and 9, place one digit in each square to find the *smallest* sum, difference, product, and quotient. Each digit must be used once in each problem. All answers must be whole numbers.

5. 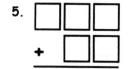   6. 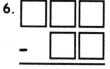   7.    8.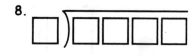

1-11   Writing Word Problems

Write a word problem for each answer below. Be sure your problems require the use of the mathematical operation(s) in parentheses that follows each answer. For example, problem 1 should be an addition problem that has an answer of $248.

1. $248 (addition)

2. 56 students (subtraction)

3. 340 school lunches (multiplication)

4. 120 concert tickets (division)

5. 452 flowers (addition)

6. 109 volunteers (subtraction)

7. 1,012 hours (multiplication)

8. 14 photographs (division)

9. 12 hours; $72 (addition and multiplication)

10. 1,896 miles; 474 miles (addition and division)

1-12 Writing Word Problems with Specific Phrases

The phrases below are common in mathematics word problems. The phrases hint at which operations—addition, subtraction, multiplication, or division—should be used to solve the problem. Create a word problem of your own for each phrase below. Be sure to include an answer key.

1. . . . in all . . .

2. . . . left over . . .

3. . . . divided by . . .

4. . . . the sum of . . .

5. . . . take away . . .

6. . . . the product of . . .

7. . . . more than . . .

8. . . . less than . . .

9. . . . arranged in ten sections . . .

10. . . . six times as many . . .

© 2002 by John Wiley & Sons, Inc.

1-13   Using the Order of Operations to Form Calculator Words

Every digit on a calculator display can be turned upside down to resemble a letter as shown in the chart below.

Numbers   0123456789

Letters   Ol2EhS9L86

These upside-down numbers may be used to form words or names. Use the order of operations to find the numerical answers to each problem and enter the answers in Column A. Then turn your calculator upside down and record the word the upside-down digits form in Column B. The first problem is done for you.

		A	B
1.	$2 + 4 \times 8$	34	hE
2.	$7 \times 100 + 8 \times 9 - 1$		
3.	$86 \times 64 + 3 \times 53$		
4.	$10 + 72 \times 7$		
5.	$(30 + 30) \times 15 - (5 \times 3 + 2)$		
6.	$8 \times 5 \times (4 + 5) \times 2 + 90 - 2$		
7.	$63 \div 9 \times 7 + 2$		
8.	$5 \times 4 \times (16 + 1) - 3$		
9.	$48 \div (4 + 2) + 3(6 - 2 \times 2)$		
10.	$(76 + 14) \times 5 \times 10 + 12 \times 10 - 2 \times 3$		
11.	$3 \times 11 + 3(3 + 7)(4 + 8 + 9)$		
12.	$4000 - (200 - 7)$		
13.	$100 + 5 + 60 \times 60$		
14.	$10(17 \times 5 \times 2 + 5 + 60 \times 10) - 5 \times 3$		
15.	$5(36 \div 4 \times 2 \times 81) + 5 \times 10 - 2 \times 3$		
16.	$50 \times 100 \div 2 + 12 \times 100 + 5 \times 2 - 6$		

1-14   Equations and Order of Operations, 1

Use the numbers 1, 2, and 3 to complete each equation below. Use each number once in each equation. Be sure to follow the order of operations. **Note:** Some equations may have more than one answer.

1. ____ × (____ + ____) = 8

2. (____ × ____) – ____ = 5

3. (____ + ____) ÷ ____ = 2

4. (____ – ____) × ____ = 3

5. ____ × (____ + ____) = 9

6. (____ × ____) + ____ = 7

7. (____ × ____) ÷ ____ = 6

8. ____ × (____ – ____) = 1

For problems 9 through 12, use the numbers 1, 2, 3, and 4 to complete the equations. Use each number only once and be sure to use the order of operations.

9. (____ × ____) × (____ + ____) = 36

10. (____ + ____) ÷ (____ – ____) = 3

11. (____ ÷ ____) × (____ – ____) = 2

12. (____ × ____) – (____ + ____) = 1

Using the numbers 1, 2, 3, and 4, create three equations of your own similar to the ones you just completed. Use each number only once in each equation and be sure to follow the order of operations. Share your equations with a friend.

© 2002 by John Wiley & Sons, Inc.

Name _____   Date _____

1-15 Equations and Order of Operations, II

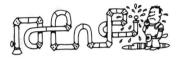

Use the numbers 1, 2, 3, and 5 to complete the equations below. Use each number once in each equation. Be sure to follow the order of operations. **Note:** Some equations may have more than one answer.

1. ____ + (____ − ____) + ____ = 7

2. (____ × ____) − (____ + ____) = 12

3. (____ − ____) − (____ − ____) = 1

4. (____ × ____) ÷ (____ − ____) = 5

5. (____ + ____) ÷ (____ − ____) = 8

6. (____ × ____) × (____ + ____) = 36

7. (____ − ____) × ____ − ____ = 3

8. (____ × ____) − (____ + ____) = 0

9. ____ + [(____ − ____) × ____] = 9

10. (____ + ____) ÷ ____ × ____ = 4

11. ____ × [(____ × ____) + ____] = 35

12. [(____ − ____) × ____] × ____ = 15

Using the numbers 1, 2, 4, and 7, create three equations of your own similar to the ones you just completed. Use each number once in each equation and follow the order of operations. Share your equations with a friend.

1-16 Finding Patterns and Missing Numbers

Each number in the following problems is placed in a square or circle according to a pattern. Determine the pattern and find the missing number in the figure. Then explain the pattern. **Note:** Some problems may have more than one answer. The first problem is done for you.

1.

2	1
3	5

6	19
4	5

3	11
6	7

5	⑦
2	3

The answer is 7. The pattern: Multiply the numbers in the first column, then subtract the number in the lower right-hand corner from the product.

2.

1	2
9	3

3	4
14	2

2	5
28	4

2	3
	4

_____

_____

_____

3.

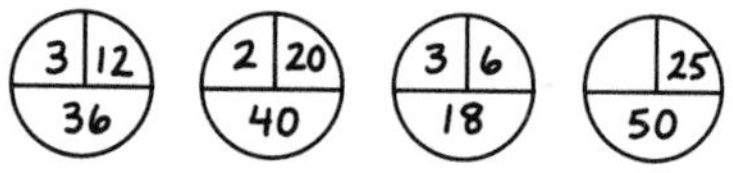

(3 | 12 / 36)   (2 | 20 / 40)   (3 | 6 / 18)   (| 25 / 50)

_____

_____

_____

4.

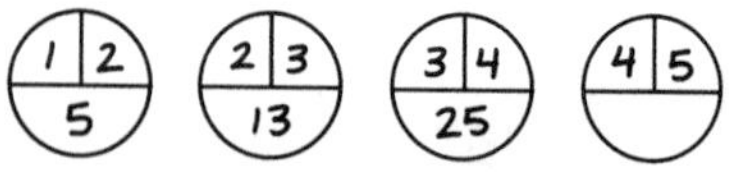

(1 | 2 / 5)   (2 | 3 / 13)   (3 | 4 / 25)   (4 | 5 /)

_____

_____

_____

5.

1	2
4	2

2	3
6	4

3	4
8	6

4	5
10	

_____

_____

_____

Name _____ **Date** _____

1-16 Finding Patterns and Missing Numbers (Continued)

6.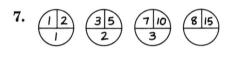

_____

_____

_____

7.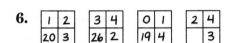

_____

_____

_____

8.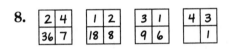

_____

_____

_____

9.

_____

_____

_____

10.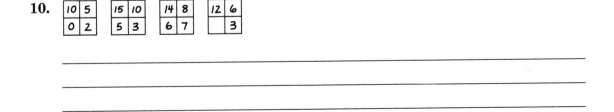

_____

_____

_____

1-17   Finding Place Value:
Ones to Billions

Write the following numbers in their numerical form. Then write the number for the place value shown. Match the letter of each place value number with its number at the bottom of the page and complete the message. The first problem is done for you.

1. Seventy-two thousand, four hundred eighty-three = _____72,483_____ tens digit = __8__ = C

2. Forty-five thousand, nine hundred = _____ thousands digit = _____ = M

3. Two hundred fifty-six thousand, three hundred ten = _____ hundred thousands digit = _____ = A

4. Thirty-eight million, three hundred eighty-four thousand, six hundred one = _____ hundred thousands digit = _____ = T

5. Three hundred forty-five million, two hundred six thousand, three hundred twenty-one = _____ ten millions digit = _____ = N

6. Four hundred sixty-eight million, two hundred twenty-two thousand, seven hundred fifteen = _____ tens digit = _____ = H

7. Five hundred fifteen thousand, seven hundred sixty-three = _____ hundreds digit = _____ = E

8. Seven billion, nine hundred eighty million, three hundred forty-five thousand, six hundred two = _____ hundred millions digit = _____ = P

9. Thirty billion, six hundred nine thousand, two hundred ten = _____ millions digit = _____ = I

10. Two hundred forty-six billion, nine hundred eighty-seven million, twenty-three = _____ billions digit = _____ = L

It's important to know your ___ ___ ___ _C_ ___   ___ ___   ___ ___ ___ ___ .
                               9 6 2 8 7   0 4   5 2 3 1

Try this challenge. Take the digits in order beneath the message and write the word name of the number they form. _____

Name _____   Date _____

1-18   A Place Value Crossnumber Puzzle

Use the clues to complete the crossnumber puzzle. The first problem "Across" is done for you.

Across

1. The number of hundreds in 23,700
3. The number halfway between 6 tens and 7 tens
4. The number of hundreds in 3,500
5. One hundred one thousand, four hundred sixty
6. 3 tens less than 94
7. 1 ten and 1 less than the number halfway between 78 thousand and 79 thousand
8. 3 tens and 5 ones more than seventy-nine thousand five hundred
10. 15 tens less than 246

11. Seven hundred ten thousand, two hundred thirty-eight
13. The largest two-digit number
14. Ten less than the smallest three-digit number
15. The number of hundreds in 83,000

Down

2. The number of tens in 3,410
3. Six thousand, three hundred four
4. Two less than thirty-four thousand
5. The number of hundreds in 1,478,900
9. The number of tens in 57,800
12. 30 tens less than 533

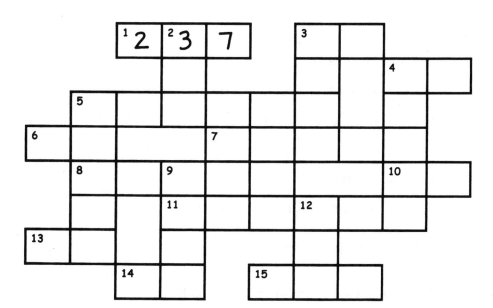

27

1-19   Rounding Whole Numbers

Round the following numbers to the place indicated.

1. Round 1,378 to the nearest hundred.   _____

2. Round 6,014 to the nearest ten.   _____

3. Round 73 to the nearest ten.   _____

4. Round 8,649 to the nearest thousand.   _____

5. Round 57,106 to the nearest ten thousand.   _____

6. Round 1,650 to the nearest hundred.   _____

7. Round 78,653 to the nearest ten.   _____

8. Round 1,415,789 to the nearest hundred thousand.   _____

9. Round 79,284 to the nearest thousand.   _____

10. Round 82 to the nearest ten.   _____

11. Round 3,384 to the nearest hundred.   _____

12. Round 51,801 to the nearest hundred.   _____

13. Round 1,471 to the nearest thousand.   _____

14. Round 33,251 to the nearest ten thousand.   _____

15. Round 4,563,274 to the nearest million.   _____

16. Round 17,468,292 to the nearest hundred thousand.   _____

17. Round 1,500 to the nearest thousand.   _____

18. Round 21,410 to the nearest ten.   _____

19. Round 62,354 to the nearest ten thousand.   _____

20. Round 234,516 to the nearest hundred thousand.   _____

Find the sum of the rounded numbers.   _____

If your sum is 24,505,520, your rounding is most likely correct.

1-20 Identifying Names of Very Large Numbers

The names of very large numbers are written below. Use the clue after the name to write the number of zeroes the number contains. The first one is done for you.

1. one decillion—the product of eleven and three. Number of zeroes: __33__

2. one sexdecillion—one more than half the number of pennies in a dollar. Number of zeroes: _____

3. one googol—a perfect score on a test. Number of zeroes: _____

4. one billion—the largest one-digit number. Number of zeroes: _____

5. one quadrillion—one less than a special "sweet" teenage birthday. Number of zeroes: _____

6. one septillion—the number of cupcakes in two dozen. Number of zeroes: _____

7. one duodecillion—four times ten, minus one. Number of zeroes: _____

8. one nonillion—the tens digit is three and the units digit is three less than the tens digit. Number of zeroes: _____

9. one quintillion—two times the quantity of five plus four. Number of zeroes: _____

10. one vigintillion—one less than the product of eight times eight. Number of zeroes: _____

1-20 Identifying Names of Very Large Numbers (Continued)

11. one quattuordillion—the sum of three and two, times nine. Number of zeroes:

    _____

12. one novemdecillion—six times two times five. Number of zeroes: _____

13. one undecillion—the tens digit is the number of sides of a triangle, the ones digit
    is twice the tens digit. Number of zeroes: _____

14. one octodecillion—three times nine, plus the product of three and ten. Number
    of zeroes: _____

15. one septendecillion—six times ten, minus six. Number of zeroes: _____

16. one trillion—the product of three and four. Number of zeroes: _____

17. one tredecillion—three dozen plus one-half dozen. Number of zeroes: _____

18. one octillion—three times the number of legs of an octopus, plus three. Number
    of zeroes: _____

19. one sextillion—three plus the product of two and nine. Number of zeroes:

    _____

20. one quindecillion—two less than half of a hundred. Number of zeroes: _____

Name _____   **Date** _____

1-21   Using Rules for Divisibility

Divisibility rules are helpful for finding factors, reducing fractions, and finding common denominators. Following are the most useful.

For a number to be divisible by

2, the number must end in 2,4,6,8, or 0.

3, the sum of the digits must be divisible by 3.

4, the number formed by the last two digits must be divisible by 4.

5, the number must end in 0 or 5.

6, the number must be divisible by 2 and 3.

8, the number formed by the last three digits of the number can be divided by 8.

9, the sum of the digits must be divisible by 9.

10, the number must end in 0.

12, the number must be divisible by both 3 and 4.

Directions: Use the rules of divisibility above to complete the chart.

- Place an X in the box if the number on the left is divisible by the number on the top of the chart. Notice that there are several rows and columns and that the first row is completed for you.
- Find the sum of the numbers you have marked in each row.
- Match the sum with a phrase in the box.
- Record the phrase on the line in the order that the sums appear from the top of the chart to the bottom. The first row is done for you. Note that the necessary punctuation and capitalization have been included.

3 — Rearrange the digits	21 — subtract the smaller
8 — Take any number	27 — more digits.
11 — you now have,	29 — having two or
12 — The difference	35 — will always be
14 — in any order.	42 — Of the two numbers
17 — from the larger.	59 — divisible by nine.

Take any number _____

_____

_____

1-21 Using Rules for Divisibility (Continued)

Divisible by

	Number	2	3	4	5	6	8	9	10	12	Sum
1	75		X		X						8
2	80										
3	156										
4	237										
5	256										
6	1,020										
7	1,326										
8	1,340										
9	1,755										
10	2,223										
11	7,368										
12	46,440										

1-22 Rules for Determining Divisibility by 7 and 11

The tests for finding if a number is divisible by 7 or 11 are somewhat longer than other divisibility tests. However, they are still useful.

To test for divisibility by 7:
- Drop the units digit.
- Subtract two times the units digit from the remaining number.
- If the difference is divisible by 7, then the original number is divisible by 7.

To test for divisibility by 11:
- Add the alternate digits beginning with the first digit.
- Add alternate digits beginning with the second digit.
- Subtract the smaller sum from the larger.
- If the difference is divisible by 11, then the original number is divisible by 11.

Directions: Use the divisibility rules for 7 and 11 to complete the chart. Place an X in the column under "7" if the number is divisible by 7, an X in the column under "11" if the number is divisible by 11, or an X in the column under "neither" if the number is not divisible by 7 or 11.

When you have completed the chart, find the sum of the numbers that are divisible by 7, the sum of the numbers that are divisible by 11, and the sum of the numbers that are divisible by neither 7 nor 11.

Describe how the sums are related. _____

_____

_____

_____

Name _____   Date _____

1-22 Rules for Determining Divisibility by 7 and 11 (Continued)

	Divisible by			
	Number	**7**	**11**	**neither**
1	121			
2	237			
3	256			
4	455			
5	616			
6	623			
7	3,080			
8	3,386			
9	3,682			
10	4,087			
11	4,477			
12	8,784			

Name _____   Date _____

1-23 Finding Factors of Numbers

List all the factors of each number below in numerical order from the least to the greatest. Place one factor over each blank. You will notice letters beneath some blanks. At the bottom of the page, write the letter above its corresponding factor to reveal a message. The first problem is done for you.

1. 6: { _1_ , _2_ , _3_ , _6_ }
                 B

2. 16: { ___, ___, ___, ___, ___ }
                      O

3. 24: { ___, ___, ___, ___, ___, ___, ___, ___ }
                                   U

4. 27: { ___, ___, ___, ___ }
              R

5. 28: { ___, ___, ___, ___, ___, ___ }
                        T

6. 30: { ___, ___, ___, ___, ___, ___, ___, ___ }
                        I

7. 33: { ___, ___, ___, ___ }
              A

8. 36: { ___, ___, ___, ___, ___, ___, ___, ___, ___ }
                             C

9. 38: { ___, ___, ___, ___ }
              M

10. 39: { ___, ___, ___, ___ }
               S

11. 40: { ___, ___, ___, ___, ___, ___, ___, ___ }
                                  F

12. 44: { ___, ___, ___, ___, ___, ___ }
                        Y

13. 45: { ___, ___, ___, ___, ___, ___ }
                        N

14. 46: { ___, ___, ___, ___ }
               E

15. 50: { ___, ___, ___, ___, ___, ___ }
                   V

___ ___ ___   ___ ___   ___   ___ ___ ___ ___ ___ ___
 8 15 23   6 13   11   10 11 9 14 8   3

___ ___   ___ ___ ___ ___ ___   ___ ___ ___ ___ ___ ___ .
 8 10   23 5 23 3 22   15 12 19 2 23 3
                                            B

1-24 Finding the Greatest Common Factor

Find the greatest common factor (GCF) of each pair of numbers from the Factor Bank below. Record the letter of the GCF in the space provided at the bottom of the page to read the message. **Note:** Some factors will be used more than once.

1. 15, 18	GCF = _____	**13.** 14, 21	GCF = _____
2. 12, 18	GCF = _____	**14.** 13, 130	GCF = _____
3. 4, 36	GCF = _____	**15.** 12, 51	GCF = _____
4. 13, 26	GCF = _____	**16.** 36, 90	GCF = _____
5. 39, 65	GCF = _____	**17.** 48, 120	GCF = _____
6. 36, 40	GCF = _____	**18.** 36, 45	GCF = _____
7. 30, 38	GCF = _____	**19.** 16, 24	GCF = _____
8. 9, 20	GCF = _____	**20.** 25, 80	GCF = _____
9. 9, 24	GCF = _____	**21.** 27, 99	GCF = _____
10. 12, 30	GCF = _____	**22.** 24, 36	GCF = _____
11. 8, 24	GCF = _____	**23.** 36, 66	GCF = _____
12. 8, 20	GCF = _____	**24.** 81, 91	GCF = _____

```
                          Factor Bank
          1—F     2—N     3—A     4—O     5—H     6—C
    7—R     8—T     9—E     12—G     13—M     18—Y     24—B
```

Letter of GCF: __   ___ ___ ___ ___ ___ ___   ___ ___ ___ ___ ___ ___
Problem Number: 1   2   3   4   5   6   7   8   9 10 11 12 13

                ___ ___ ___   ___ ___   ___ ___ ___   ___ ___ ___.
                14 15 16   17 18   19 20 21   22 23 24

Name _____   Date _____

1-25 Euclid's Method for Finding the Greatest Common Factor

Euclid was a Greek mathematician who lived about 350 to 300 B.C. He developed a method, or algorithm, to find the greatest common factor (GCF) of two numbers. Instead of listing the factors of each number and finding the largest number that is common to both, he used the following steps:

1. Divide the larger number by the smaller.
2. Divide the divisor in Step 1 by the remainder in Step 1.
3. Repeat Step 2 until there is no remainder.
4. The last divisor is the GCF of the original numbers.

Directions: Find the GCF of each pair of numbers using Euclid's method.

1. 312, 648   GCF = _____

2. 208, 464   GCF = _____

3. 153, 333   GCF = _____

4. 400, 720   GCF = _____

5. 105, 180   GCF = _____

6. 215, 610   GCF = _____

7. 168, 231   GCF = _____

8. 54, 237   GCF = _____

Find the sum of the greatest common factors of problems 1 through 8. How does this sum compare to the greatest common factor of 519 and 865?

_____

_____

Name _____   Date _____

1-26 Perfect, Abundant, and Deficient Numbers

The ancient Greeks believed everything could be explained through the study of numbers and their properties. Greek mathematicians classified numbers according to the sum of a number's factors, excluding the number itself. They categorized numbers as being abundant, deficient, or perfect.

An *abundant* number is less than the sum of its factors, excluding itself. 12 is an abundant number because 12 is less than the sum of its factors, $1 + 2 + 3 + 4 + 6$, which equals 16.

A *deficient* number is greater than the sum of its factors, excluding itself. 10 is deficient because 10 is greater than the sum of its factors, $1 + 2 + 5$, which equals 8.

A *perfect* number is equal to the sum of its factors, excluding itself. 6 is perfect because 6 equals the sum of its factors, $1 + 2 + 3$.

Directions: For the numbers that follow, determine if each is abundant, deficient, or perfect. Circle the letter under the appropriate column for each number. Write the circled letters in order, starting with the first problem, on the lines below to complete the statement.

	Number	Abundant	Deficient	Perfect
1.	1	S	A	O
2.	2	O	L	F
3.	4	M	W	T
4.	7	E	A	E
5.	8	T	Y	N
6.	11	I	S	M
7.	14	A	D	H
8.	15	Y	E	A
9.	16	V	F	B
10.	18	I	E	E
11.	20	C	P	T
12.	21	W	I	E
13.	23	R	E	T
14.	24	N	H	O
15.	28	E	F	T

Prime numbers are ____ ____ ____ ____ ____ ____

____ ____ ____ ____ ____ ____ ____ ____ .

© 2002 by John Wiley & Sons, Inc.

1-27 Classifying Numbers as Prime or Composite

Pierre de Fermat (1601–1665) was a French lawyer who explored math as a hobby. Much of his work was in the study of prime numbers.

A *prime number* has only two factors, 1 and the number. A *composite number* has more than two factors. The number 1 is the only number that is neither prime nor composite.

Directions: The list below contains prime and composite numbers. If a number is prime, circle the letter in the same row under the "Prime" column. If a number is composite, circle the letter in the same row under the "Composite" column. After circling the letters, write them in order on the spaces at the bottom of this page, starting with problem one. You will find another name for Fermat.

	Number	Prime	Composite
1.	5	T	A
2.	6	M	H
3.	9	A	E
4.	11	P	W
5.	15	O	R
6.	17	I	M
7.	19	N	A
8.	25	N	C
9.	27	U	E
10.	29	O	M
11.	31	F	B
12.	37	A	E
13.	41	M	R
14.	43	A	N
15.	49	O	T
16.	51	H	E
17.	53	U	S
18.	57	E	R
19.	59	S	T

__ __ __   __ __ __ __ __ __   __ __

__ __ __ __ __ __ __ __ __

1-28 Expressing Composite Numbers as the Product of Primes

A *theorem* is a fact or idea that can be shown to be true. An important theorem about prime and composite numbers states that every composite number can be expressed as the product of prime numbers in only one way.

Directions: Fourteen composite numbers are shown below. Write each as the product of prime numbers, recording the prime factors in order from the smallest to the largest. Then write the letter that corresponds to the factor in the space provided at the bottom of the page. Your answer will name the theorem noted above. The first problem is done for you.

1. 14 = __2__ × __7__
             O

2. 18 = ___ × ___ × ___
          E

3. 20 = ___ × ___ × ___
             M

4. 22 = ___ × ___
         A

5. 24 = ___ × ___ × ___ × ___
            T

6. 102 = ___ × ___ × ___
            H

7. 155 = ___ × ___
          U

8. 169 = ___ × ___
          N

9. 205 = ___ × ___
           C

10. 207 = ___ × ___ × ___
             L

11. 259 = ___ × ___
           D

12. 285 = ___ × ___ × ___
             F

13. 860 = ___ × ___ × ___ × ___
               R

14. 870 = ___ × ___ × ___ × ___
               I

___ ___ ___   ___ ___ ___ ___ ___ ___ ___ ___ ___ ___
 2 17 3   19 31 13 37 11 5 3 13 2 11 23

___ ___ ___ _O_ ___ ___ ___   _O_ ___
 2 17 3 7 43 3 5   7 19

___ ___ ___ ___ ___ ___ ___ ___ ___ ___
 11 43 29 2 17 5 3 2 29 41

Name _____   **Date** _____

1-29 Identifying Emirps

An *emirp* is a special type of prime number. If the digits of an emirp are reversed, the resulting number is also prime.

The number 13 is an emirp. It is prime and if its digits are reversed, it is 31, which is also prime.

The number 29 is not an emirp. It is prime, but if its digits are reversed, the new number is 92, which is not prime.

Directions: A list of prime numbers appears below. If the number is an emirp, circle the letters on the same line under the "Yes" column. If the number is not an emirp, circle the letters on the same line under the "No" column. After circling the letters, write them in order, starting with problem one, in the spaces at the end of the activity. Place one letter in each space. You will learn an interesting fact about the word "emirp."

		Yes	**No**
1.	11	EM	AP
2.	23	RI	IR
3.	89	ME	PI
4.	101	SP	IS
5.	19	AN	RI
6.	37	ME	IT
7.	53	ET	SP
8.	41	ER	EL
9.	67	FA	LE
10.	61	CE	DB
11.	17	AC	CA
12.	59	NE	KW
13.	79	AR	RO
14.	43	OT	DS

___ ___ ___ ___ ___ ___ ___

___ ___ ___ ___ ___ ___ ___ ___ ___ ___

___ ___ ___ ___ ___ ___ ___ .

Name _____   Date _____

1-30 Examples of Goldbach's Conjecture

Christian Goldbach, a German mathematician, is best remembered for his contribution to number theory in 1742. He stated that "Every even number greater than 4 can be written as the sum of two odd prime numbers." This statement is now known as Goldbach's Conjecture.

With the aid of computers, Goldbach's Conjecture has been shown to hold true for millions of even numbers. It has never been proven false. However, no one has ever been able to prove that it will always be true for all even numbers larger than 4.

Directions: Express each number below as the sum of two odd prime numbers. Sometimes more than one solution is possible. Try to find all solutions. The first problem is done for you. *Note:* 1 is not a prime number.

1. 6 = 3 + 3

2. 8 = ____ + ____

3. 10 = ____ + ____
   or ____ + ____

4. 12 = ____ + ____

5. 14 = ____ + ____
   or ____ + ____

6. 16 = ____ + ____
   or ____ + ____

7. 18 = ____ + ____
   or ____ + ____

8. 20 = ____ + ____
   or ____ + ____

9. 22 = ____ + ____
   or ____ + ____
   or ____ + ____

10. 28 = ____ + ____
    or ____ + ____

11. 36 = ____ + ____
    or ____ + ____
    or ____ + ____
    or ____ + ____

12. 48 = ____ + ____
    or ____ + ____
    or ____ + ____
    or ____ + ____
    or ____ + ____

13. 50 = ____ + ____
    or ____ + ____
    or ____ + ____
    or ____ + ____

14. 54 = ____ + ____
    or ____ + ____
    or ____ + ____
    or ____ + ____
    or ____ + ____

15. 62 = ____ + ____
    or ____ + ____
    or ____ + ____

16. 70 = ____ + ____
    or ____ + ____
    or ____ + ____
    or ____ + ____
    or ____ + ____

Name _____   **Date** _____

1-31 Finding the Least Common Multiple

You can find the least common multiple (LCM) of two numbers in two ways. One is to list the multiples of each number until a common multiple is found. The other is to find the product of two numbers and divide the product by the greatest common factor.

Directions: Find the least common multiple of the pairs of numbers and place it in the space provided. Find the sum of the LCMs of each column. Find the LCM of the two sums.

Column 1		Column 2	
1. 5, 15	LCM = _____	2, 4	LCM = _____
2. 12, 18	LCM = _____	8, 12	LCM = _____
3. 6, 9	LCM = _____	16, 36	LCM = _____
4. 10, 15	LCM = _____	15, 20	LCM = _____
5. 15, 21	LCM = _____	7, 9	LCM = _____
6. 30, 40	LCM = _____	28, 56	LCM = _____
	Sum = _____		Sum = _____

LCM of the sums = _____

1-32 Finding the Squares and Cubes of Numbers

Find and record the square and cube of each number. Then follow the directions at the bottom of this page to find a message about the squares and cubes of numbers.

	Square	Cube			Square	Cube
1. 3	_____	_____	**8.** 8		_____	_____
2. 10	_____	_____	**9.** 13		_____	_____
3. 12	_____	_____	**10.** 4		_____	_____
4. 6	_____	_____	**11.** 14		_____	_____
5. 7	_____	_____	**12.** 11		_____	_____
6. 2	_____	_____	**13.** 5		_____	_____
7. 9	_____	_____				

Match your answers with the corresponding letters in the Numbers and Letters Bank below. Then write the letters on the lines at the bottom of the page in order of the problems. For example, for problem one, write the letters of the answer of the squared number, then the letters for the answer of the cubed number. Do the same for problem two.

<table>
<tr><th colspan="5">Numbers and Letters Bank</th></tr>
<tr><td>1000—SC</td><td>100—DE</td><td>16—UM</td><td>343—EF</td><td>64—ER</td></tr>
<tr><td>9—RE</td><td>2197—DN</td><td>729—US</td><td>8—ST</td><td>121—OR</td></tr>
<tr><td>81—TO</td><td>1728—TE</td><td>196—AL</td><td>25—WE</td><td>216—AS</td></tr>
<tr><td>512—AI</td><td>2744—SF</td><td>169—SE</td><td>36—SW</td><td>49—TH</td></tr>
<tr><td>4—IR</td><td>144—AR</td><td>1331—PO</td><td>125—RS</td><td>27—NE</td></tr>
</table>

When you are done, break the letters into words and you will find the message.

_____

_____

_____

1-33 Simplifying Expressions with Exponents

Simplify each expression below. Match your answer to the corresponding number and letter in the Answer Bank at the bottom of the page. Write this letter in the space after the answer. Starting with the first problem, write the letters, in order, on the lines at the bottom of the page. When you are done, break the letters into words and you will learn an important fact about exponents. The first problem is done for you.

1. $4^2 + 2^2 =$ ___20___ ___A___
2. $4^2 + 2^3 =$ _____ _____
3. $5^3 =$ _____ _____
4. $7^2 - 5^2 =$ _____ _____
5. $9^2 =$ _____ _____
6. $7^3 =$ _____ _____
7. $8^3 =$ _____ _____
8. $2^4 =$ _____ _____
9. $2^3 =$ _____ _____
10. $2^5 =$ _____ _____
11. $10^0 =$ _____ _____
12. $4^2 + 4^2 =$ _____ _____
13. $6^3 =$ _____ _____
14. $4^2 =$ _____ _____
15. $11^2 =$ _____ _____
16. $5^2 - 3^2 =$ _____ _____
17. $4^2 - 2^3 =$ _____ _____
18. $3^0 =$ _____ _____

19. $4^3 =$ _____ _____
20. $5^1 - 2^2 =$ _____ _____
21. $8^2 + 6^2 =$ _____ _____
22. $2^3 + 2^3 =$ _____ _____
23. $4^2 - 2^2 - 2^2 =$ _____ _____
24. $4^2 + 7^2 =$ _____ _____
25. $3^5 =$ _____ _____
26. $2^5 - 4^2 =$ _____ _____
27. $12^2 =$ _____ _____
28. $3^4 =$ _____ _____
29. $7^2 - 5^2 - 2^2 =$ _____ _____
30. $13^2 =$ _____ _____
31. $6^2 - 2^2 =$ _____ _____
32. $3^2 - 2^3 =$ _____ _____
33. $3^3 - 5^2 - 4^0 =$ _____ _____
34. $5^2 - 3^0 =$ _____ _____
35. $8^2 - 2^5 - 4^2 =$ _____ _____

Answer Bank

A—20	M—343	S—243	B—512	N—24	T—32
E—16	O—1	U—81	H—216	P—64	W—100
I—65	Q—144	Y—125	L—169	R—8	Z—121

A _____

_____

_____

1-34 Using Scientific Notation

Scientific notation is used to express very large numbers. Most large numbers are not written in words or digits because they are simply "too big." Scientific notation is used instead.

Here are some tips for writing scientific notation:

- The first factor is greater than or equal to one and is less than ten.
- The second factor is a power of 10 and is written in exponential form.
- To write numbers with exponents, count the number of places to the right of the first non-zero number. This number is the exponent.

Directions: Write each of the following numbers in scientific notation. The first problem is done for you.

1. Our sun has a diameter of 864,000 miles. _____ 8.64×10^5 _____

2. The temperature of the sun's surface is about 11,000° F. _____ Its inner core may reach temperatures of 35 million degrees. _____

3. The largest planet of our solar system is Jupiter. Its diameter is about 89,000 miles. _____

4. The smallest planet of our solar system is Pluto with a diameter of about 1,400 miles. _____

5. The diameter of the Earth is about 8,000 miles. _____

6. Mercury is the planet closest to the sun. It is about 36 million miles from the sun. _____

7. Mercury is also the fastest moving planet at a speed of 107,000 miles per hour.

    _____

8. The slowest moving planet is Pluto at about 10,600 miles per hour.

    _____

9. The moon, Earth's natural satellite, is about 238,900 miles from the Earth. _____ The moon has a diameter of about 2,160 miles.

    _____

10. Asteroids, or minor planets, are solid chunks of rock that may be very small or quite large. Ceres, the largest asteroid, is about 600 miles across.

    _____

11. A galaxy is a group of billions of stars held together by gravity. There are about 50 billion galaxies in the universe. _____

12. We live in a galaxy called the Milky Way, which contains about 200 billion stars.

    _____

1-35 Converting Scientific Notation to Standard Form

To get an idea of how useful scientific notation is for writing large numbers, rewrite the numbers expressed in scientific notation in standard form.

1. 1.7×10^5 = _____

2. 6.0×10^4 = _____

3. 3.5×10^8 = _____

4. 7.34×10^6 = _____

5. 8.7×10^{12} = _____

6. 9.45×10^3 = _____

7. 6.8×10^{10} = _____

8. 4.58×10^5 = _____

9. 6.217×10^8 = _____

10. 5.704×10^9 = _____

11. 2.04×10^7 = _____

12. 7.0×10^1 = _____

Write three problems of your own in which numbers expressed in scientific notation must be rewritten in standard form. Be sure to have an answer key. Share your problems with a friend.

_____

_____

_____

1-36 Finding Missing Numbers in Patterns and Sequences

Find the missing numbers in the sequences of problems 1 through 11, and record them in the spaces provided. Note that a letter appears beneath some numbers. Write the letter that corresponds to each number at the bottom of the page. A hint to determining the missing numbers in problem 12 will be revealed. The first problem is done for you.

1. 1, 2, 3, 4, __5__ , __6__ , __7__ , . . .
N

2. 2, 4, 6, 8, _____, _____, _____, . . .
M

3. 2, 4, 8, 16, _____, _____, _____, . . .
R

4. 2, 3, 5, 7, _____, _____, _____, . . .
P

5. 8, 16, 24, 32, _____, _____, _____, . . .
T

6. 6, 9, 12, 15, _____, _____, _____, . . .
E

7. 5, 1, 6, 2, 7, _____, _____, _____, . . .
B$$O

8. 1, 8, 27, 64, _____, _____, _____, . . .
W$$A

9. 1, 1, 2, 3, 5, _____, _____, _____, . . .
S$$D

10. 1, 5, 14, 30, 55, _____, _____, _____, . . .
UL

Hint for problems 11 and 12: Spell the numbers.

11. 2, 3, 10, 12, 13, 20, _____, _____, _____, . . .
HI

12. 2, 4, 6, 30, 32, 34, _____, _____, _____, . . .

An additional hint for solving problem 12:

56	22	24	13	24	N 7	140	14	3	24	128	13

343	128	24		13	17	24	204	204	24	21	

125	23	56	22	4	140	56		343	N 7		24 .

© 2002 by John Wiley & Sons, Inc.

Name _____ Date _____

1-37 Writing About Numbers

We use numbers in "countless" ways every day. Write a short article about the ways you use numbers. Following are some examples of the ways numbers are used:

- Counting: 1, 2, 3, 4, 5 . . .
- Quantity: 12 eggs in a dozen
- Cost: $9.95
- Distance: 738 miles; 395 kilometers
- Size: The circle has a diameter of 20 feet. The field is 5 acres.
- Height: 5 feet 8 inches tall
- Weight: 120 pounds
- Time: 2:45 P.M.
- Position: She's third in line.
- Identification: His student number is 1074.

Of course, there are many other ways we use numbers each day. Along with the examples above, include as many in your article as you can.

Notes

_____

_____

_____

_____

_____

_____

_____

_____

1-38 Solving Tricky Math Problems

The problems below are "tricky" and require a lot of thinking. Solve the problems. **Note:** All of the problems deal with whole numbers.

1. Arrange the digits 2 and 3 to obtain the largest one-digit number. _____

2. Use the number 11 twice to obtain 121. _____

3. Express 100 by using 10 and a single digit. _____

4. Use only the numbers 4 and 5 to obtain the smallest whole number. _____

5. Express 25 in another way by using the digits 5 and 2. _____

6. Express 27 by using two threes. _____

7. Express the number 1 by using 4 and 0. _____

8. Use two slanted lines to represent the number 5. _____

9. When does 12 = 1? _____

10. Any number can be used 4 times to equal 0. Find the arrangement.

   _____

1-39 Scrambled Math Words

Unscramble the "scrambled" math terms on the left. *Note:* Each word relates to a whole number.

1. dad _____

2. mus _____

3. eroz _____

4. eon _____

5. strubcat _____

6. totienqu _____

7. dropuct _____

8. tpumlily _____

9. crefenfide _____

10. viddie _____

11. trafoc _____

12. visidro _____

13. slup _____

14. tipmulle _____

15. nopentex _____

16. perim _____

17. copsomite _____

18. blodue _____

19. dorun _____

20. suqare _____

1-40   Matching Signs and Symbols

Signs and symbols play an important part in mathematics. They are a type of short-hand, provided you know their meaning.

Directions: Math words and phrases are listed in the column on the left. Math symbols are listed in the column on the right. Write the letter of the math symbol before the word or phrase it represents. Find the message by writing the letter over the number of the math word or phrase that appears at the bottom of the page. The first one is done for you.

Math Word or Phrase	Symbol
1. __N__ addition	G. @
2. _____ subtraction	T. =
3. _____ multiplication	L. >
4. _____ division	I. ≈
5. _____ is equal to	O. x^a
6. _____ is approximately equal to	M. φ
7. _____ is not equal to	H. × or •
8. _____ is greater than	B. ( )
9. _____ is less than	U. ≤
10. _____ is greater than or equal to	F. –
11. _____ is less than or equal to	A. [ ]
12. _____ at	C. $
13. _____ number or pound	S. ÷
14. _____ parentheses	N. +
15. _____ braces	E. #
16. _____ empty set	Y. ≠
17. _____ x to the power	R. <
18. _____ dollar sign	P. ≥

```
__  __  __    __  __  __  __  N   __  __    __  __
 5   3  13    13   4   4  13   1  18  13    17   2

__  __  __    __  __  __  N   __  __    __  __
15   8   8     5   3   6   1  12   4     6   4

N   __  __  __  __  __  __      —
 1  11  16  14  13   9   4

__  __  __  __  __  __  __  __  __  __
10   7   5   3  15  12  17   9  15   4
```

Section 2

FRACTIONS, DECIMALS, AND PERCENTS

2-1   Finding Equivalent Fractions

For each fraction find an equivalent fraction in the Fraction Bank. **Note:** Not all fractions will be used. Write the equivalent fractions and their corresponding letters in the spaces provided. Then record the letters in order, starting with the first problem, in the spaces at the end of this activity. If you match the fractions correctly, the letters will spell a message. The first problem is done for you.

1. $\frac{1}{2} = \frac{8}{16}$ <u>F</u>

2. $\frac{7}{8} =$ ____ ____

3. $\frac{2}{3} =$ ____ ____

4. $\frac{3}{5} =$ ____ ____

5. $\frac{1}{4} =$ ____ ____

6. $\frac{2}{9} =$ ____ ____

7. $\frac{6}{7} =$ ____ ____

8. $\frac{4}{11} =$ ____ ____

9. $\frac{3}{4} =$ ____ ____

10. $\frac{3}{10} =$ ____ ____

11. $\frac{5}{8} =$ ____ ____

12. $\frac{1}{9} =$ ____ ____

13. $\frac{9}{10} =$ ____ ____

14. $\frac{8}{9} =$ ____ ____

15. $\frac{4}{5} =$ ____ ____

16. $\frac{7}{15} =$ ____ ____

17. $\frac{5}{12} =$ ____ ____

18. $\frac{1}{6} =$ ____ ____

19. $\frac{6}{11} =$ ____ ____

20. $\frac{4}{9} =$ ____ ____

21. $\frac{5}{6} =$ ____ ____

22. $\frac{3}{8} =$ ____ ____

23. $\frac{2}{7} =$ ____ ____

24. $\frac{5}{7} =$ ____ ____

25. $\frac{7}{13} =$ ____ ____

2-1   Finding Equivalent Fractions
(Continued)

Fraction Bank

R. $\frac{21}{24}$ A. $\frac{12}{40}$ M. $\frac{4}{17}$ J. $\frac{9}{26}$ T. $\frac{25}{100}$

O. $\frac{2}{12}$ F. $\frac{8}{16}$ I. $\frac{6}{27}$ O. $\frac{18}{21}$ Q. $\frac{9}{23}$

A. $\frac{32}{36}$ E. $\frac{3}{27}$ R. $\frac{28}{35}$ N. $\frac{12}{33}$ Y. $\frac{9}{55}$

F. $\frac{18}{33}$ P. $\frac{54}{60}$ S. $\frac{40}{96}$ U. $\frac{17}{42}$ W. $\frac{20}{45}$

S. $\frac{75}{100}$ A. $\frac{6}{9}$ O. $\frac{27}{72}$ C. $\frac{15}{25}$ R. $\frac{30}{48}$

D. $\frac{33}{40}$ T. $\frac{28}{60}$ B. $\frac{20}{21}$ S. $\frac{28}{52}$ K. $\frac{32}{45}$

H. $\frac{35}{42}$ M. $\frac{17}{35}$ L. $\frac{4}{14}$ G. $\frac{23}{27}$ E. $\frac{60}{84}$

F __ __ __ __ __ __ __ __   __ __ __ __

__ __ __ __ __ __   __ __   __ __ __ __ __ __ .

Name _____   Date _____

2-2   Simplifying Fractions

Match the fraction on the left with its simplified form on the right. Write the letter of the fraction on the line after the simplified form. When you are done, write the letters in order, starting from the top, to complete the statement below.

T.	$\frac{8}{16}$	$\frac{5}{6}$	_____
W.	$\frac{9}{12}$	$\frac{2}{3}$	_____
I.	$\frac{15}{18}$	$\frac{7}{27}$	_____
M.	$\frac{5}{5}$	$\frac{1}{9}$	_____
N.	$\frac{3}{27}$	$\frac{11}{18}$	_____
E.	$\frac{18}{32}$	$\frac{1}{3}$	_____
O.	$\frac{4}{12}$	$\frac{3}{4}$	_____
S.	$\frac{6}{30}$	$\frac{2}{9}$	_____
S.	$\frac{12}{48}$	$\frac{1}{4}$	_____
I.	$\frac{14}{54}$	$\frac{1}{2}$	_____
R.	$\frac{21}{33}$	$\frac{8}{9}$	_____
L.	$\frac{22}{36}$	$\frac{9}{16}$	_____
T.	$\frac{16}{18}$	$\frac{7}{11}$	_____
S.	$\frac{10}{15}$	1	_____
E.	$\frac{18}{81}$	$\frac{1}{5}$	_____

A simplifed fraction _____ _____   _____ _____

_____ _____ _____ _____ _____   _____ _____ _____ _____ _____.

2-3 Improper Fractions and Mixed Numbers

Match each improper fraction and mixed number on the left to its equivalent form on the right. Write the letter of each improper fraction or mixed number on the line after its equivalent form. When you are done matching, write the letters in order, starting from the top, to complete the statement below.

E. $\frac{22}{9}$	$\frac{59}{8}$	_____
O. $\frac{9}{3}$	$\frac{15}{4}$	_____
W. $4\frac{2}{3}$	$\frac{62}{7}$	_____
N. $\frac{33}{10}$	$6\frac{1}{3}$	_____
I. $3\frac{3}{4}$	$\frac{33}{7}$	_____
M. $\frac{22}{3}$	3	_____
D. $4\frac{5}{7}$	$\frac{75}{8}$	_____
O. $\frac{27}{5}$	$\frac{14}{3}$	_____
R. $9\frac{4}{5}$	$\frac{8}{1}$	_____
M. $7\frac{3}{8}$	$5\frac{2}{5}$	_____

© 2002 by John Wiley & Sons, Inc.

2-3 Improper Fractions and Mixed Numbers (Continued)

S. $\frac{39}{6}$ $5\frac{1}{2}$ ____

R. $9\frac{3}{8}$ $\frac{27}{4}$ ____

U. $\frac{51}{9}$ $3\frac{3}{10}$ ____

E. $\frac{38}{6}$ $5\frac{2}{3}$ ____

B. $4\frac{3}{11}$ $7\frac{1}{3}$ ____

L. $\frac{44}{8}$ $\frac{47}{11}$ ____

H. 8 $2\frac{4}{9}$ ____

E. $6\frac{3}{4}$ $\frac{49}{5}$ ____

X. $8\frac{6}{7}$ $6\frac{1}{2}$ ____

Improper fractions should always be expressed as

_____ _____ _____

_____ .

2-4 Comparing Fractions and Mixed Numbers

Compare the fractions and mixed numbers below and determine if the first is greater than (>), less than (<), or equal to (=) the second. Circle the correct symbol. After you are done, write the letters underneath the circled symbols in order, starting with the first problem, to complete the statement below.

1. $\frac{7}{8}$ > < = $\frac{3}{4}$
   F B C

2. $\frac{2}{3}$ > < = $\frac{15}{18}$
   O I S

3. $\frac{4}{7}$ > < = $\frac{7}{9}$
   U N T

4. $\frac{4}{5}$ > < = $\frac{24}{30}$
   R E D

5. $2\frac{3}{4}$ > < = $2\frac{4}{5}$
   T C A

6. $\frac{3}{10}$ > < = $\frac{6}{20}$
   B R O

7. $\frac{16}{19}$ > < = $\frac{34}{38}$
   I M W

8. $\frac{3}{4}$ > < = $\frac{7}{10}$
   M I S

9. $\frac{5}{16}$ > < = $\frac{3}{8}$
   R O A

10. $\frac{4}{6}$ > < = $\frac{5}{8}$
    N I U

11. $\frac{1}{6}$ > < = $\frac{1}{7}$
    D N E

12. $3\frac{5}{6}$ > < = $3\frac{3}{4}$
    E S T

13. $\frac{5}{8}$ > < = $\frac{7}{10}$
    W N M

14. $\frac{3}{3}$ > < = $\frac{12}{12}$
    U C O

15. $\frac{7}{8}$ > < = $\frac{4}{5}$
    M H P

16. $\frac{3}{8}$ > < = $\frac{2}{5}$
    O I R

17. $3\frac{2}{3}$ > < = $3\frac{3}{4}$
    D N E

18. $\frac{7}{10}$ > < = $\frac{5}{6}$
    R A L

19. $\frac{3}{5}$ > < = $\frac{4}{7}$
    T I W

20. $\frac{5}{6}$ > < = $\frac{11}{12}$
    E O P

21. $\frac{14}{15}$ > < = $\frac{4}{7}$
    R U A

22. $6\frac{7}{12}$ > < = $6\frac{4}{7}$
    S T N

A good strategy for comparing fractions is to

___ ___ ___ ___ ___   ___ ___ ___ ___ ___ ___ ___

___ ___ ___ ___ ___ ___ ___ ___ ___ ___ ___ ___ ___ ___ ___ ___.

2-5 Ordering Fractions

Write the fractions in each row from smallest to largest on the line beneath the row. Be sure to write their accompanying letters with them. Then write the letter of each fraction in order in the spaces at the bottom of the page to complete the statement.

R. $\dfrac{13}{24}$ T. $\dfrac{3}{4}$ W. $\dfrac{1}{2}$ I. $\dfrac{5}{8}$

1.

E. $\dfrac{3}{4}$ U. $\dfrac{11}{12}$ E. $\dfrac{2}{3}$ Q. $\dfrac{5}{6}$

2.

I. $\dfrac{1}{3}$ A. $\dfrac{11}{15}$ L. $\dfrac{23}{30}$ V. $\dfrac{3}{5}$

3.

T. $\dfrac{7}{10}$ N. $\dfrac{3}{5}$ E. $\dfrac{1}{3}$ F. $\dfrac{5}{6}$

4.

T. $\dfrac{3}{4}$ C. $\dfrac{5}{8}$ A. $\dfrac{7}{12}$ R. $\dfrac{9}{16}$

5.

N. $\dfrac{3}{4}$ O. $\dfrac{2}{3}$ I. $\dfrac{5}{8}$ S. $\dfrac{7}{9}$

6. _____

A good strategy for ordering fractions is to find common denominators and

__ __ __ __ __ __ __ __ __ __ __ __ __ __ __

__ __ __ __ __ __ __ __ __ .

2-6   Writing Word Names for Fractions

Write the word name for each fraction and mixed number. After writing each word name, write the indicated letter in the space at the end of the line. Then write the letters in order, starting with the first problem, to complete the statement. The first problem is done for you.

1. $\frac{1}{5}$ _____one fifth_____ seventh letter <u>T</u>

2. $\frac{3}{7}$ _____ second letter ___

3. $\frac{5}{6}$ _____ fourth letter ___

4. $\frac{1}{2}$ _____ sixth letter ___

5. $4\frac{6}{7}$ _____ fifth letter ___

6. $\frac{7}{8}$ _____ tenth letter ___

7. $\frac{10}{13}$ _____ sixth letter ___

8. $\frac{3}{10}$ _____ eighth letter ___

9. $5\frac{2}{3}$ _____ ninth letter ___

10. $\frac{3}{4}$ _____ seventh letter ___

2-6 Writing Word Names for Fractions
(Continued)

11. $9\frac{3}{5}$ _____   tenth letter   ___

12. $\frac{1}{3}$ _____   eighth letter   ___

13. $\frac{5}{8}$ _____   first letter   ___

14. $8\frac{3}{7}$ _____   eleventh letter   ___

15. $2\frac{1}{9}$ _____   fourth letter   ___

16. $\frac{9}{22}$ _____   thirteenth letter   ___

17. $\frac{3}{1}$ _____   first letter   ___

18. $\frac{5}{14}$ _____   seventh letter   ___

19. $\frac{17}{20}$ _____   first letter   ___

The word *fraction* is derived from __t_ ___ ___   ___ ___ ___ ___

___ ___ ___ ___   ___ ___ ___ ___ ___ ___ ___, which means "to break."

2-7   Fractions in Everyday Use

Complete the story below by filling in the blanks with a fraction, mixed number, or word related to fractions. Choose answers that will make the story realistic. Compare your completed story with the story of a friend.

Sheila's Busy Day

Sheila woke up at _____ to eight. Like most days, this one promised

to be busy. She rose quickly and hurried to get ready for school. She had

_____ hour before school started. Each of her classes was 45 minutes

or _____ of an hour long. She had three classes before lunch and

three after. Lunch divided her school day into two _____.

   After school Sheila had track practice for _____ hours. She was a

runner. After stretching she liked to warm up by jogging _____ times

around the track.

   When track practice was done, Sheila would ride her bike _____

miles to her piano teacher's house. Her lesson would last _____ hour.

   By the time Sheila arrived home, it was time for dinner. After dinner, she usually

spent _____ hours on homework, and then had _____

hours for talking on the phone with friends or watching TV. Sheila's day was a full

one.

2-8 Adding and Subtracting Fractions and Mixed Numbers Crossnumber Puzzle

Solve each problem and complete the puzzle. Be sure to simplify all answers. When you write your answers in the puzzle, each digit and fraction should occupy one box. Number 6 Across is done for you as an example.

Across

2. $3\frac{1}{3} + 3\frac{1}{4} + 2\frac{1}{6} =$ _____

6. $11\frac{2}{7} + 4\frac{1}{3} = 15\frac{13}{21}$ _____

7. $1\frac{4}{7} + \frac{2}{9} =$ _____

9. $22\frac{4}{5} - \frac{2}{3} =$ _____

11. $25\frac{1}{2} - 15\frac{2}{4} =$ _____

12. $14\frac{1}{6} + \frac{3}{10} =$ _____

16. $1\frac{1}{5} + 2\frac{9}{40} =$ _____

Down

1. $\frac{3}{5} + \frac{1}{15} =$ _____

2. $9\frac{4}{5} - 1\frac{1}{6} =$ _____

3. $\frac{5}{8} - \frac{5}{24} =$ _____

4. $15\frac{1}{4} - \frac{1}{4} =$ _____

5. $13\frac{2}{3} - 2\frac{1}{2} =$ _____

8. $12\frac{1}{4} + \frac{3}{5} =$ _____

10. $6\frac{1}{8} + 4\frac{5}{12} + \frac{1}{4} =$ _____

13. $3\frac{3}{10} + 1\frac{4}{15} =$ _____

14. $4\frac{1}{8} + 2\frac{3}{10} =$ _____

15. $\frac{1}{6} + \frac{7}{10} =$ _____

17. $\frac{1}{3} - \frac{5}{21} =$ _____

2-8   Adding and Subtracting Fractions and Mixed Numbers Crossnumber Puzzle (Continued)

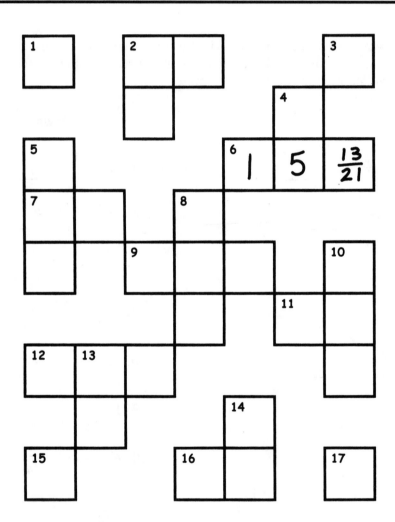

2-9 Subtracting Mixed Numbers, with Regrouping

Fill in the boxes with the correct number to complete the subtraction problems. Be sure your answers are simplified.

1. $5\frac{1}{3} = 5\frac{5}{\square} = \square\frac{\square}{\square}$
    $- 3\frac{4}{5} = 3\frac{12}{\square} = 3\frac{12}{\square}$
    $\phantom{- 3\frac{4}{5} = 3\frac{12}{\square} = } \square\frac{8}{\square}$

2. $7\frac{2}{5} = 7\frac{8}{\square} = 6\frac{\square}{\square}$
    $- 2\frac{3}{4} = 2\frac{15}{\square} = 2\frac{15}{\square}$
    $\phantom{- 2\frac{3}{4} = 2\frac{15}{\square} = } 4\frac{13}{\square}$

3. $11\frac{2}{9} = 11\frac{4}{\square} = \square\frac{22}{18}$
    $- 6\frac{5}{6} = 6\frac{\square}{18} = 6\frac{\square}{18}$
    $\phantom{- 6\frac{5}{6} = 6\frac{\square}{18} = } 4\frac{7}{\square}$

4. $8\frac{3}{\square} = 8\frac{6}{14} = 7\frac{\square}{14}$
    $- 7\frac{9}{14} = 7\frac{9}{\square} = 7\frac{9}{\square}$
    $\phantom{- 7\frac{9}{14} = 7\frac{9}{\square} = } \dfrac{\square}{14}$

5. $\square\frac{1}{8} = \square\frac{\square}{56} = 8\frac{\square}{56}$
    $- 6\frac{2}{7} = 6\frac{\square}{56} = 6\frac{16}{\square}$
    $\phantom{- 6\frac{2}{7} = 6\frac{\square}{56} = } \square\frac{47}{\square}$

6. $21\frac{3}{8} = 21\frac{\square}{24} = \square\frac{33}{24}$
    $- \square\frac{5}{6} = \square\frac{\square}{24} = \square\frac{\square}{24}$
    $\phantom{- \square\frac{5}{6} = \square\frac{\square}{24} = } 10\frac{13}{24}$

7. $\square = 7\frac{3}{\square}$
    $- 3\frac{2}{\square} = 3\frac{2}{\square}$
    $\phantom{- 3\frac{2}{\square} = } \square\frac{1}{3}$

8. $12\frac{2}{9} = 12\frac{\square}{18} = \square\frac{\square}{18}$
    $- \square\frac{13}{18} = \square\frac{13}{18} = \square\frac{13}{18}$
    $\phantom{- \square\frac{13}{18} = \square\frac{13}{18} = } 3\frac{\square}{18} = 3\frac{1}{\square}$

2-9 Subtracting Mixed Numbers, with Regrouping (Continued)

9. $8\frac{3}{16} = 8\frac{3}{16} = \boxed{}\frac{\boxed{}}{16}$

   $-\boxed{}\frac{1}{4} = \boxed{}\frac{4}{16} = \boxed{}\frac{4}{16}$

   $\overline{}$

   $4\frac{\boxed{}}{16}$

10. $19\frac{5}{12} = 19\frac{5}{12} = 18\frac{\boxed{}}{12}$

    $-11\frac{3}{\boxed{}} = 11\frac{\boxed{}}{\boxed{}} = 11\frac{\boxed{}}{\boxed{}}$

    $\overline{}$

    $\boxed{}\frac{\boxed{}}{12} = \boxed{}\frac{\boxed{}}{3}$

11. $13\frac{2}{15} = 13\frac{4}{\boxed{}} = 12\frac{34}{\boxed{}}$

    $-8\frac{5}{6} = 8\frac{\boxed{}}{30} = 8\frac{\boxed{}}{30}$

    $\overline{}$

    $\boxed{}\frac{9}{30} = \boxed{}\frac{\boxed{}}{\boxed{}}$

12. $10\frac{\boxed{}}{\boxed{}} = 10\frac{\boxed{}}{\boxed{}} = 9\frac{13}{\boxed{}}$

    $-7\frac{1}{2} = 7\frac{5}{10} = 7\frac{5}{10}$

    $\overline{}$

    $2\frac{\boxed{}}{10} = 2\frac{\boxed{}}{\boxed{}}$

Name _____   Date _____

2-10 Fractions and Magic Squares

In a magic square the sum of the numbers in each row, column, and diagonal equals the same number. This number is called the magic number. The magic square in the example has a magic number of $3\frac{3}{4}$. Complete the magic squares that follow.

Example:

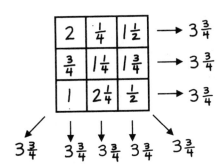

1.

	$1\frac{1}{12}$	
$\frac{3}{4}$		$\frac{5}{6}$

The magic number is $3\frac{1}{4}$.

2.

$\frac{7}{8}$		$1\frac{3}{8}$	
		1	$\frac{3}{8}$
$1\frac{1}{2}$	$1\frac{7}{8}$		$\frac{5}{8}$
$\frac{1}{8}$			

The magic number is $4\frac{1}{4}$.

3.

$\frac{1}{2}$			$3\frac{2}{3}$	
	$1\frac{1}{3}$	$3\frac{1}{2}$	$2\frac{1}{3}$	$\frac{1}{3}$
	$4\frac{1}{6}$	$2\frac{1}{6}$		$3\frac{1}{6}$
	2	$\frac{5}{6}$	3	
$1\frac{5}{6}$		$2\frac{5}{6}$		

The magic number is $10\frac{5}{6}$.

2-11   Multiplying Simple Fractions, 1

Multiply the fractions below. Be sure to simplify your answers.

1. $\dfrac{1}{2} \times \dfrac{3}{4} \times \dfrac{2}{3} =$ _____

2. $\dfrac{2}{5} \times \dfrac{7}{8} \times \dfrac{5}{6} =$ _____

3. $\dfrac{2}{3} \times \dfrac{1}{5} \times \dfrac{5}{8} =$ _____

4. $\dfrac{4}{7} \times \dfrac{7}{12} \times \dfrac{3}{4} =$ _____

5. $\dfrac{8}{9} \times \dfrac{3}{4} \times \dfrac{1}{4} =$ _____

6. $\dfrac{1}{6} \times \dfrac{3}{8} \times \dfrac{2}{3} =$ _____

7. $\dfrac{3}{5} \times \dfrac{5}{15} \times \dfrac{10}{12} \times \dfrac{3}{4} =$ _____

8. $\dfrac{5}{12} \times \dfrac{2}{7} \times \dfrac{9}{10} \times \dfrac{7}{18} =$ _____

9. $\dfrac{4}{5} \times \dfrac{5}{8} \times \dfrac{7}{20} \times \dfrac{10}{21} =$ _____

10. $\dfrac{7}{9} \times \dfrac{10}{14} \times \dfrac{7}{10} \times \dfrac{3}{7} =$ _____

Add your answers and simplify. If your sum is $1\dfrac{1}{2}$, you have most likely multiplied correctly.

2-12 Multiplying Simple Fractions, II

Create multiplication problems of simple fractions to equal each answer below. The first problem is done for you.

1. $\dfrac{5}{18} = \dfrac{5}{6} \times \dfrac{1}{3}$

2. $\dfrac{2}{7}$

3. $\dfrac{7}{36}$

4. $\dfrac{1}{2}$

5. $\dfrac{35}{48}$

6. $\dfrac{3}{10}$

7. $\dfrac{1}{14}$

8. $\dfrac{2}{13}$

9. $\dfrac{4}{9}$

10. 1

11. $1\dfrac{1}{2}$

12. $2\dfrac{1}{3}$

13. $3\dfrac{3}{4}$

14. $6\dfrac{2}{5}$

15. $1\dfrac{7}{8}$

16. $2\dfrac{1}{6}$

17. $2\dfrac{7}{10}$

18. $6\dfrac{2}{3}$

19. $5\dfrac{5}{8}$

20. $3\dfrac{1}{8}$

Name _____   **Date** _____

2-13 Multiplying Fractions and Mixed Numbers

Match each problem on the left with its simplified answer on the right. Write the answer on the space after the problem. Matching problems and answers correctly will reveal the name of an animal's collective group. For example, a group of sheep is called a flock. The first problem is done for you.

1. $2\frac{1}{2} \times 1\frac{1}{3} = \quad 3\frac{1}{3}$ business: _____   ferrets $1\frac{7}{10}$ knot

2. $10 \times 1\frac{1}{10} = $ _____: wolves $3\frac{1}{8}$ host

3. $\frac{2}{3} \times 2\frac{11}{20} = $ _____: toads 9 troop

4. $3\frac{3}{4} \times \frac{2}{3} = $ _____: elks $9\frac{5}{8}$ bed

5. $5\frac{2}{3} \times 4\frac{1}{2} = $ _____: fish $5\frac{1}{2}$ clutch

6. $1\frac{1}{2} \times 2\frac{1}{3} = $ _____: bees 27 gaggle

7. $2\frac{2}{3} \times 1\frac{3}{4} = $ _____: lions $2\frac{2}{15}$ army

8. $2\frac{3}{4} \times 3\frac{1}{3} = $ _____: whales $8\frac{1}{2}$ band

9. $1\frac{4}{5} \times 15 = $ _____: geese $9\frac{1}{6}$ pod

2-13 Multiplying Fractions and Mixed Numbers (Continued)

10. $1\frac{1}{4} \times 2\frac{1}{2}$ = _____ :   sparrows $3\frac{1}{3}$ business

11. $2\frac{2}{3} \times \frac{4}{5}$ = _____ :   frogs $19\frac{1}{2}$ brace

12. $6\frac{3}{8} \times 1\frac{1}{3}$ = _____ :   gorillas $2\frac{1}{2}$ gang

13. $2\frac{1}{3} \times 2\frac{5}{8}$ = _____ :   peacocks   11 pack

14. $2 \times 2\frac{3}{4}$ = _____ :   chicks $6\frac{1}{4}$ tribe

15. $3\frac{3}{5} \times 2\frac{1}{2}$ = _____ :   kangaroos $3\frac{1}{2}$ hive

16. $1\frac{3}{4} \times 5\frac{1}{2}$ = _____ :   clams $16\frac{1}{2}$ bevy

17. $2\frac{1}{4} \times 8\frac{2}{3}$ = _____ :   ducks $25\frac{1}{2}$ school

18. $3\frac{1}{3} \times 1\frac{7}{8}$ = _____ :   goats   12 herd

19. $6\frac{3}{4} \times 2\frac{4}{9}$ = _____ :   swans $6\frac{1}{8}$ muster

20. $2\frac{1}{2} \times 4\frac{4}{5}$ = _____ :   cattle $4\frac{2}{3}$ pride

Name _____   **Date** _____

2-14 Dividing Simple Fractions

Divide the fractions and be sure to simplify all answers. Write the letter of the problem above its answer to complete the statement below.

P. $\dfrac{3}{5} \div \dfrac{6}{7} =$ _____

L. $\dfrac{2}{3} \div \dfrac{3}{4} =$ _____

O. $\dfrac{1}{2} \div \dfrac{3}{8} =$ _____

E. $\dfrac{7}{8} \div \dfrac{14}{24} =$ _____

T. $\dfrac{6}{11} \div \dfrac{3}{22} =$ _____

R. $\dfrac{4}{5} \div \dfrac{4}{9} =$ _____

C. $\dfrac{2}{5} \div \dfrac{13}{15} =$ _____

D. $\dfrac{9}{10} \div \dfrac{4}{5} =$ _____

O. $\dfrac{1}{7} \div 7 =$ _____

H. $\dfrac{7}{8} \div \dfrac{5}{9} =$ _____

S. $\dfrac{7}{15} \div \dfrac{5}{24} =$ _____

F. $\dfrac{8}{9} \div \dfrac{4}{7} =$ _____

I. $\dfrac{3}{16} \div \dfrac{6}{7} =$ _____

V. $\dfrac{14}{15} \div \dfrac{7}{12} =$ _____

A. $\dfrac{11}{16} \div \dfrac{22}{27} =$ _____

R. $\dfrac{7}{10} \div \dfrac{21}{25} =$ _____

O. $\dfrac{3}{8} \div 9 =$ _____

I. $\dfrac{12}{25} \div \dfrac{3}{20} =$ _____

E. $\dfrac{7}{18} \div \dfrac{14}{15} =$ _____

R. $\dfrac{8}{15} \div \dfrac{6}{35} =$ _____

C. $6 \div \dfrac{10}{13} =$ _____

I. $\dfrac{3}{20} \div \dfrac{18}{45} =$ _____

To divide fractions, you must multiply by the

_____ _____ _____ _____ _____ _____ _____ _____ _____ _____
$\dfrac{5}{6}$ $\dfrac{5}{12}$ $\dfrac{6}{13}$ $3\dfrac{1}{5}$ $\dfrac{7}{10}$ $3\dfrac{1}{9}$ $1\dfrac{1}{3}$ $7\dfrac{4}{5}$ $\dfrac{27}{32}$ $\dfrac{8}{9}$

_____ _____ _____ _____ _____
$\dfrac{1}{24}$ $1\dfrac{5}{9}$ 4 $1\dfrac{23}{40}$ $1\dfrac{1}{2}$

_____ _____ _____ _____ _____ _____ _____ .
$1\dfrac{1}{8}$ $\dfrac{7}{32}$ $1\dfrac{3}{5}$ $\dfrac{3}{8}$ $2\dfrac{6}{25}$ $\dfrac{1}{49}$ $1\dfrac{4}{5}$

© 2002 by John Wiley & Sons, Inc.

Dividing Fractions
and Mixed Numbers

Divide the problems on the left and match them with their answers on the right. Write the answer on the space after each problem. Matching problems and answers correctly will also match the name of the animal with the name of its young. For example, young ducks are called ducklings. The first problem is done for you.

1. $3\frac{3}{4} \div \frac{3}{5} = $ _____ $6\frac{1}{4}$ joey: _____   kangaroo   12 baby

2. $18 \div 2\frac{2}{5} = $ _____ :   zebra $3\frac{2}{3}$ nestling

3. $6\frac{2}{3} \div \frac{2}{3} = $ _____ :   hawk   25 spat

4. $5\frac{1}{3} \div \frac{4}{9} = $ _____ :   monkey $1\frac{17}{28}$ elver

5. $3\frac{1}{3} \div 2\frac{4}{5} = $ _____ :   eagle $\frac{2}{3}$ fry

6. $17\frac{1}{2} \div \frac{7}{10} = $ _____ :   oyster $1\frac{13}{17}$ calf

7. $1\frac{1}{2} \div 1\frac{7}{8} = $ _____ :   turkey $1\frac{1}{9}$ gosling

8. $19\frac{1}{4} \div 5\frac{1}{4} = $ _____ :   bird $7\frac{1}{2}$ colt

9. $2\frac{3}{4} \div 1\frac{1}{2} = $ _____ :   swan $2\frac{1}{4}$ cub

10. $2\frac{3}{11} \div 3\frac{1}{3} = $ _____ :   beaver $1\frac{4}{21}$ eaglet

11. $7\frac{1}{2} \div 4\frac{1}{4} = $ _____ :   elephant $\frac{4}{5}$ poult

12. $1\frac{2}{3} \div 1\frac{1}{2} = $ _____ :   goose $\frac{15}{22}$ kit

13. $5\frac{5}{8} \div 2\frac{1}{2} = $ _____ :   tiger $6\frac{1}{4}$ joey

14. $4\frac{2}{7} \div 2\frac{2}{3} = $ _____ :   eel $1\frac{5}{6}$ cygnet

15. $6\frac{1}{4} \div 9\frac{3}{8} = $ _____ :   fish   10 eyas

75

2-16 Dividing Mixed Numbers

Using the digits given, create mixed-number division problems that result in the provided answer. The problems are partially done for you.

1. Use each of the digits 1, 2, 3, 4, 5, and 6 only once to complete the following.

$$1\frac{\Box}{\Box} \div \Box\frac{5}{6} = \frac{21}{34}$$

2. Use each of the digits 1, 2, 3, 7, 8, and 9 only once to complete the following.

$$\Box\frac{8}{\Box} \div 2\frac{\Box}{\Box} = \frac{7}{9}$$

3. Use each of the digits 2, 3, 5, 7, 8, and 9 only once to complete the following.

$$9\frac{\Box}{\Box} \div 2\frac{\Box}{\Box} = 3\frac{83}{104}$$

2-17 Fraction Crossnumber Puzzle–All Operations

Solve each problem and complete the puzzle. Be sure to simplify all answers. When you write your answers in the puzzle, each digit and fraction should occupy one box. Number 4 Across is done for you as an example.

Across

3. $2\frac{7}{8} \times 3\frac{1}{3} =$ _____

4. $15\frac{3}{5} - 2\frac{3}{10} = \underline{13\frac{3}{10}}$

6. $12 \div \frac{2}{5} =$ _____

8. $\frac{2}{5} \div \frac{1}{3} =$ _____

10. $2\frac{1}{12} + 4\frac{7}{8} =$ _____

14. $1\frac{9}{16} \div \frac{3}{8} =$ _____

15. $35\frac{2}{5} + 75\frac{6}{10} =$ _____

17. $6 \div 1\frac{1}{3} =$ _____

Down

1. $4\frac{1}{3} + 6\frac{2}{3} =$ _____

2. $\frac{3}{5} - \frac{1}{2} =$ _____

3. $84\frac{7}{9} + 5\frac{4}{9} =$ _____

5. $15\frac{5}{6} \div 5 =$ _____

7. $12\frac{4}{5} \times \frac{5}{8} =$ _____

8. $3\frac{1}{4} - 1\frac{1}{2} =$ _____

9. $5 - 3\frac{1}{24} =$ _____

11. $\frac{1}{5} \div \frac{2}{3} =$ _____

12. $25\frac{1}{4} - 10\frac{3}{4} =$ _____

13. $3\frac{1}{5} \times 3\frac{7}{16} =$ _____

16. $\frac{3}{5} + \frac{2}{3} =$ _____

18. $\frac{2}{5} + \frac{1}{6} =$ _____

2-17 Fraction Crossnumber Puzzle–All Operations (Continued)

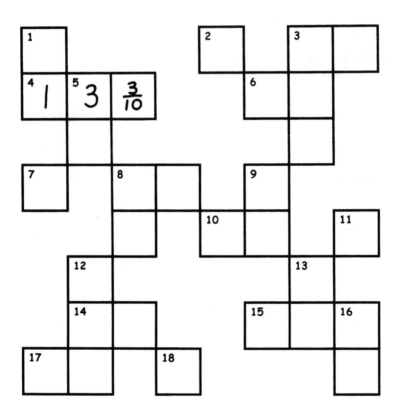

2-18 Using Decimal Word Names

Write the letter of the word name in the space before the decimal number so that the name and number match. When you are done, read the letters down from the top. If your answers are correct, you will have spelled the name of the first European mathematician to use decimal fractions. The year was 1585.

1. _____ 0.75   S. sixty-two and fifty-three hundredths

2. _____ 0.753   E. five hundred three ten-thousandths

3. _____ 0.003   O. five and three tenths

4. _____ 5.3   N. five hundredths

5. _____ 0.053   S. seventy-five hundredths

6. _____ 62.53   T. sixty-two thousand seven hundred fifty-three hundred-thousandths

7. _____ 0.62753   I. sixty-two and seven hundred fifty-three thousandths

8. _____ 0.0503   V. five and three hundredths

9. _____ 5.03   I. seven hundred fifty-three thousandths

10. _____ 62.753   N. fifty-three thousandths

11. _____ 0.05   M. three thousandths

Now write the letter of the word name before the decimal number it matches to find the region of Europe in which this man was born.

12. _____ 1.06   E. four thousand three ten-thousandths

13. _____ 0.003   A. forty-three and forty-three thousandths

14. _____ 43.043   S. one hundred six ten-thousandths

15. _____ 0.1   F. one and six hundredths

16. _____ 43.003   N. one tenth

17. _____ 0.4003   L. three thousandths

18. _____ 1.063   R. one and sixty-three thousandths

19. _____ 0.0106   D. forty-three and three thousandths

2-19 Decimal Place Value

Study the example and write the place value of each bold digit of the problems that follow. Then write the indicated letter of the answer of each problem in order, starting with the first problem, to complete the statement below. The first problem is done for you.

2.378942 = 2 ones, 3 tenths, 7 hundredths, 8 thousandths, 9 ten-thousandths, 4 hundred-thousandths, 2 millionths

1.	0.47521	thousandths	sixth letter	a
2.	0.8927546	_____	third letter	___
3.	7.4035	_____	sixth letter	___
4.	0.4572	_____	eighth letter	___
5.	3.00476874	_____	second letter	___
6.	8.04	_____	second letter	___
7.	0.4620	_____	first letter	___
8.	0.2634	_____	sixth letter	___
9.	4.60764312	_____	fifth letter	___
10.	0.24891062	_____	first letter	___
11.	0.4897	_____	first letter	___
12.	23.07	_____	first letter	___
13.	0.0078	_____	sixth letter	___
14.	9.724916	_____	first letter	___
15.	1.94745615	_____	first letter	___
16.	234.06	_____	second letter	___
17.	0.9286	_____	ninth letter	___
18.	4.623	_____	third letter	___
19.	0.009	_____	fifth letter	___
20.	16.142	_____	first letter	___
21.	0.92	_____	sixth letter	___
22.	15.6097340	_____	third letter	___

The word *decimal* is derived from "decem," _a_   ___ ___ ___ ___ ___

___ ___ ___ ___   ___ ___ ___ ___   ___ ___ ___ ___ ___

___ ___ ___ .

Name _____   Date _____

2-20 Comparing Decimals

Compare each pair of decimals and write the appropriate sign, greater than (>), less than (<), or equal to (=), between them.

After you have written the signs, write the letter of the larger decimal of each pair in order, starting with the first problem, to complete the statement below. If the decimals of any pair are equal, do not write either of the letters.

1. 0.643 _____ 0.65
     S   U

2. 2.602 _____ 2.603
     E   N

3. 1.84 _____ 1.8392
     D   R

4. 74.8404 _____ 74.84114
        V   E

5. 0.734 _____ 0.7340
     E   U

6. 2.874 _____ 2.88
     T   R

7. 23.0492 _____ 2.30492
       S   U

8. 0.26461 _____ 0.264600
      T   S

9. 46.045 _____ 46.45
      U   A

10. 3.5009 _____ 3.509
       R   N

11. 11.02 _____ 1.202
       D   A

12. 13.64 _____ 13.639
       P   T

13. 0.2790 _____ 0.0279
       L   S

14. 3.8 _____ 3.800
      O   C

15. 0.6408 _____ 0.641
       H   A

16. 1.00538 _____ 1.0054
       O   C

17. 0.61 _____ 0.6007
      E   O

18. 9.40 _____ 9.400
      U   H

19. 0.0041 _____ 0.0400
       L   V

20. 12.427 _____ 12.0427
       A   R

21. 64.25 _____ 64.205
       L   W

22. 8.7592 _____ 8.76
       I   U

23. 0.0620 _____ 0.062
       G   S

24. 3.045 _____ 3.0400
       E   H

To compare decimals you must

___ ___ ___ ___ ___ ___ ___ ___ ___ ___ ___ ___

___ ___ ___ ___ ___ ___   ___ ___ ___ ___ ___ ___.

81

2-21 Ordering Decimals

Arrange the decimals in order from smallest to largest. When you are done, write the letter of each decimal, in order, to complete the statement.

L. 0.753	**E.** 0.080	**A.** 0.0401	**D.** 1.007
A. 0.023	**T.** 0.00600	**R.** 0.805	**I.** 0.15
O. 0.8	**O.** 0.00620	**S.** 0.7539	**E.** 0.1
A. 0.306	**M.** 0.230	**N.** 0.045	**I.** 0.754
G. 0.06020	**R.** 0.04	**R.** 10.01	**C.** 0.10124
D. 0.09	**E.** 3.0	**R.** 0.034	**N.** 0.76

_____

_____

_____

_____

Understanding place value is necessary

___ ___ ___ ___ ___ ___ ___ ___ ___

___ ___ ___ ___ ___ ___ ___ ___ ___ ___

___ ___ ___ ___ ___ .

Name _____   Date _____

2-22 Rounding Decimals

Round each decimal to the place indicated. Then follow the directions at the bottom of the page.

1. Round 0.473 to the nearest tenth. _____

2. Round 7.0463 to the nearest hundredth. _____

3. Round 0.804 to the nearest whole number. _____

4. Round 3.5621 to the nearest hundredth. _____

5. Round 0.709649 to the nearest thousandth. _____

6. Round 0.8069472 to the nearest ten-thousandth. _____

7. Round 217.623 to the nearest hundredth. _____

8. Round 2.938 to the nearest hundredth. _____

9. Round 31.098 to the nearest whole number. _____

10. Round 0.683 to the nearest tenth. _____

11. Round 50.069 to the nearest hundredth. _____

12. Round 0.48392 to the nearest ten-thousandth. _____

13. Round 0.20156 to the nearest thousandth. _____

14. Round 10.4039767 to the nearest hundred-thousandth. _____

15. Round 0.4962 to the nearest hundredth. _____

16. Round 48.36952 to the nearest ten-thousandth. _____

17. Round 39.52 to the nearest whole number. _____

18. Round 11.876 to the nearest hundredth. _____

19. Round 254.750 to the nearest hundredth. _____

20. Round 0.999 to the nearest whole number. _____

Add the last digit of each answer. If your sum is 85, you have most likely rounded correctly.

2-23 Expressing Fractions as Decimals

The cards of a math game are given on the next page. The game is similar to Bingo, but fractions are called instead of numbers and letters. The game card also differs. Each card contains decimals.

The rules are simple. When a fraction is called, the player crosses out the decimal on the card that is equivalent to each fraction. The object is to cross out five decimals in a row vertically, horizontally, or diagonally. **Note:** Decimal equivalents of fractions may appear on more than one card.

Assume that the following fractions have been called.

$$\frac{1}{4} \quad \frac{5}{6} \quad \frac{1}{6} \quad \frac{7}{10} \quad \frac{1}{8} \quad \frac{3}{20} \quad \frac{1}{2}$$

$$\frac{17}{100} \quad \frac{2}{3} \quad \frac{7}{8} \quad \frac{1}{20} \quad \frac{4}{10} \quad \frac{3}{8} \quad \frac{4}{5}$$

$$\frac{1}{3} \quad \frac{3}{10} \quad \frac{5}{8} \quad \frac{9}{10} \quad \frac{1}{5} \quad \frac{3}{100} \quad \frac{3}{4} \quad \frac{1}{10}$$

Which card wins? Show how the win was achieved by circling the decimal equivalents of the fractions. Draw a line through the five in a row.

Name _____   Date _____

2-23 Expressing Fractions as Decimals
(Continued)

Card 1

0.66	0.2	$0.8\overline{3}$	0.05	0.01
0.125	0.375	0.6	0.4	0.25
0.37	0.15	0.625	0.03	1
0.3	0.35	0.1	$0.\overline{6}$	0.28
0.18	0.45	0.5	1.5	0.8

Card 2

0.37	0.1	0.375	0.7	0.5
0.45	0.75	0.35	0.625	1.5
0.25	0.66	$0.\overline{3}$	0.03	0.15
0.18	0.6	1	0.28	0.8
0.01	0.9	0.05	0.17	0.4

Card 3

0.875	0.15	1	0.3	0.4
0.37	0.8	0.125	0.28	0.17
$0.1\overline{6}$	1.5	0.375	0.7	0.6
0.45	0.5	0.01	$0.8\overline{3}$	0.66
0.18	0.35	0.9	0.2	0.1

2-24 Expressing Decimals as Fractions

Match the decimal with its equivalent fraction. Write the letter of the fraction on the space before its equivalent decimal. After matching, write the letters in order, starting from the top, to complete the statement below.

1. _____ 0.63   R. $\frac{11}{20}$

2. _____ 1.3   I. $\frac{3}{4}$

3. _____ 0.55   H. $\frac{1}{2}$

4. _____ 0.75   P. $5\frac{16}{25}$

5. _____ 0.005   H. $1\frac{3}{10}$

6. _____ 0.60   S. $\frac{1}{200}$

7. _____ 0.225   O. $\frac{9}{40}$

8. _____ 5.64   C. $\frac{63}{100}$

9. _____ 0.500   T. $\frac{3}{5}$

10. _____ 0.875   L. $5\frac{9}{20}$

11. _____ 1.03   E. $\frac{7}{8}$

12. _____ 0.57   U. $\frac{1}{25}$

13. _____ 5.45   C. $\frac{57}{100}$

14. _____ 5.4   S. $\frac{3}{25}$

15. _____ 0.087   I. $\frac{1}{5}$

16. _____ 0.2   R. $1\frac{3}{100}$

17. _____ 0.04   A. $5\frac{2}{5}$

18. _____ 0.120   V. $\frac{87}{1000}$

© 2002 by John Wiley & Sons, Inc.

In 1593, ____ ____ ____ ____ ____ ____ ____ ____ ____ ____

____ ____ ____ ____ ____ ____ ____, a German mathematician, was the first European to use a decimal point for decimal fractions.

2-25 Adding and Subtracting Decimals

Find the missing decimals and complete the addition and subtraction problems. Write the letter of each problem above its answer to complete the statement below.

P. 42.4
    + ____
    71.0

S. 54.8
    + ____
    127.37

G. 0.158
    + ____
    0.821

A. 29.47
    + ____
    30.302

T. _____ + 3.88 = 5.48

I. 0.2487 + _____ = 1.0077

E. 19.53 + _____ = 62.3

E. _____ + 0.463 = 3.363

T. _____ + 6.732 = 7.636

E. 7.42 + _____ = 8.3164

D. _____ + 16.83 = 46.38

M. 53.72 + _____ = 142.42

A. 45.296 + _____ = 53.336

L. 3.34
    - ____
    1.69

B. 6.010
    - ____
    2.94

N. 5.20
    - ____
    3.47

L. 75.07
    - ____
    17.49

I. 0.525 – _____ = 0.386

M. 8.0 – _____ = 3.103

U. 4.5 – _____ = 4.12

C. 9.4 – _____ = 6.3255

D. _____ – 0.892 = 2.514

N. _____ – 15.218 = 20.829

I. _____ – 0.7621 = 19.2779

O. 0.084 – _____ = 0.037

S. 22.046 – _____ = 11.3136

To add and subtract decimals, the

29.55	0.8964	3.0745	0.759	4.897	8.04	57.58			
28.6	0.047	0.139	1.73	1.60	10.7324	88.7	0.38	72.57	0.904
3.07	42.77	0.832	1.65	20.04	0.663	36.047	2.9	3.406	

2-26 Adding and Subtracting Decimals—A Magic Square

In a magic square the sum of the numbers in each row, column, and diagonal equals the same number. This number is called the magic number. The magic square in the example has a magic number of 1.5. Complete the magic squares that follow.

Example:

0.8	0.1	0.6
0.3	0.5	0.7
0.4	0.9	0.2

→ 1.5
→ 1.5
→ 1.5

1.5 1.5 1.5 1.5 1.5

1.

3.2		2.4
		0.8

The magic number is 6.

2.

0.8	11.2		9.6
12			
	4	12.8	
6.4			10.4

The magic number is 27.2.

3.

10.2		0.6	4.8	9
13.8			8.4	9.6
	3.6	7.8		13.2
	7.2	11.4		
		15		5.4

The magic number is 39.

2-27 Making Change

Given the cost and payment, determine the amount of change necessary. Then determine the fewest dollars and coins for making the change. (Avoid using the $2 bill, which is uncommon.) The first problem is done for you.

1. Cost: $19.95   Payment: $20   Change: _____ $.05 = 1 _____
   nickel

2. Cost: $4.79   Payment: $10   Change: _____

3. Cost: $21.23   Payment: $30   Change: _____

4. Cost: $3.64   Payment: $5   Change: _____

5. Cost: $10.57   Payment: $11   Change: _____

6. Cost: $35.07   Payment: $40   Change: _____

7. Cost: $7.29   Payment: $20   Change: _____

8. Cost $44.67   Payment: $60   Change: _____

9. Cost: $62.23   Payment: $70   Change: _____

10. Cost: $11.65   Payment: $20   Change: _____

11. Cost: $83.57   Payment: $100   Change: _____

12. Cost: $26.91   Payment: $30   Change: _____

2-28 Multiplying Decimals

Multiply the decimals. If your answer extends beyond the thousandths place, round your answer to the nearest thousandth. Write the letter of the problem above its answer to complete the message below.

C.   2.3
    ×7.1

P.   0.42
    ×0.57

O. 0.62
    × 7.7

T.   96
    ×3.4

L.   0.871
    × 3.9

N.   5.12
    × 8.7

D.   63.8
    × 7.5

E.   5.47
    ×0.83

L.   0.926
    × 0.38

C.   70.2
    ×0.86

H.   6.25
    × 6.9

E.   2.39
    ×0.71

R.   14.6
    × 9.3

T.   0.806
    × 0.045

Y.   6.47
    ×   39

M.   0.984
    ×0.067

E. 8.046 × 0.082 = _____

A. 4.753 × 0.076 = _____

I. 0.9204 × 0.063 = _____

O. 47.34 × 0.207 = _____

C. 8.029 × 0.0063 = _____

T. 0.06041 × 0.073 = _____

I. 5.407 × 0.368 = _____

R. 0.462 × 0.806 = _____

When multiplying decimals, you must position ____ ____ ____
                                             326.4 43.125 0.660

____ ____ ____ ____ ____ ____ ____
478.5 1.697 16.33 1.990 0.066 0.361 3.397

____ ____ ____ ____ ____
0.239 4.774 0.058 44.544 0.036

____ ____ ____ ____ ____ ____ ____ ____ ____.
60.372 9.799 135.78 0.372 4.540 0.051 0.004 0.352 252.33

2-29 Dividing Decimals by Whole Numbers and Decimals

Divide the decimals. Write the letter of the problem above its answer to complete the statement below. If necessary, round your answer to the hundredths place.

T. $9\overline{)2.79}$ K. $6\overline{)84.12}$ H. $0.5\overline{)2.560}$ I. $0.9\overline{).8106}$

O. $0.7\overline{)64.38}$ N. $54\overline{)38.88}$ R. $64\overline{)1.344}$ F. $0.04\overline{)5.792}$

A. $0.07\overline{)1.652}$ B. $0.04\overline{)0.0132}$ O. $2.3\overline{)12.88}$ M. $7.2\overline{)36.648}$

N. $0.50\overline{)22}$ E. $0.44\overline{)8.80}$ T. $0.16\overline{)8}$ A. $0.25\overline{)0.300}$

M. $0.84\overline{)5.46}$ E. $0.67\overline{)1.49}$ O. $7.3\overline{)48.20}$ E. $0.49\overline{)2.3}$

W. $0.56\overline{)3.89}$ U. $0.28\overline{)6.64}$ E. $0.94\overline{)6}$

L. $0.073\overline{)67.1}$ T. $0.087\overline{)48.3}$

When dividing by decimals, you must multiply the divisor by a power ____ ____
                                                                    5.6 144.8

___ ___ ___   ___ ___   ___ ___ ___ ___   ___ ___
0.31 6.38 44   50 91.97   6.5 23.6 14.02 4.69 0.90 555.17

___   ___ ___ ___ ___ ___   ___ ___ ___ ___ ___ ___.
1.2   6.95 5.12 6.60 919.18 20 0.72 23.71 5.09 0.33 2.22 0.021

91

2-30 Finding the Largest and Smallest Sums, Differences, Products, and Quotients—Decimals

Use the digits 1, 2, 3, and 4 to fill in each box to find the *largest* sum, difference, product, and quotient for the problems below. Each digit must be used once in each problem. You may insert decimal points as needed.

1.

2.

3.

4.

Use the digits 1, 2, 3, and 4 to fill in each box to find the *smallest* sum, difference, product, and quotient for the problems below. Each digit must be used once in each problem, and each answer must be larger than 0. You may insert decimal points as needed.

5.

6.

7.

8.

Name _____   **Date** _____

2-31 Decimals–All Operations

Start with the number given for each problem, then follow the instructions to find the answer. Round each answer to the nearest hundredth. **Note:** Do not apply the order of operations.

1. Start with 27.4. Add 3. Subtract 0.854. Multiply by 0.46. Divide by 0.3.

   Final Answer: _____

2. Start with 9.09. Divide by 0.9. Multiply by 3.04. Subtract 0.0675. Add 2.1.

   Final Answer: _____

3. Start with 0.08. Multiply by 6.7. Add 7.5. Subtract 4.002. Divide by 0.08.

   Final Answer: _____

4. Start with 29.67. Subtract 16.806. Multiply by 3.4. Divide by 40. Add 8.69.

   Final Answer: _____

5. Start with 0.004. Multiply by 87. Add 0.69. Divide by 0.25. Subtract 2.16.

   Final Answer: _____

Start with the Final Answer to the first problem, add it to the Final Answer of the second, subtract the Final Answer of your third, multiply by the Final Answer of your fourth, and divide by the Final Answer of your fifth. If the answer you now have is 135.69, your math is most likely correct.

2-32 Writing Decimal Word Problems

Use the information below to write decimal word problems. You may use any operation and add more information if you wish. Be sure to provide an answer key for your problems. When you are done, share your problems with a friend.

1. Ray works after school three days per week for four hours each day. He earns $6.50 per hour. On Saturdays he works four hours for $7.00 per hour.

2. Maria's math tests for the quarter were 92, 90.5, 86.5, 88, and 94. To attain an "A" on her report card in math, Maria must average at least a 90.

3. Will drove 440.8 miles on a tank of gasoline. The gas tank of his car holds 20 gallons. A gallon of gasoline costs $1.89.

4. It rained a lot in Sunville this past spring. It rained 4.7 inches in April. It rained 6.03 inches in May. It rained 5.98 inches in June. The usual total rainfall for these three months is 6.42 inches.

5. Mount Everest is 29,028 feet in elevation. Mount McKinley is about 0.7 times as tall.

6. The distance from Ashland to Harrisville is 52.4 miles. The distance from Harrisville to Smithton is 2.6 times greater.

7. Tom has been working odd jobs around his neighborhood in an effort to earn enough money to buy a stereo system for $169.99. He has earned $75 for cutting grass, $15.75 for baby-sitting, and $12.00 for taking care of the Wilsons' dog while they were on vacation.

Now create three problems of your own.

2-33 Fractions and Decimals Crossword Puzzle

Complete the crossword puzzle.

Across

2. The place value of 7 in 7,001,000.6.

5. A proper fraction is part of a _____.

7. A fraction whose numerator is greater than the denominator.

8. The place value of 4 in 3.4162.

11. The place value of 9 in 49,876.2.

12. The number of pennies in a dollar: one _____.

13. The place value of 2 in 321.67.

14. A fraction whose numerator is less than the denominator.

17. Ten dimes equal one _____.

18. Two or more fractions that represent the same value.

19. This coin is one tenth of a dollar.

20. A fraction is a _____ of something.

21. $\frac{10}{10}$ is equal to _____.

23. A part of one's earnings paid to the government is a _____.

24. 0.375 is an example of a _____.

25. To _____ a fraction means to write it in simplest form.

Down

1. A coin worth one hundredth of a dollar.

2. The place value of 8 in 0.246158.

3. The place value of 3 in 8,421.763.

4. The numerator of the fraction $\frac{4}{5}$.

6. $3\frac{2}{3}$ is an example of a _____ number.

9. This type of number has a numerator and denominator.

10. It is used every day and is based on 10.

14. The decimal system may be called a _____ system (two words).

15. 4 is the _____ of $\frac{1}{4}$.

16. The place value of 1 in 2.81.

22. The denominator of $\frac{4}{5}$.

2-33 Fractions and Decimals
Crossword Puzzle (Continued)

2-34 Fractions and Decimals– Finding Patterns

Find the missing numbers in each pattern below.

1. $2, 1, \frac{1}{2}, \frac{1}{4}, \frac{1}{8}$, _____, _____, _____

2. $1, 0.1, 0.01, 0.001$, _____, _____, _____

3. $\frac{1}{2}, \frac{2}{3}, \frac{3}{4}$, _____, _____, _____

4. $0.5, 0.\overline{3}, 0.25, 0.2$, _____, _____, _____

5. $0, 0.1, 0.1, 0.2, 0.3, 0.5, 0.8, 1.3$, _____, _____, _____

6. $\frac{1}{2}, \frac{1}{3}, \frac{1}{4}, \frac{1}{9}, \frac{1}{8}$, _____, _____, _____

7. $0.125, 0.25, 0.375, 0.5$, _____, _____, _____

8. $1, \frac{1}{4}, \frac{1}{9}, \frac{1}{16}, \frac{1}{25}$, _____, _____, _____

9. $0.2, 0.4, 0.6, 0.8, 1$, _____, _____, _____

10. $\frac{1}{2}, \frac{1}{3}, \frac{1}{5}, \frac{1}{7}, \frac{1}{11}$, _____, _____, _____

2-35 Ratio and Proportion

Solve each proportion and write each ratio. (The facts used in the problems are amazing but true!)

1. Prairie dog colonies can cover huge areas of land. A colony of prairie dogs in Texas spanned an area of about 24,000 square miles, which is twice the size of Belgium. What is the area of Belgium?

   _____

   _____

2. You can find out how far away a thunderstorm is if you count the seconds between the time you see the lightning flash and hear the thunder. Sound travels at a rate of 1,096 feet per second. How far is the storm if three seconds elapse between the time you see the lightning and hear the thunder? (Round your answer to the nearest hundredth mile. 5,280 feet = 1 mile.)

   _____

   _____

3. Fleas are the world's highest leapers for their body size. A flea that leaps 7.5 inches leaps about 130 times its height. What is the height of this flea? Round your answer to the nearest hundredth.

   _____

   _____

4. One person in 200 is allergic to bee and wasp venom. If 1,000 people are stung by bees and wasps, about how many would suffer allergic reactions?

   _____

   _____

5. After they reach the age of 18 years, humans lose more than 1,000 brain cells a day. According to this statistic, about how many brain cells might a 20-year-old human lose during the month of June?

   _____

   _____

2-35 Ratio and Proportion (Continued)

6. If all the cells in the average human body were placed end to end, they would stretch 620 miles. If all the nerve cells in a human body were laid end to end, they would stretch for about 47 miles. What is the ratio of the length of all the cells in the human body to the length of nerve cells?

_____

_____

7. A fast human can run about 28 mph. The cheetah is the fastest mammal over short distances, able to run at a rate of 65 mph. Write a ratio of the speed of a fast human to the speed of the cheetah.

_____

_____

8. The average adult breathes about 1,056 pints of air every minute. Adult lungs hold about 5.28 pints of air. Write the ratio of air breathed per minute to air held in the average adult's lungs. Express your answer in simplest form.

_____

_____

9. If the inner surfaces of an adult human's lungs were laid out flat, their total area would be about 1,938 square feet. The area of a tennis court (for playing doubles) is 2,808 square feet. Write the ratio of the area of the lungs to the area of a tennis court. Express your answer in simplest form.

_____

_____

10. Pike's Peak, one of the most famous mountain peaks in Colorado, is 14,110 feet high. Assume that a man is 6 feet tall. Write a ratio of the man's height to the elevation of Pike's Peak. Express your answer in simplest form.

_____

_____

2-36 Matching Fraction, Decimal, and Percent Equivalencies

Connect each pair of equivalent values with a straight line. Then find the square, equilateral triangle, and pentagon. **Hint:** Every value will be used only once.

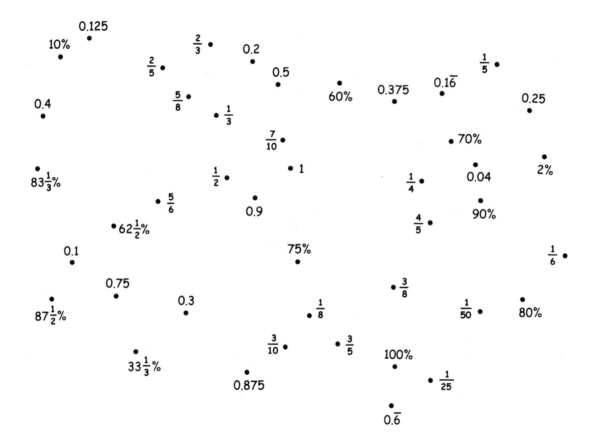

2-37 Ordering Fractions, Decimals, and Percents

Write the numbers in each row in order from smallest to largest on the line beneath the row. Be sure to write their accompanying letters with them. Then write the letter of each number in order in the spaces at the bottom of this page to complete the statement. Correct answers will reveal an important relationship among fractions, decimals, and percents.

E. 2.83   C. 23%   B. 1   N. $\frac{3}{4}$ A. 0.283

1. _____

R. $\frac{1}{4}$ I. $\frac{6}{20}$ T. 1.75   T. 85%   W. 0.176

2. _____

E. 14.5%   I. 0.27   N. $\frac{2}{5}$ N. 0.148   T. $\frac{7}{10}$

3. _____

S. 62%   O. $\frac{20}{25}$ M. 0.60   E. $\frac{8}{20}$ R. $\frac{3}{7}$

4. _____

H. $\frac{2}{3}$ A. 50%   C. $\frac{130}{250}$ E. 0.4   F. 1.30%

5. _____

H. $\frac{2}{9}$ R. $\frac{3}{2}$ O. 11.20%   T. 0.148   E. $1\frac{1}{4}$

6. _____

Every fraction, decimal, and percent ____ ____ ____   ____ ____

____ ____ ____ ____ ____ ____ ____ ____   ____ ____ ____

____ ____ ____ ____ ____ ____   ____ ____ ____   ____ ____ ____ ____

____ ____ ____ ____ ____ ____ ____.

2-38 Finding Percents of Numbers

Find the percent of each number. Write the letter of the problem above its answer to complete the statement below.

U. 75% of 80 =   _____   S. 18% of 100 =   _____

E. 84% of 64 =   _____   R. 42% of 96 =   _____

F. 50% of 82 =   _____   D. 35% of 78 =   _____

T. 29% of 55 =   _____   N. 62% of 46 =   _____

U. 37% of 126 =   _____   R. 47% of 158 =   _____

E. 71% of 842 =   _____   R. 98% of 200 =   _____

C. 26% of 504 =   _____   H. 86% of 396 =   _____

T. 39% of 300 =   _____   A. 48% of 1,024 =   _____

D. 79% of 1,226 =   _____   O. 25.5% of 76 =   _____

F. 5.5% of 68 =   _____   E. 42.5% of 84 =   _____

E. 36.25% of 88 =   _____   E. 62.75% of 36 =   _____

O. 75% of 14.8 =   _____   N. 92% of 42.6 =   _____

P. 45% of 67.5 =   _____   W. 64% of 52.5 =   _____

Your ___ ___ ___ ___ ___ ___   ___ ___ ___
      22.59 3.74 41 11.1 74.26 15.95 33.6 491.52 18

___ ___ ___   ___ ___ ___ ___ ___ ___ ___
19.38 39.192 53.76 340.56 60 46.62 968.54 196 35.7 27.3

___ ___ ___ ___ ___ ___ ___ .
30.375 597.82 40.32 131.04 31.9 28.52 117

2-39 Finding What Percent a Number Is of Another Number

Solve each problem. Your answer will equal the average life expectancy (in years) of the animal that follows the problem.

1. What percent of 80 is 4? _____ *rabbit*

2. What percent of 900 is 108? _____ *leopard*

3. What percent of 200 is 6? _____ *mouse*

4. 18 is what percent of 150? _____ *dog*

5. 2 is what percent of 10? _____ *horse*

6. 3 is what percent of 50? _____ *chipmunk*

7. What percent of 140 is 21? _____ *lobster*

8. What percent of 45 is 9? _____ *gorilla*

9. What percent of 31 is 31? _____ *box turtle*

10. 11 is what percent of 110? _____ *pig*

11. 6 is what percent of 15? _____ *Asian elephant*

12. 63 is what percent of 350? _____ *black bear*

13. What percent of 180 is 12.6? _____ *kangaroo*

14. What percent of 50 is 5? _____ *squirrel*

15. 15 is what percent of 125? _____ *cat*

16. 1.2 is what percent of 8? _____ *lion*

17. What percent of 18 is 0.18? _____ *opossum*

18. 5.6 is what percent of 80? _____ *red fox*

19. 1.3 is what percent of 13? _____ *giraffe*

20. What percent of 90 is 22.5? _____ *grizzly bear*

2-40 Finding the Number When a Percent of It Is Known

Solve each problem. Your answer will equal the top running speed in miles per hour of the animal that follows the problem.

1. 30% of what number is 21? _____ *cheetah*

2. 15.25 is 25% of what number? _____ *pronghorn antelope*

3. 12.5% of what number is 6.25? _____ *lion*

4. 43.2 is 90% of what number? _____ *quarter horse*

5. 20% of what number is 9? _____ *elk*

6. 86 is 200% of what number? _____ *coyote*

7. $16.\overline{6}$% of what number is 7? _____ *gray fox*

8. 32 is 80% of what number? _____ *greyhound*

9. 60% of what number is 21? _____ *rabbit*

10. 20 is 62.5% of what number? _____ *giraffe*

11. $83.\overline{3}$% of what number is 25? _____ *domestic cat*

12. 7 is 25% of what number? _____ *human*

13. 40% of what number is 10? _____ *elephant*

14. 4.5 is 30% of what number? _____ *wild turkey*

15. 75% of what number is 9? _____ *squirrel*

16. 1.1 is 10% of what number? _____ *pig*

17. 10% of what number is 0.9? _____ *chicken*

18. 0.017 is 10% of what number? _____ *giant tortoise*

19. 0.09 is 60% of what number? _____ *three-toed sloth*

20. 150% of what number is 0.045? _____ *garden snail*

2-41 Solving the Three Types of Percentage Problems

Solve each problem and record your answer in the space provided. The first problem is done for you.

1. 80% of what number is 36? __45__

2. 198 is what percent of 900? _____

3. What number is 3% of 15,000? _____

4. What percent of 120 is 18? _____

5. 120% of 180 is what number? _____

6. 10% of what number is 2? _____

7. What percent of 99 is 33? _____

8. 36 is 150% of what number? _____

9. 15% of what number is 135? _____

10. What number is 30% of 450? _____

11. 10% of what number is 9.9? _____

12. 20% of what number is 32? _____

13. 9 is what percent of 24? _____

14. 12.2 is what percent of 48.8? _____

15. 42 is 75% of what number? _____

Now write the answers of the problems above the spaces labeled by the number of the problem. The first problem is done for you. When you are done, you should find that five percent problems are created. Not all of them are correct. Identify the incorrect ones by writing False after them.

_____ of _____ = _____   _____
  4   12   8

_____ of _____ = __45__   _____
  7   10   1

_____ of _____ = _____   _____
  14   9   5

_____ of _____ = _____   _____
  13   15   6

_____ of _____ = _____   _____
  2   3   11

2-42 Percent of Increase and Decrease

Find the percent of increase and decrease based upon these "famous firsts." Round your answers to the nearest percent.

1. The first roller coaster was introduced at Coney Island, New York in 1884. It traveled at a rate of six miles per hour. In 1927, also at Coney Island, the Cyclone, the first "high speed" roller coaster, was introduced. The Cyclone traveled at speeds up to 60 miles per hour. Find the percent of increase in the speed of the first roller coaster to the Cyclone.

   _____

   _____

2. Texas Instruments introduced the first electronic pocket calculator in 1971. It could add, subtract, multiply, and divide. It sold for $149. Now a pocket calculator that performs similar functions sells for $5. Find the percent of decrease.

   _____

   _____

3. The first microwave oven for home use was manufactured in 1952 and sold for $1,295. Now microwave ovens sell for as low as $79. Find the percent of decrease.

   _____

   _____

4. In 1988 Lewis C. Thompson of Washington, D.C. was the first person to win more than $1 million from a slot machine. He collected $1.1 million in a jackpot payoff after playing eight quarters. Find the percent of increase from his eight-quarter investment.

   _____

   _____

5. The first airplane flight was made at Kitty Hawk, North Carolina in 1903. Wilbur Wright was at the controls and remained aloft for 12 seconds. Three other flights took place that day, with the longest lasting for 59 seconds. Find the percent of increase of the time aloft between the first flight and the longest flight.

   _____

   _____

2-42 Percent of Increase and Decrease
(Continued)

6. The flights mentioned in problem 5 varied in distance traveled. The first flight covered 120 feet. The longest of the next three flights covered 852 feet. Find the percent of increase of the distance traveled between the first and longest flights.

_____

_____

7. Noah Webster compiled the first *Dictionary of the English Language* in 1806. Webster's dictionary was 408 pages long. Today, a version of Webster's dictionary contains 1,575 pages. Find the percent of increase.

_____

_____

8. Home Insurance Company of New York built the first skyscraper, a ten-story building in Chicago, in 1885. Today, the Sears Building in Chicago stands 110 stories high. Find the percent of increase.

_____

_____

9. Congress established the first speed limit for highway traffic in 1974. The limit was 55 miles per hour. This limit was repealed in 1995, and several states promptly raised their speed limits to 65 miles per hour or more. Find the percent of increase from 55 miles per hour to 65 miles per hour.

_____

_____

10. In 1895 King Camp Gillette invented the first safety razors to be successfully marketed. The razors sold for $5 each. Disposable razors are now sold for as little as $0.39 each. Find the percent of decrease.

_____

_____

2-43 Percents and Discount

Find the discount and final cost of the items below. If necessary, round your answer to the nearest cent.

1. **CD**
   Original Cost: $19.95
   Discount Amount: _____
   Discount: 30%
   Final Cost: _____

2. **13-inch color TV**
   Original Cost $129.99
   Discount Amount: _____
   Discount: 25%
   Final Cost: _____

3. **Movie video**
   Original Cost: $18.95
   Discount Amount: _____
   Discount: 50%
   Final Cost: _____

4. **Mountain bike**
   Original Cost: $389.49
   Discount Amount: _____
   Discount: 15%
   Final Cost: _____

5. **Pair of blue jeans**
   Original Cost: $27.99
   Discount Amount: _____
   Discount: 35%
   Final Cost: _____

6. **Wrist watch**
   Original Cost: $69.79
   Discount Amount: _____
   Discount: 20%
   Final Cost: _____

7. **Sneakers**
   Original Cost: $95.89
   Discount Amount: _____
   Discount: 5%
   Final Cost: _____

8. **Calculator**
   Original Cost: $99.98
   Discount Amount: _____
   Discount: 15%
   Final Cost: _____

9. **Carry-all bag**
   Original Cost: $19.69
   Discount Amount: _____
   Discount: 35%
   Final Cost: _____

10. **Computer system**
    Original Cost: $1,029.95
    Discount Amount: _____
    Discount: 25%
    Final Cost: _____

Round each of the Discount Amounts and Final Costs to the nearest whole number. Find the sum of all the Discounts. Find the sum of all the Final Costs. Subtract the total of the Discounts from the total of the Final Costs.

Total Final Costs: _____

– Total Discounts: _____

_____

What percent of the Final Costs is the Total Discounts? _____

2-44 Percents and Sales Tax

Find the amount of sales tax and final cost (price plus sales tax) for each item below. If necessary, round your answers to the nearest hundredth (penny).

1. **Cordless phone**   Price: $64.99   Sales Tax: 6%
    Sales Tax: _____   Final Cost: _____

2. **Portable radio**   Price: $59.99   Sales Tax: 5%
    Sales Tax: _____   Final Cost: _____

3. **Video game**   Price: $69.99   Sales Tax: 6%
    Sales Tax: _____   Final Cost: _____

4. **Wrist watch**   Price: $39.95   Sales Tax: 4%
    Sales Tax: _____   Final Cost: _____

5. **Camera**   Price: $84.99   Sales Tax: 5%
    Sales Tax: _____   Final Cost: _____

6. **Duffel carry bag**   Price: $39.49   Sales Tax: 4.5%
    Sales Tax: _____   Final Cost: _____

7. **Binoculars**   Price: $139.95   Sales Tax: 5.5%
    Sales Tax: _____   Final Cost: _____

8. **Computer printer**   Price: $149.99   Sales Tax: 3.5%
    Sales Tax: _____   Final Cost: _____

9. **Stereo system**   Price: $159.95   Sales Tax: 4.5%
    Sales Tax: _____   Final Cost: _____

10. **19-inch color TV**   Price: $169.99   Sales Tax: 4.25%
    Sales Tax: _____   Final Cost: _____

Assume a shopper bought all of the items above. Round the final cost of each item to the nearest dollar and add. If your sum is $1,025, your math is likely to be correct.

2-45 Fractions, Decimals, and Percents—Word Problems

Here are some word problems with a new twist. The answers to the problems appear below. You must determine which answer(s) belong with which problems. Write the answers on the spaces after the problems.

40%	60%	65%	80%	$11.91
$13.63	$35	$40	$45	$48.75
Computer Center		Discount Dave		Good Buys

1. John estimates that he will need 20 gallons of paint to paint his house. If he used 7 gallons, what percent of the job needs to be completed?

   _____

2. A personal computer regularly sells for $2,350 but is on sale at 10% off at Computer Center. Good Buys sells the same computer for $2,600, but it is on sale at one fifth off. At which store is the computer less expensive and by how much?

   _____

3. One fifth of the 300 tickets to the school play have been sold. What percent of the tickets have not been sold yet?

   _____

4. Myanza purchased a camera and saved $10. If this is a savings of 25%, what was the original price of the camera?

   _____

5. Discount Dave is offering a great buy on cordless phones that regularly cost $69.97. He has cut the price by $20. Computer Center sells the same phone, which lists for $65 at a 25% discount. What is the lower price and which store sells the phone at the lower price?

   _____

6. Sue purchased two Super-Size Meals for $3.79 each and a cookie for $.79 at a fast-food restaurant. She had one $1-off coupon for each Super-Size Meal she bought. How much change should Sue receive from $20?

   _____

7. Juanita was driving to visit a friend who lived 275 miles away. She decided to stop for dinner after she had driven 110 miles. What percent of the trip was completed?

   _____

8. A VCR regularly sells for $60. This week it is on sale at 25% off. What is the sale price?

   _____

9. Good Buys sells $15 CDs at a 20% discount. Discount Dave sells the same CDs for $15.88, but this week Discount Dave is running a special on CDs, which are one fourth off their regular price. What store sells the CDs at the lower price and what is the lower price?

   _____

10. Sam is a member of the school swimming team. At a recent event the team scored 81 points, of which Sam scored 32 points. What percent of the team's points did the other team members score?

   _____

Section 3

MEASUREMENT

Name _____   Date _____

3-1 Measuring Line Segments with Rulers (Inches)

Use a ruler to measure the following line segments. **Note:** You will need a ruler divided into 16ths of an inch.

1. AE = _____

2. HK = _____

3. BE = _____

4. BH = _____

5. FJ = _____

6. DE = _____

7. GK = _____

8. CJ = _____

9. HI = _____

10. JK = _____

11. Without using your ruler, which of the line segments—1, 2, 3, or 4—to the right *appears* to be longest? _____ Which *appears* to be shortest? _____ Now measure the segments. Which is longest? _____ Which is shortest? _____

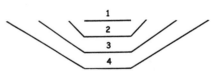

Explain why the lengths are not what they appear to be.

_____

_____

12. Without using your ruler, which, if any, of the line segments—$\overline{AE}$, $\overline{BF}$, $\overline{CF}$, or $\overline{DF}$—to the right *appears* to be the shortest? _____ Now measure the segments. What did you find? _____

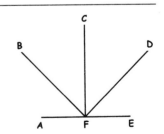

Explain your findings.

_____

_____

3-2 Units of Length in the English System

Match the unit of measurement on the left with its equivalent unit on the right. Write the letter that follows the equivalent unit in the space after the measure. When you are done, write the letters in order, starting with the first problem, to complete the statement. The first problem is done for you.

12 inches = 1 foot	40 rods = 1 furlong
3 feet = 1 yard	5,280 feet = 1 mile
5.5 yards = 1 rod	1,760 yards = 1 mile

1. 2 feet = ___24___ inches __L__   6,336 **N**

2. 2,640 feet = _____ mile _____   15,840 **T**

3. 3 rods = _____ yards _____   3 **C**

4. 48 inches = _____ feet _____   2 **R**

5. 3 miles = _____ feet _____ $\frac{1}{2}$ **E**

6. 100 yards = _____ furlong _____ $52\frac{1}{2}$ **B**

7. 2 yards = _____ inches _____   1,584 **Y**

8. 6 rods = _____ yards _____ $\frac{2}{3}$ **T**

9. 24 inches = _____ yard _____   440 **E**

10. 4 miles = _____ yards _____   33 **F**

11. 33 feet = _____ rods _____   6 **R**

12. 20 rods = _____ furlong _____ $16\frac{1}{2}$ **N**

3-2   Units of Length in the English System (Continued)

13. $\frac{1}{4}$ mile = _____ yards _____   24 **L**

14. $17\frac{1}{2}$ yards = _____ feet _____ $\frac{1}{2}$ **E**

15. 4 rods = _____ feet _____   320 **R**

16. 1 mile = _____ rods _____   7,040 **H**

17. 4 inches = _____ foot _____   3,960 **E**

18. $\frac{3}{4}$ mile = _____ feet _____   66 **A**

19. 8 rods = _____ inches _____   72 **O**

20. $49\frac{1}{2}$ feet = _____ rods _____   4 **G**

21. 1 furlong = _____ feet _____ $\frac{1}{3}$ **L**

22. $\frac{1}{2}$ foot = _____ inches _____   660 **O**

23. $1\frac{1}{5}$ mile = _____ feet _____   1,980 **S**

24. 3 furlongs = _____ feet _____ $\frac{5}{11}$ **H**

The length of an inch was established during the reign of King Edward II of England.

Edward declared that the inch was equal to the _L_ __ __ __ __ __ __ __

__ __ __ __ __   __ __ __ __ __ __   __ __ __ __ __.

3-3 Units of Weight in the English System

Match the unit of measurement on the left with its equivalent unit on the right. Write the letter that follows the equivalent unit in the space after the measure. When you are done, write the letters in order, starting with the first problem, to complete the statement. The first problem is done for you.

> 27.3 grains ≈ 1 dram
> 16 drams = 1 ounce
> 16 ounces = 1 pound
> 100 pounds = 1 short hundredweight (U.S.)
> 2,000 pounds = 1 ton (U.S.)

1. 48 ounces = ____3____ pounds __T__   8 **R**

2. 6 pounds = _____ ounces _____   9 **U**

3. 8 drams ≈ _____ grains _____   3,494.4 **O**

4. $\frac{1}{2}$ ton = _____ hundredweights _____ $\frac{1}{2}$ **Y**

5. 1,500 pounds = _____ ton _____   30,000 **D**

6. 1 pound = _____ drams _____   32 **P**

7. 160 ounces = _____ hundredweight _____   96 **H**

8. $\frac{1}{2}$ ounce = _____ drams _____   10 **A**

9. 15 tons = _____ pounds _____   3 **T**

© 2002 by John Wiley & Sons, Inc.

3-3 Units of Weight in the English System (Continued)

10. 245.7 grains ≈ _____ drams _____ $\frac{1}{16}$ **S**

11. 0.32 hundredweight = _____ pounds _____   218.4 **E**

12. $\frac{1}{2}$ pound ≈ _____ grains _____   256 **O**

13. $5\frac{1}{2}$ pounds = _____ ounces _____   1,600 **T**

14. 4 ounces = _____ pound _____ $\frac{3}{4}$ **V**

15. 1 dram = _____ ounce _____ $\frac{3}{10}$ **S**

16. 218.4 grains ≈ _____ ounce _____ $\frac{1}{10}$ **I**

17. 6 hundredweights = _____ ton _____ $\frac{1}{4}$ **S**

18. 0.05 ton = _____ ounces _____   128 **E**

19. $\frac{1}{2}$ pound = _____ drams _____ $\frac{1}{5}$ **M**

20. 320 ounces = _____ hundredweight _____   88 **I**

$\underline{\text{T}}$ ___ ___   ___ ___ ___ ___ ___ ___ ___ ___ ___ ___ ___

___ ___ ___ ___ ___ ___ includes weights and measures based on a pound

containing 16 ounces.

3-4 Units of Liquid Measure in the English System

Match the unit of measurement on the left with its equivalent unit on the right. Write the letter that follows the equivalent unit in the space after the measure. **Note:** Some answers will be used more than once and some will not be used at all.

When you are done, write the letters in order, starting with the first problem, to complete the statement. The first problem is done for you.

3 teaspoons = 1 tablespoon	2 cups = 1 pint
2 tablespoons = 1 fluid ounce	2 pints = 1 quart
8 fluid ounces = 1 cup	4 quarts = 1 gallon

1. 16 fluid ounces = __1__ pint __G__ $3\frac{1}{2}$ **O**

2. 1 gallon = _____ pints _____   16 **N**

3. 6 quarts = _____ gallons _____   1 **G**

4. 3 cups = _____ pints _____   2 **C**

5. 7 pints = _____ quarts _____   8 **A**

6. 1 gallon = _____ cups _____ $\frac{1}{4}$ **E**

7. 9 teaspoons = _____ tablespoons _____ $\frac{1}{16}$ **M**

8. 8 fluid ounces = _____ quart _____   4 **H**

9. 6 pints = _____ gallon _____ $1\frac{1}{2}$ **L**

10. 2 tablespoons = _____ cup _____ $\frac{3}{4}$ **Q**

11. $\frac{1}{2}$ gallon = _____ cups _____   6 **D**

Name _____   Date _____

3-4   Units of Liquid Measure in the English System (Continued)

---

12. 12 fluid ounces = _____ cups _____

13. 1 quart = _____ gallon _____

14. 1.5 quarts = _____ cups _____

15. 14 quarts = _____ gallons _____

16. 1 pint = _____ fluid ounces _____

17. 1 cup = _____ quart _____

18. 1 quart = _____ cups _____

19. 7 tablespoons = _____ ounces _____

20. 16 tablespoons = _____ cup _____

21. 1.5 pints = _____ cups _____

22. $\frac{1}{2}$ gallon = _____ pints _____

23. 4 tablespoons = _____ cup _____

24. $\frac{1}{2}$ pint = _____ fluid ounces _____

25. $\frac{3}{4}$ gallon = _____ pints _____

$\frac{1}{8}$ **U**

3 **S**

$\frac{1}{2}$ **B**

12 **R**

Just as language changes over time, so do the units we use for measurement. Once most people knew that 63 _G_ ___ ___ ___ ___ ___ ___

___ ___ ___ ___ ___ ___ ___ ___ ___ ___

___ ___ ___ ___ ___ ___ ___ ___.

3-5   Using the English System of Measurement

Write T after the statement if the statement is true or F if the statement is false. If it is false, correct it on the line below.

1. If 2 pints = 1 quart, then 2 pints = $\frac{1}{2}$ gallon. ____

   _____

2. If 1 gallon = 4 quarts, then 1 gallon = 16 cups. ____

   _____

3. If $\frac{2}{3}$ foot = 8 inches, then $\frac{2}{3}$ foot = $\frac{1}{6}$ of a yard. ____

   _____

4. If 4 quarts = 8 pints, then 4 quarts = 64 fluid ounces. ____

   _____

5. If 2 tablespoons = 1 fluid ounce, then 2 tablespoons = $\frac{1}{4}$ cup. ____

   _____

6. If $\frac{1}{2}$ mile = 2,640 feet, then $\frac{1}{2}$ mile = 880 yards. ____

   _____

7. If 8 fluid ounces = $\frac{1}{2}$ pint, then 8 fluid ounces = $\frac{1}{4}$ quart. ____

   _____

8. If 1 rod = 5.5 yards, then 1 rod = 178 inches. ____

   _____

9. If 1 league = 3 miles, then $\frac{1}{2}$ league = 7,820 feet. ____

   _____

10. If 1 acre = 4,840 square yards, and 9 square feet = 1 square yard, then 1 acre = 34,520 square feet. ____

   _____

Name _____   **Date** _____

3-6 Converting Units in the Metric System, I

Match the unit of measurement on the left with its equivalent unit on the right. Write the letter that follows the equivalent unit in the space after the measure. **Note:** Some answers will be used more than once.

When you are done, write the letters in order, starting with the first problem, to complete the statement below. The first problem is done for you.

> Basic Units: meter, liter, gram
> Example: 1 meter = 10 decimeters
>   1 meter = 100 centimeters
>   1 meter = 1,000 millimeters
>   1 dekameter (or deca-) = 10 meters
>   1 hectometer = 100 meters
>   1 kilometer = 1,000 meters

1. 100 meters = ____1____ hectometer __I__   1 **I**

2. 1 meter = _____ decimeters _____   89 **F**

3. 40 milliliters = _____ centiliters _____   10 **N**

4. 32 liters = _____ milliliters _____   100 **M**

5. 3.2 grams = _____ milligrams _____   4 **T**

6. 1 centimeter = _____ millimeters _____   32,000 **E**

7. 89 centiliters = _____ liter _____   3,200 **R**

8. 4,000 meters = _____ kilometers _____   0.89 **A**

9. 1,000 grams = _____ kilogram _____   40 **O**

10. 0.4 liters = _____ centiliters _____   400 **L**

3-6 Converting Units in the Metric System, I (Continued)

11. 1 dekagram = _____ grams _____   8.9 **S**

12. 890 meters = _____ kilometer _____   320 **Y**

13. 4 meters = _____ centimeters _____   32 **U**

14. 8,900 milliliters = _____ liters _____

15. 32 centimeters = _____ millimeters _____

16. 890 centimeters = _____ meters _____

17. 40 liters = _____ dekaliters _____

18. 0.32 kilometers = _____ centimeters _____

19. 1 meter = _____ centimeters _____

20. 4 dekagrams = _____ grams _____

21. 0.89 meters = _____ centimeters _____

22. 3.2 meters = _____ decimeters _____

23. 1 centiliter = _____ milliliters _____

24. 10 millimeters = _____ centimeter _____

25. 0.04 meters = _____ centimeters _____

26. 89 milliliters = _____ centiliters _____

The official name of the Metric System of measurement is the

I __ __ __ __ __ __ __ __ __ __ __ __ __

__ __ __ __ __   __ __   __ __ __ __ __.

© 2002 by John Wiley & Sons, Inc.

3-7 Converting Units in the Metric System, II

Write T after the statement if the statement is true or F if the statement is false. If a statement is false, correct it on the line below. **Hint:** The number of false statements is the same as the number of millimeters in a centimeter.

1. 1 meter = 1,000 centimeters ____

   _____

2. 2 liters = 200 hectoliters ____

   _____

3. 17 milliliters = 1.7 centiliters ____

   _____

4. 0.5 meters = 50 centimeters ____

   _____

5. 35 centigrams = 3.5 milligrams ____

   _____

6. 42 kilometers = 42,000 meters ____

   _____

7. 58 centiliters = 0.058 liters ____

   _____

8. 1.2 dekagrams = 12 hectograms ____

   _____

9. 5.5 kilograms = 150 grams ____

   _____

10. 15 deciliters = 150 milliliters ____

   _____

11. 1,200 millimeters = 120 centimeters = 12 meters ____

   _____

12. 2 kilograms = 200 hectograms = 2,000 centigrams ____

   _____

13. 300 milliliters = 30 centiliters = 3 deciliters = 0.3 liters ____

   _____

14. 2 grams = 0.2 dekagrams = 0.02 hectograms = 0.002 kilograms ____

   _____

15. 550 centimeters = 55 meters = 5.5 dekameters = 0.55 hectometers = 0.055 kilometers ____

   _____

3-8   Using Metric Units of Weight

Suppose you had four weights—a 1-kilogram weight, a 3-kilogram weight, a 9-kilogram weight, a 27-kilogram weight—and a scale pan.

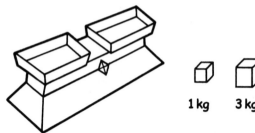
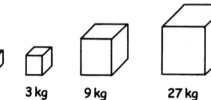

1 kg   3 kg   9 kg   27 kg

You could correctly weigh objects of every whole number of kilograms from 1 to 40. Use the lines below to show how you could weigh the different weights. (The numbers 1 through 40 represent the weights.) The solution to weighing a 5-kilogram object is done for you. The 9-kilogram weight is placed on one side of the scale, the 1-kilogram weight, 3-kilogram weight, and the object is placed on the other. **Note:** In the example, the weight of the 5-kilogram object is in bold.

1: _____   2: _____   3: _____

4: _____   5: _9 = 1 + 3 + **5**_   6: _____

7: _____   8: _____   9: _____

10: _____   11: _____   12: _____

13: _____   14: _____   15: _____

16: _____   17: _____   18: _____

19: _____   20: _____   21: _____

22: _____   23: _____   24: _____

25: _____   26: _____   27: _____

28: _____   29: _____   30: _____

31: _____   32: _____   33: _____

34: _____   35: _____   36: _____

37: _____   38: _____   39: _____

40: _____

3-9   Computing Units of Measure (English and Metric)

Solve each problem. Regroup where necessary and write your answer in the largest possible units.

1. 1 yard 10 inches
        +1 yard 6 inches

2. 4 gallons 2 quarts
        −1 gallon 3 quarts

3. 2 pounds 13 ounces
        +4 pounds 12 ounces

4. 1 gallon 3 quarts
        +   2 quarts

5. 10 centimeters 4 millimeters
        + 1 centimeter 9 millimeters

6. 12 pounds 5 ounces
        − 6 pounds 7 ounces

7. 14 yards 3 feet
        − 4 yards 1 foot

8. 2 feet 7 inches
        ×   6

9. 7 liters
        −   2 milliliters

10. 3)10 yards

11. 3)3 kiloliters 3 hectoliters

12. 2 pints 7 fluid ounces
        ×   3

13. 3 pounds 4 ounces
        ×   6

14. 4)17 pounds 4 ounces

15. 2)20 fluid ounces

16. 15 millimeters
        × 4

3-10 Making Sense of Measurement

Since the United States uses both the English and Metric systems of measurement, it is sometimes necessary to convert units between the two systems. Use the following conversions to solve the problems.

1 inch ≈ 2.54 centimeters	1 centimeter ≈ 0.39 inch
1 yard ≈ 0.91 meter	1 meter ≈ 1.09 yards
1 mile ≈ 1.61 kilometers	1 kilometer ≈ 0.62 mile
1 quart ≈ 0.95 liter	1 liter ≈ 1.06 quarts
1 pound ≈ 0.45 kilogram	1 kilogram ≈ 2.20 pounds

1. A teenager who weighs 67 kilograms is not considered to be underweight. Express this weight in pounds.

2. The average ostrich is 9 feet tall and weighs 345 pounds. Express this height in meters and weight in kilograms.

3. The first recorded Olympiad took place in Greece in 776 B.C. It consisted of a 200-yard foot race near the city of Olympia. Express this length in meters.

4. The highest point in North America is Mount McKinley (Alaska) at 20,320 feet. Express this height in kilometers rounded to the nearest kilometer.

5. A file card measures 3 inches by 5 inches. Express these dimensions in centimeters.

© 2002 by John Wiley & Sons, Inc.

3-10 Making Sense of Measurement
(Continued)

6. The deepest lake in the world is Lake Baykal in Asia with a depth of 5,315 feet. Express this depth in meters rounded to the nearest meter.

_____

7. At the Olympics, both men and women swim the backstroke, breaststroke, butterfly, and freestyle in events ranging from 50 meters to 1,500 meters. Express these distances in feet.

_____

8. Would a car traveling at 90 kilometers per hour be speeding if the speed limit were 60 miles per hour? Express kilometers per hour in terms of miles per hour.

_____

9. A foreign car dealer claims that a car has a fuel economy rate of 8 kilometers per liter. Express this in miles per gallon.

_____

10. A cookie recipe calls for $\frac{1}{4}$ pound of butter. Express this weight in grams.

_____

11. To stay healthy, people need to drink $2\frac{1}{2}$ quarts of water each day. Express this capacity in liters.

_____

12. A washing machine uses about 50 gallons of water for each load of wash. Express this amount in liters.

_____

3-11   Converting Units of Time

Match the unit of time on the left with its equivalent unit on the right. Write the letter that follows the equivalent unit in the space after the unit. **Note:** Some answers will be used more than once and some will not be used at all.

   When you are done, write the letters in order, starting with the first problem, to complete the statement below. Look for the abbreviations of a city and a state in the statement. The first problem is done for you.

1. 30 minutes = $\frac{1}{2}$ hour _I_	90 **A**
2. June has _____ days _____	50 **E**
3. 3 weeks = _____ days _____	40 **G**
4. $1\frac{1}{2}$ hours = _____ minutes _____	$\frac{2}{3}$ **H**
5. 30 years = _____ months _____	$\frac{1}{2}$ **I**
6. 40 minutes = _____ hour _____	$\frac{1}{3}$ **K**
7. $\frac{1}{2}$ century = _____ years _____	21 **L**
8. $\frac{1}{2}$ hour = _____ minutes _____	100 **M**
9. 5 years = _____ decade _____	30 **N**
10. 6 hours = _____ minutes _____	24 **O**
11. 6 months = _____ year _____	2 **P**
12. 15 minutes = _____ hour _____	$\frac{1}{4}$ **S**
13. 3 decades = _____ years _____	360 **T**

14. 1 day = _____ hours _____

15. 2 years = _____ months _____

16. $1\frac{1}{4}$ days = _____ hours _____

17. 1,800 seconds = _____ hour _____

18. 2.5 years = _____ months _____

19. 48 hours = _____ days _____

20. 9 decades = _____ years _____

Hint: Be sure to look for the abbreviations in the statement.

If it is 9 A.M. __I__ ____ ____ ____, ____ ____ ____ ____   ____ ____   ____ ____

____ ____ ____ ____   ____ ____   ____ ____.

Name _____   Date _____

3-12 Using Time Cards

The time cards below record the number of hours and the rate of pay for three employees of the XYZ Company. According to company policy, employees receive time and a half for each hour over 40 hours they work each week.

Complete the time cards. Refer to the clock to help you with your calculations.

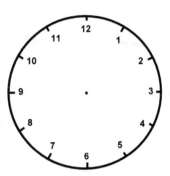

1. **Jose**
   Wage: $7.50 per hour

Day	Time on the Job		Total Hours
Mon.:	8:00 to 12:15	1:00 to 5:30	_____
Tues.:	7:30 to 12:00	1:00 to 4:15	_____
Wed.:	7:45 to 12:10	1:25 to 5:00	_____
Thurs.:	6:00 to 11:00	12:30 to 5:30	_____
Fri.:	8:00 to 1:00	1:30 to 6:00	_____
	Total Hours Worked This Week		_____
	Overtime Hours Worked		_____
	Money Earned		_____

2. **Peter**
   Wage: $6.40 per hour

Day	Time on the Job		Total Hours
Mon.:	1:00 to 5:30	7:30 to 10:00	_____
Tues.:		5:30 to 10:00	_____
Wed.:	7:30 to 1:15		_____
Thurs.:		5:30 to 10:00	_____
Sat.:	6:00 to 12:00	1:00 to 5:00	_____
	Total Hours Worked This Week		_____
	Overtime Hours Worked		_____
	Money Earned		_____

Name _____   Date _____

3-12 Using Time Cards (Continued)

3. **Callie**
   Wage: $7.00 per hour

Day	Time on the Job		Total Hours
Mon.:	7:00 to 10:30	12:00 to 4:00	_____
Tues.:	5:45 to 10:00	11:00 to 3:15	_____
Wed.:	8:00 to 12:30	1:30 to 6:15	_____
Thurs.:	6:15 to 12:00	1:30 to 4:00	_____
Fri.:	8:00 to 1:45		_____
Sat.:		4:00 to 10:15	_____
	Total Hours Worked This Week		_____
	Overtime Hours Worked		_____
	Money Earned		_____

Will the person who is paid the highest wage always earn the most money? Give an example to support your answer.

_____

_____

_____

_____

_____

Name _____   **Date** _____

3-13 Converting Fahrenheit to Celsius

Use the formulas that follow to convert the degrees Fahrenheit to degrees Celsius. Then record and label the Celsius temperatures on the thermometer on the right.

$$C = \left(\frac{F-32}{9}\right) \times 5 \quad \text{or} \quad C = (F - 32) \div 1.8$$

1. 98.6° F, average human temperature

   C = _____

2. 32° F, freezing temperature of water

   C = _____

3. 68° F, room temperature on winter day

   C = _____

4. 158° F, hot faucet water

   C = _____

5. 5° F, a very cold winter day

   C = _____

6. 95° F, a hot summer day

   C = _____

7. 50° F, a cool day

   C = _____

8. 176° F, hot soup

   C = _____

9. 14° F, frozen ice cream

   C = _____

10. 212° F, boiling point of water

    C = _____

11. 140° F, broiled steak

    C = _____

12. 77° F, a pleasant day

    C = _____

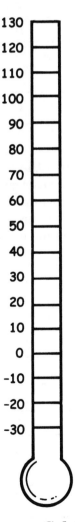

130
120
110
100
90
80
70
60
50
40
30
20
10
0
-10
-20
-30

Degrees Celsius

131

3-14 Converting Celsius to Fahrenheit

Because wind can make the air feel colder on a person's body than the actual temperature, winter weather reports provide information about the wind chill factor. The chart below contains wind chill temperatures (what the temperature of the air feels like) for different wind speeds and actual temperatures.

Wind Chill Table

Actual Temperature °C	−1°	−6.6°	−12°	−18°
Wind Speed (miles per hour)	Wind Chill Temperature			
10	−9°	−16°	−23°	−30°
20	−15.5°	−23.3°	−31°	−39.4°
30	−19°	−28°	−36°	−45°
40	−20.5°	−29.4°	−38.3°	−47°

Note that if the temperature is −12° C and the wind is traveling at a rate of 30 mph, the temperature would feel as if it is −36° C. Using the information in the table above, and the formulas below, complete the chart that follows by converting the degrees Celsius to Fahrenheit. Then answer the questions. **Note:** Round your answers to the nearest whole number.

$$F = (C \times 1.8) + 32 \qquad F = \frac{9C}{5} + 32$$

Wind Chill Table

Actual Temperature °F				
Wind Speed (miles per hour)	Wind Chill Temperature			
10				
20				
30				
40				

3-14 Converting Celsius to Fahrenheit (Continued)

1. If the temperature is 0° F and the wind speed is 20 mph, what is the wind chill in degrees F? _____

2. If the temperature is 30° F and the wind speed is 10 mph, what is the wind chill in degrees F? _____

3. What combinations of actual temperature and wind speed result in a wind chill of –53° F? _____

   _____

4. If the wind speed is 10 mph and the wind chill is 3° F, what is the actual temperature in degrees F? _____

5. If the wind chill is –33° F and the actual temperature is 10° F, what is the wind speed? _____

3-15 Measurement and Language

Listed below are well-known phrases and titles that include some type of measure. Fill in the blanks with a unit or phrase of measurement. Some clues are provided.

1. A _____ hat. (*an item worn by cowboys and cowgirls*)

2. A _____ weakling. (*think of a well-known advertisement for bodybuilding.*)

3. The heavy box weighs a _____ .

4. "_____ Minutes" (*TV show*)

5. _____ (*a movie about a spaceflight with an out-of-control computer*)

6. A _____ of coffee.

7. The Longest _____ (*movie*)

8. Fahrenheit _____ (*book*)

9. _____ Leagues Under the Sea (*book*)

10. The batter swung and missed the ball by a _____. (*a very long distance*)

11. A cat is said to have _____ lives.

12. Service available around the clock is _____.

13. Give him an _____ and he'll take a _____.

14. An _____ of prevention is worth a _____ of cure.

15. Another day, another _____.

16. Not a _____ too soon.

17. _____ cents for one, a _____ for another.

18. 13 cookies make a baker's _____.

19. All in a _____ work.

20. He feels great, like he's _____ tall.

Name _____ Date _____

3-16 A Measurement Crossword Puzzle

Complete the crossword puzzle.

Across

5. A test used to measure intelligence.

8. Amount of water an eyedropper holds.

13. It travels at a rate of about 186,000 miles per second.

14. Measure of computer memory.

15. A metric unit slightly longer than a yard.

17. Basic unit of capacity in the Metric System.

19. A system of measurement based on ten (two words).

20. A foot race of 26 miles.

22. This unit of exchange may vary from country to country.

25. 1,760 of these equal one mile.

27. A period of 1,000 years.

30. One hour equals 360 of these.

31. An instrument used to measure tempo (in music).

33. A prefix that means "one thousand."

34. The world is divided into 24 of these (two words).

35. It is used to measure angles.

Down

1. Measures time with grains of sand.

2. Instrument used to measure weight (especially in science).

3. Rhythmical beat of one's heart.

4. Basic unit of mass in the Metric System.

6. This unit of capacity is slightly less than a liter.

7. Scale on which water freezes at 0°.

9. The length of time it takes the Earth to rotate on its axis.

10. Scale on which water boils at 212°.

11. A count of the U.S. population, every ten years.

12. An instrument used to measure radiation (two words).

16. Another name for a thousand.

18. A prefix that means "one tenth."

21. T is the abbreviation of this unit of weight.

23. 500 (or 480) sheets of paper.

24. A measure of firewood.

25. The length of time it takes the Earth to revolve around the sun.

26. The metric unit of length that is a little less than a half inch.

28. A unit of measure for gems.

29. A group of 12 items.

31. Unit of length equal to about 1.6 kilometers.

32. The number of days in this month varies.

3-16 A Measurement
Crossword Puzzle (Continued)

3-17 Measurement Puzzlers

Identify the measurement puzzlers. The first one is done for you.

1. 4 = C in a P   4 cups in a pint _____

2. 12 = I in a F   _____

3. 10 = Y in a D   _____

4. 500 = S of P in a R   _____

5. O = F P of W on C S   _____

6. 16 = F O in a P   _____

7. 29 = D in F in a L Y   _____

8. 2,000 = P in a T   _____

9. 4 = S in a Y   _____

10. 4 = T Z in the 48 S   _____

11. 100 = P in a D   _____

12. 3 = S and you're O   _____

13. 98.6 = normal H B T   _____

14. 12 = M in a Y   _____

15. 60 = M in an H   _____

16. 100 = C in a M   _____

17. 10 = C in a M   _____

18. 3 = D in an A C   _____

19. 16 = O in a P   _____

20. 9 = I of a B G   _____

3-18 Measurements Used in Outer Space

The universe is a big place (probably infinite, though no one knows for sure) and astronomers use big units to measure it. Solve the following problems.

1. An *astronomical unit* is 93 million miles, based on the Earth's average distance from the sun. Astronomical units are often used to measure distances within our solar system. Calculate the distance of the planets from our sun in astronomical units. Round your answers to the nearest hundredth.

Planet	Distance from Sun	Astronomical Unit
Mercury	36 million miles	_____
Venus	67 million miles	_____
Earth	93 million miles	1.00
Mars	142 million miles	_____
Jupiter	483 million miles	_____
Saturn	887 million miles	_____
Uranus	1,783 million miles	_____
Neptune	2,794 million miles	_____
Pluto	3,666 million miles	_____

2. The distances between stars are so great that astronomers measure them with light years. A *light year* is the distance that light travels in one Earth year. Light travels about 186,000 miles per second. About how many miles is a light year? Round your answer to the nearest billion.

_____

© 2002 by John Wiley & Sons, Inc.

Name _____   **Date** _____

3-18 Measurements Used in Outer Space (Continued)

3. Along with light years, astronomers use parsecs to measure great distances in space. A *parsec* is equal to 3.26 light years. Calculate the distances of the following stars from our sun in parsecs. Round your answers to the nearest hundredth.

Star	Light Years Distance from Sun	Parsecs
Alpha Centauri	4.3	_____
Sirius	8.7	_____
Arcturus	40	_____
Capella	45	_____
Betelgeuse	520	_____

4. Astronomers refer to the brightness of a star as its *magnitude*. Magnitude 1 stars include most of the brightest stars able to be seen by the naked eye. Magnitude 6 stars are the faintest. A magnitude 1 star is 2.512 times brighter than a magnitude 2 star, which is 2.512 times brighter than a magnitude 3 star, and so on. Answer the questions below. Round your answers to the nearest thousandth.

How many times brighter is a magnitude 1 star than a:

magnitude 3 star? _____

magnitude 4 star? _____

magnitude 5 star? _____

magnitude 6 star? _____

3-19   Tools of Measurement

Use the clues to write the name of the measuring tool in the puzzle. Place one letter in each blank, noting the letters that correspond to the boxes. Then, starting with the first answer, write the "boxed" letters in order to complete the statement. The first problem is done for you.

1. Used to measure the speed of a car or truck.

2. Used to measure the winning time of a race.

3. Used to measure the air pressure of a car's tires.

4. Used to measure time.

5. Used to measure the amount of rainfall.

6. Used to measure air pressure.

7. Used to measure the passing of days.

8. Used to measure a person's hearing.

9. Used to measure the "beat," or tempo, of music.

10. Used to measure the power of earthquakes.

11. Used to measure the degrees of angles.

12. Used to measure the flow of water.

13. Used to measure length.

14. Used to record the number of miles a car travels.

15. Used to measure temperature.

16. Used to measure the speed of the wind.

17. Used to measure altitude.

18. Used to measure weight.

© 2002 by John Wiley & Sons, Inc.

3-19 Tools of Measurement (Continued)

1 [S] P E E D O M E T E R

2 _ _ _ [ ] _ _ _ _ _

3 _ _ _ [ ] _ _ _ _ _

4 [ ] _ _ _ _

5 _ _ _ [ ] _ _ _ _

6 _ [ ] _ _ _ _ _

7 _ _ [ ] _ _ _

8 _ _ _ [ ] _ _ _ _

9 _ _ _ _ _ [ ]

10 _ _ _ [ ] _ _ _ _ _

11 _ _ _ [ ] _ _ _ _

12 _ _ _ _ [ ] _ _ _ _

13 _ [ ] _ _ _

14 _ _ _ [ ] _ _ _

15 _ _ [ ] _ _ _ _ _

16 _ [ ] _ _ _ _ _

17 _ _ [ ] _ _ _ _ _

18 [ ] _ _ _ _

Accurate measurement depends upon using S_ __ __ __ __ __ __ __

__ __ __ __ __ __ __ __ __ __ __ __ __ __.

3-20 Measurement Trivia

Complete these statements on measurement.

1. The _____ is used to express the amount of energy released at the focus of an earthquake.

2. _____ invented the temperature scale that uses 32° for the freezing point of water and 212° for its boiling point. _____ invented the temperature scale that uses 0° for the freezing point of water and 100° for its boiling point.

3. –459.67° F and –273.15° C are known as _____.

4. In the United States, Standard Time plus one hour results in _____.

5. In computer memory, a byte can store 1 character, for example, the letter "a." A kilobyte equals 1,000 bytes. A _____ equals one million bytes, and a _____ equals one billion bytes.

6. _____ is the scale used to describe wind speeds from calm to hurricane force.

7. A _____ is used to measure ring size.

8. Sailors use _____ to describe the depth of water. One of these units is equal to _____ feet.

9. The weight of precious stones is measured in _____.

10. 43,560 square feet, or 4,840 square yards, equals one _____.

11. A _____ is a unit of length used in sea and air navigation that equals about _____ feet.

12. Firewood is often sold in a _____, which equals a stack of wood 4 feet by 4 feet by 8 feet.

Section 4

GEOMETRY

4-1 Geometry Crossword Puzzle

Complete the crossword puzzle.

Across

2. Set of all points.

4. Two lines that lie in the same plane and do not intersect.

5. The figure formed by two rays that have the same endpoint.

6. Another name for the two rays of an angle.

8. An undefined term of geometry.

11. Instrument used to measure an angle.

14. Point that divides a segment into two congruent parts.

15. Instrument used to measure a line segment.

17. The common endpoint of the two rays of an angle.

18. Geometric figure consisting of two points on a line and all the points between them.

20. Part of a line that has only one endpoint.

22. An angle whose measure is between 90° and 180°.

23. An angle whose measure is 180°.

24. Geometric figure represented by a dot.

Down

1. A homophone for plain.

3. Two lines that intersect to form right angles.

6. Two lines that do not lie in the same plane and do not intersect.

7. The distance between the endpoints of a segment.

9. Points that lie on the same line.

10. Two or more angles that have the same measure.

12. An angle whose measure is between 0° and 90°.

13. The unit for measuring angles.

16. An angle whose measure is 90°.

19. A segment has two of these.

21. Points that lie on the same plane.

4-1   Geometry Crossword Puzzle
(Continued)

Name _____   Date _____

4-2   Identifying Types of Angles

Use the diagrams on the left to identify each angle in the group as *acute, right,* or *obtuse*. Circle the letters in the appropriate column. Then write the answers in order, starting with the first problem, to complete the statement below. **Note:** The letters of problems 1 through 9 should be placed in the first set of blanks, and the letters of problems 10 through 20 should be placed in the second set of blanks. Place one letter per blank.

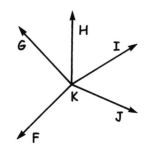

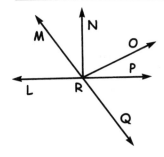

	Acute	Right	Obtuse
1. ∠AEC	li	ac	sm
2. ∠AEB	ut	tt	al
3. ∠CED	us	le	la
4. ∠BED	ab	sh	me
5. ∠BEC	an	or	om
6. ∠AED	tm	gl	in
7. ∠HKJ	ea	su	gs
8. ∠GKH	ha	re	an
9. ∠FKG	an	rp	gl
10. ∠FKJ	gl	ef	ob
11. ∠IKJ	tu	of	mo
12. ∠HKI	su	re	sl
13. ∠GKI	op	th	sw
14. ∠FKI	an	es	hi
15. ∠MRL	ch	ha	ni
16. ∠LRN	ne	me	rp
17. ∠MRP	ty	de	an
18. ∠NRP	gr	sb	ee
19. ∠MRN	lu	es	ne
20. ∠QRN	es	le	nt

The word *acute* is taken from the Latin word ___ ___ ___ ___ ___ ___

___ ___ ___ ___ ___ ___ ___   ___ ___ ___ ___ ___ . The word *obtuse* is taken

from the Latin word ___ ___ ___ ___ ___ ___ ___   ___ ___ ___ ___ ___

___ ___ ___ ___ ___ ___   ___ ___ ___ ___ ___ ___ .

147

4-3   Measuring Angles with a Protractor, I

Find the measure of each angle below. Then arrange the angles from smallest to largest, copying the letters after each. Write the letters in order on the line at the end of the activity to reveal an important fact. Problem number 12, which is the angle with the smallest measure, is done for you.

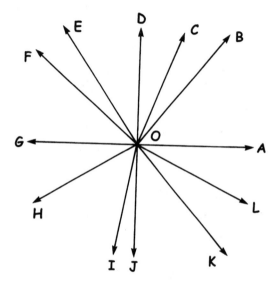

1. m∠BOL = ____	th		**9.** m∠EOC = ____	wi
2. m∠GOH = ____	re		**10.** m∠DOH = ____	t
3. m∠BOC = ____	ua		**11.** m∠GOF = ____	a
4. m∠JOK = ____	pr		**12.** m∠IOJ = __11__	yo
5. m∠KOD = ____	a		**13.** m∠IOE = ____	r
6. m∠AOG = ____	or		**14.** m∠JOA = ____	ap
7. m∠AOH = ____	ct		**15.** m∠DOF = ____	o
8. m∠BOK = ____	ro			

Fact: _Y_ _o_ __ __ __ __ __ __ __ __

___ ___ ___ ___ ___ ___ ___ ___ ___ ___ ___ ___ ___ ___ ___.

4-4 Measuring Angles with a Protractor, II

Find the measure of each angle below. Then arrange the angles from smallest to largest, copying the letters after each. Write the letters in order on the line at the end of the activity to find an important message. You will have to divide the letters to form words. The fourth problem, which is the angle with the smallest measure, is done for you. **Note:** Capital letters are shown where needed in the message.

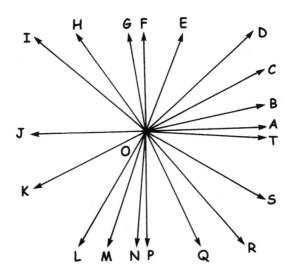

1. m∠ROT = _____	swa	**12.** m∠LOP = _____	deg
2. m∠EOR = _____	lem	**13.** m∠GOK = _____	ius
3. m∠POT = _____	yCl	**14.** m∠BOC = _____	bol
4. m∠NOP = __5__	The	**15.** m∠HOJ = _____	sin
5. m∠EOI = _____	edb	**16.** m∠FOG = _____	sym
6. m∠FOP = _____	est	**17.** m∠EOQ = _____	his
7. m∠HOQ = _____	kAl	**18.** m∠DOR = _____	aud
8. m∠EOJ = _____	Pto	**19.** m∠JOT = _____	mag
9. m∠KOS = _____	yin	**20.** m∠GOM = _____	wor
10. m∠EOF = _____	for	**21.** m∠POS = _____	tro
11. m∠GOI = _____	ree	**22.** m∠AOE = _____	duc

Message: The _____

_____ .

4-5 Calculating the Measures of Angles in a Diagram

Find the measure of each angle on the next page. Write the measure and its corresponding letter in the appropriate blanks. When you are done, write the letters in order, starting with the first problem, to complete the statement. The first problem is done for you.

30—T	55—O	65—D	90—E	140—F	150—P
40—I	60—H	75—L	125—N	145—R	165—C
					180—A

1. m∠2 =   __40__ __I__

2. m∠3 =   ____ __

3. m∠5 =   ____ __

4. m∠BEC =   ____ __

5. m∠AED =   ____ __

6. m∠BED =   ____ __

7. m∠CED =   ____ __

8. m∠GKH =   ____ __

9. m∠FKE =   ____ __

10. m∠EKJ = ____ __

11. m∠EKG = ____ __

12. m∠FKJ = ____ __

13. m∠PSQ = ____ __

14. m∠OSP = ____ __

15. m∠RSQ = ____ __

16. m∠MSN = ____ __

17. m∠LSM = ____ __

18. m∠LSN = ____ __

19. m∠XBY = ____ __

20. m∠ABZ = ____ __

21. m∠TBA = ____ __

22. m∠VBX = ____ __

23. m∠VBY = ____ __

The word *congruent* is taken from the Latin word *cogruens,* which means "to meet together." *Congruent angles* are identical and will meet together _i_ __

__ __ __ __ __   __ __ __   __ __ __ __   __ __ __

__ __ __ __ __.

4-5   Calculating the Measures of Angles in a Diagram (Continued)

For problems 1 and 2

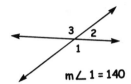

m∠1 = 140

For problem 3

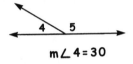

m∠4 = 30

For problems 4-7

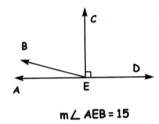

m∠AEB = 15

For problems 8-12

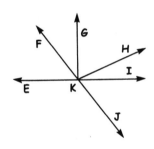

$\overrightarrow{KG} \perp \overleftrightarrow{EI}$
m∠HKI = 25
m∠FKG = 35

For problems 13-18

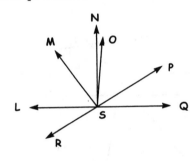

$\overrightarrow{SN} \perp \overleftrightarrow{LQ}$
m∠NSO = 5
m∠LSR = 30
∠MSN ≈ ∠LSR

For problems 19-23

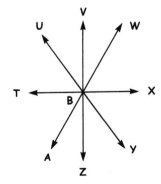

m∠TBU = 55
m∠WBX = 60
m∠ZBY = 35

4-6 Identifying Parallel and Perpendicular Lines

Study the diagram. Use a protractor and ruler to identify the parallel and perpendicular lines. List all of them on the lines below. There are two pairs of each.

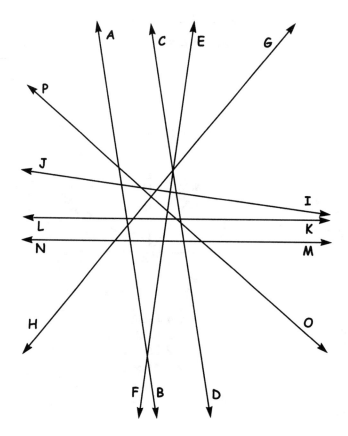

Parallel Lines:

_____

Perpendicular Lines:

_____

Look around your classroom. Identify and list three examples of parallel lines. Identify and list three examples of perpendicular lines. Write your answers on the back of this sheet.

Name _____   Date _____

4-7 Parallel Lines, Perpendicular Lines, and Angles

Study the diagram. List all of the parallel lines, perpendicular lines, right angles, acute angles, and obtuse angles. The number in parentheses indicates the number of each type of geometric figure.

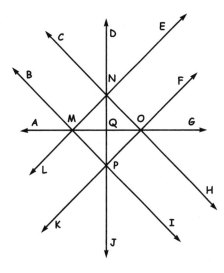

Parallel Lines (2 pairs):

_____

Perpendicular Lines (5 pairs):

_____

Right Angles (20):

_____

_____

_____

Acute Angles (16):

_____

_____

_____

Obtuse Angles (16):

_____

_____

_____

4-8 Identifying Angles Formed by Parallel Lines and Transversals

---

In the diagram, Lines 1 and 2 are parallel, and Lines 3 and 4 are parallel. Several pairs of different types of angles are formed. Some of these pairs are listed below the diagram. Identify each pair of angles on the list and write it on the appropriate line below. **Hint:** There are five pairs of each type of angle listed below.

Corresponding Angles: _____

_____

Vertical Angles: _____

_____

Alternate Interior Angles: _____

_____

Same Side Interior Angles: _____

_____

Alternate Exterior Angles: _____

_____

Same Side Exterior Angles: _____

_____

Linear Pairs: _____

_____

Name _____   Date _____

4-8 Identifying Angles Formed by Parallel Lines and Transversals

(Continued)

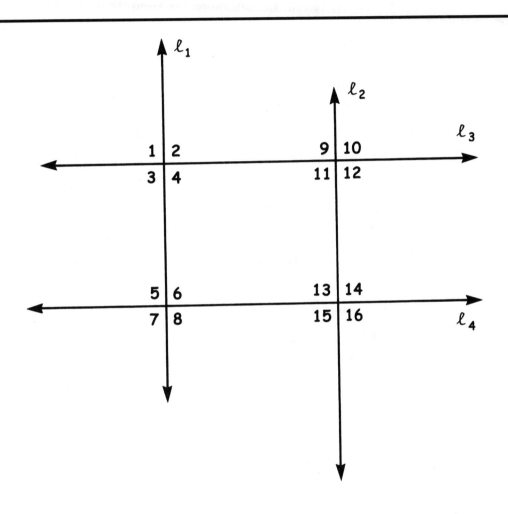

$\angle 1$ and $\angle 4$	$\angle 2$ and $\angle 8$	$\angle 4$ and $\angle 8$	$\angle 6$ and $\angle 8$	$\angle 9$ and $\angle 15$
$\angle 1$ and $\angle 5$	$\angle 2$ and $\angle 9$	$\angle 4$ and $\angle 9$	$\angle 6$ and $\angle 13$	$\angle 10$ and $\angle 11$
$\angle 1$ and $\angle 8$	$\angle 2$ and $\angle 10$	$\angle 4$ and $\angle 11$	$\angle 7$ and $\angle 14$	$\angle 11$ and $\angle 12$
$\angle 1$ and $\angle 10$	$\angle 3$ and $\angle 4$	$\angle 5$ and $\angle 13$	$\angle 7$ and $\angle 16$	$\angle 12$ and $\angle 13$
$\angle 1$ and $\angle 12$	$\angle 3$ and $\angle 5$	$\angle 5$ and $\angle 14$	$\angle 8$ and $\angle 13$	$\angle 12$ and $\angle 14$
$\angle 2$ and $\angle 4$	$\angle 3$ and $\angle 6$	$\angle 5$ and $\angle 16$	$\angle 9$ and $\angle 10$	$\angle 13$ and $\angle 16$
$\angle 2$ and $\angle 7$	$\angle 4$ and $\angle 5$	$\angle 6$ and $\angle 7$	$\angle 9$ and $\angle 13$	$\angle 14$ and $\angle 15$

4-9   Naming Polygons

Sixteen types of polygons are written in the column on the right. Place the letter of the polygon on the blank before its definition in the column on the left. To decode the message, place the letter above the same number in the blanks at the bottom of the page.

1. _____ a polygon with 3 sides
2. _____ a quadrilateral with 2 pairs of parallel sides
3. _____ a polygon with 6 sides
4. _____ a triangle with no congruent sides
5. _____ a polygon with 8 sides
6. _____ a triangle with at least 2 congruent sides
7. _____ a polygon with 4 sides
8. _____ a quadrilateral with exactly 1 pair of parallel sides
9. _____ a polygon with 10 sides
10. _____ a triangle with 3 acute angles
11. _____ a quadrilateral with 4 congruent sides
12. _____ a quadrilateral with 4 congruent sides and 4 right angles
13. _____ a polygon with 5 sides
14. _____ a quadrilateral with 4 right angles
15. _____ a triangle with 3 congruent sides
16. _____ a triangle with 1 right angle

K. scalene triangle
P. decagon
T. square
S. parallelogram
M. quadrilateral
G. trapezoid
E. equilateral triangle
O. triangle
R. rhombus
Y. pentagon
N. isosceles triangle
A. right triangle
F. rectangle
H. hexagon
L. octagon
I. acute triangle

___ ___ ___ ___ ___ ___ ___   ___ ___   ___ ___ ___ ___ ___
9   1   5   13 8   1   6   10 2   12 16 4   15 6

___ ___ ___ ___   ___ ___ ___   ___ ___ ___ ___ ___
14 11 1   7   12 3   15   8   11 15 15 4

___ ___ ___ ___   ___ ___ ___ ___ ___ ___ ___ ___ ___
12 15 11 7   9   1   5   13 8   1   6   1   2

___ ___ ___   ___ ___ ___ ___   ___ ___ ___ ___
7   15 16   6   10 6   8   7   16 6   13

___ ___ ___ ___ ___ ___
16 6   8   5   15 2

4-10 Finding the Number of Sides and Angle Measures of Regular Polygons

Complete the chart by placing the correct number in the blank next to each letter. Then place each letter above its corresponding number in the blanks at the end of the activity to complete the message. **Note:** One letter is not used.

Type of Regular Polygon	Number of Sides	Sum of Measures of Interior Angles (in Degrees)	Measure of Each Interior Angle (in Degrees)
Pentagon	X _____	G _____	P _____
Octagon	T _____	F _____	A _____
Quadrilateral	O _____	R _____	N _____
Hexagon	L _____	I _____	Y _____
Triangle	S _____	H _____	E _____
Decagon	U _____	M _____	B _____

360° is the sum of _____ _____ _____
                                    8   180   60

_____ _____ _____ _____ _____ _____ _____ _____
1,440 60   135   3   10   360   60   3

_____ _____ _____ _____ _____
  4   1,080   8   180   60

_____ _____ _____ _____ _____ _____ _____ _____
 60   5   8   60   360   720   4   360

_____ _____ _____ _____ _____ _____   _____ _____ _____ _____ _____
135 90   540   6   60   3   4   1,080   135   90   120

_____ _____ _____ _____ _____ _____ .
108   4   6   120   540   4   90

157

4-11   Words and Numbers of Triangles Crossword Puzzle

Complete the crossword puzzle.

Across

1. The side opposite the vertex angle of an isosceles triangle.

4. This triangle has three acute angles.

7. This triangle is never acute or obtuse.

9. This triangle has three sides of different lengths.

11. This triangle has one obtuse angle.

13. Name of the angle that is *not* congruent to the base angles of an isosceles triangle (two words).

14. The number of obtuse angles in a right triangle.

15. The sides adjacent to the right angle of a right triangle.

16. A word that means "have the same measure."

17. The measure of each angle of an equilateral triangle (in degrees).

18. This triangle has at least two congruent sides.

19. The two legs of a right triangle have this property.

Down

2. Every triangle has three of these.

3. This triangle has three congruent sides.

5. The two acute angles of a right triangle have this property.

6. The number of right angles in a right triangle.

8. The side opposite the right angle of a right triangle.

10. The sum of the measures of the angles in any triangle equals 180 of these.

12. The number of acute angles in an obtuse triangle.

17. Another name for the congruent legs of an isosceles triangle.

Name _____   Date _____

4-11   Words and Numbers of Triangles Crossword Puzzle (Continued)

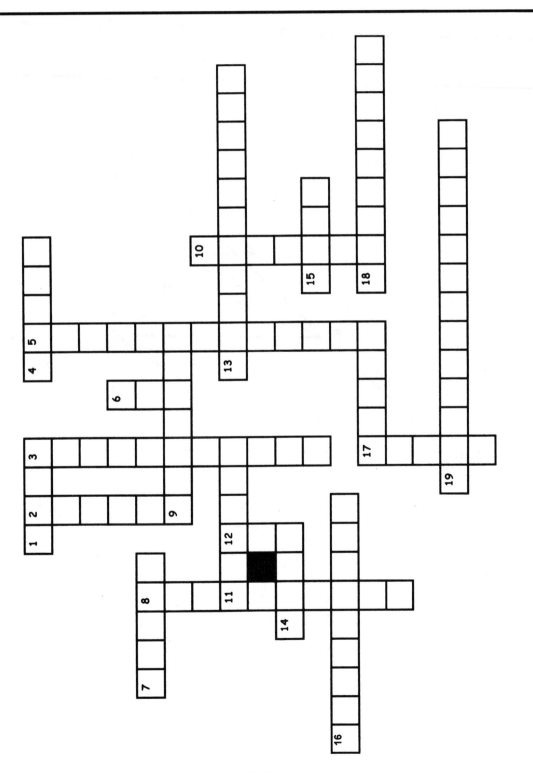

4-12 Identifying Acute, Obtuse, and Right Triangles

Study the diagram. Use a protractor and ruler to identify all of the acute, obtuse, and right triangles. Write them on the lines below. The number in parentheses indicates the number of each type of triangle.

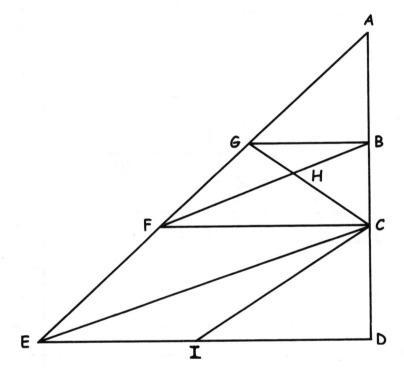

Acute (2): _____

Obtuse (10): _____

_____

Right (7): _____

_____

4-13 Classifying Triangles

Use a protractor and ruler to identify the triangle in each row that does not belong with the others. Circle that triangle, and then explain on the lines that follow why the triangle does not belong. Remember that triangles are classified by their sides and angles.

1. A.   B.   C.   D.

_____

_____

2. A.   B.   C.   D.

_____

_____

3. A.  B.   C.   D.

_____

_____

4. A.   B.   C.   D.

_____

_____

5. A.  B.   C.  D.

_____

_____

4-13 Classifying Triangles (Continued)

6. A.  B.   C.   D.

---

7. A.  B.   C.   D.

---

8. A. 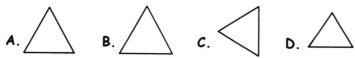 B.   C.   D.

---

9. A.  B.   C. D.

---

10. A. B. C.   D.

Name _____   Date _____

4-14 Drawing Triangles

Use a ruler and protractor to draw an example of each triangle described below. Use a separate sheet of paper for your drawings. **Note:** Some triangles may be drawn in more than one way.

1. An obtuse isosceles triangle. The length of each leg is two inches.

2. An obtuse isosceles triangle. The length of the base is two inches.

3. An acute isosceles triangle. The length of each leg is two inches.

4. An acute isosceles triangle. The length of the base is two inches.

5. A right isosceles triangle. The length of each leg is two inches.

6. A right isosceles triangle. The length of the hypotenuse is two inches.

7. An obtuse scalene triangle. The length of the shortest side is two inches.

8. A right scalene triangle. The length of the shortest leg is two inches.

9. An acute scalene triangle. The length of the side that is neither the shortest nor longest is two inches.

10. An equilateral triangle. The length of each side is two inches.

4-15 Finding the Sum of the Measures of Angles in a Triangle

The degrees of some of the angles in the four triangles below are labeled. Without using a protractor, find the measures of the angles labeled with the lower-case letter near the vertex. Then record the letter of the angle over its measure to complete the statement.

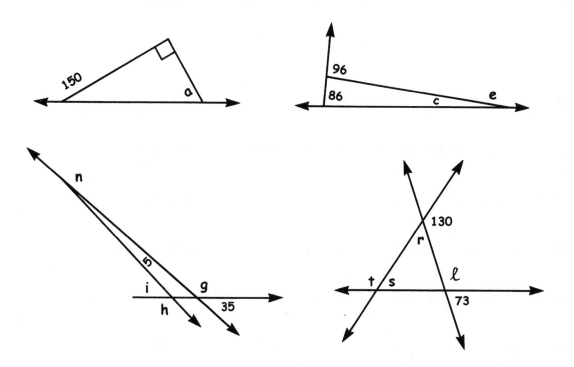

All of ____ ____ ____   ____ ____ ____ ____ ____ ____ ____ ____ ____
       123 140 170   123 50   40   60 175 145 107 170   57

____ ____ ____   ____ ____ ____ ____ ____ ____ ____.
60   50   170   57   10   60 107 170 175 170

Name _____   **Date** _____

4-16 Finding the Measures of Angles in Triangles, I

Study the diagram below. Given the following information, find the measure of each angle. **Note:** You may not use protractors.

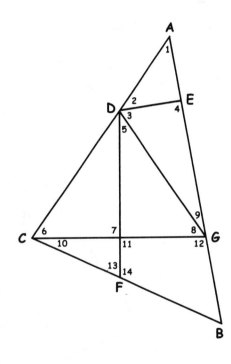

$$\overline{DC} \cong \overline{DG}$$

$$\overline{AE} \cong \overline{DE}$$

$$\overline{DF} \perp \overline{CG}$$

m∠CDF = 35

m∠AED = 88

m∠CBA = 56

1. m∠1 = _____

2. m∠2 = _____

3. m∠3 = _____

4. m∠4 = _____

5. m∠5 = _____

6. m∠6 = _____

7. m∠7 = _____

8. m∠8 = _____

9. m∠9 = _____

10. m∠10 = _____

11. m∠11 = _____

12. m∠12 = _____

13. m∠13 = _____

14. m∠14 = _____

4-17   Finding the Measures of Angles in Triangles, II

Study the diagram below. Given the following information, find the measure of each angle. **Note:** You may not use protractors.

G is the midpoint of $\overline{AB}$		D is the midpoint of $\overline{AC}$	
$\overline{AN} \perp \overline{CB}$	m∠AGD = 48	m∠ACB = 56	m∠DNA = 32
m∠GMB = 80	m∠DGC = 25	m∠DHA = 72	m∠AOC = 82

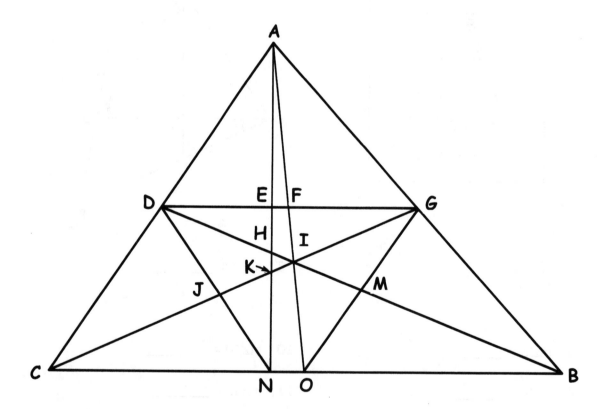

4-17   Finding the Measures of Angles in Triangles, II (Continued)

1. m∠ADG = _____

2. m∠ABC = _____

3. m∠AOB = _____

4. m∠NAO = _____

5. m∠AED = _____

6. m∠CAN = _____

7. m∠CAB = _____

8. m∠GDB = _____

9. m∠DIG = _____

10. m∠AFD = _____

11. m∠OAB = _____

12. m∠AFG = _____

13. m∠OFG = _____

14. m∠AIG = _____

15. m∠CGB = _____

16. m∠ABD = _____

17. m∠DMG = _____

18. m∠OIB = _____

19. m∠OGB = _____

20. m∠CGO = _____

21. m∠DNC = _____

22. m∠GCB = _____

23. m∠ACG = _____

24. m∠CDN = _____

25. m∠CJD = _____

26. m∠AOG = _____

27. m∠GOB = _____

28. m∠NDB = _____

29. m∠CKN = _____

30. m∠CIB = _____

4-18 Identifying Segments, Angles, and Types of Triangles

Study the diagram, then write the letter of each phrase on the right in the blank before the figure it most closely matches on the left. When you are done, write the letters in order, starting with the first problem, to complete the statement.

E is the midpoint of $\overline{CA}$

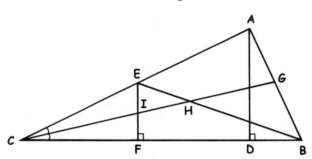

1. _____ ∠DAB and ∠DBA
2. _____ $\overline{CE}$ and $\overline{EA}$
3. _____ ∠ADB
4. _____ $\overline{CE}$
5. _____ $\overline{CG}$
6. _____ ΔCHE
7. _____ ∠CBE
8. _____ ΔHEI
9. _____ ∠ACG and ∠GCB
10. _____ $\overline{BE}$
11. _____ $\overline{AD}$
12. _____ $\overline{EF}$ and $\overline{AD}$
13. _____ $\overline{EF}$
14. _____ ∠EHG and ∠CHB
15. _____ ΔEFB
16. _____ ∠CHB
17. _____ $\overline{AD}$ and $\overline{DB}$
18. _____ ∠AGC and ∠CGB

E. a right angle
H. an acute triangle
O. an angle bisector
T. an acute angle
A. a median
L. an altitude of ΔABC
T. vertical angles
D. an obtuse angle
F. complementary angles
E. legs of a right triangle
U. a right triangle
F. an obtuse triangle
S. a linear pair
T. parallel segments
T. a hypotenuse of ΔCEF
I. a leg of ΔCFE and ΔBEF
E. congruent segments
E. adjacent congruent angles

A pedal triangle is formed by joining the ___ ___ ___ ___   ___ ___

___ ___ ___   ___ ___ ___ ___ ___ ___ ___ ___ ___ ___.

Name _____   **Date** _____

4-19 Using the Pythagorean Theorem

Match the length of the missing leg or hypotenuse of each triangle with its measure given in the box. (**Note:** a and b represent the lengths of the legs; c represents the length of the hypotenuse.) Write your answers and their corresponding letters on the blanks. Then write the letters above the problem numbers to complete the statement at the end of this activity. The first problem is done for you.

Example of a Right Triangle

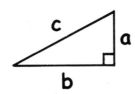

5—O	16—L	25—R
8—A	20—D	34—G
11—E	21—I	40—S
15—T	24—H	45—N

1. a = __8__   b = 15   c = 17
___A___

2. a = 10   b = ____   c = 26
____

3. a = ____   b = 48   c = 52
____

4. a = 9   b = 12   c = ____
____

5. a = 7   b = 24   c = ____
____

6. a = 9   b = ____   c = 41
____

7. a = ____   b = 28   c = 35
____

8. a = 24   b = ____   c = 51
____

9. a = 12   b = ____   c = 20
____

10. a = ____   b = 60   c = 61
____

11. a = 3   b = 4   c = ____
____

12. a = 16   b = 30   c = ____
____

The word *hypotenuse* is taken from the Greek words *hypo* and *teinein*, meaning to "stretch under." It was used by Pythagoras to describe the relationship of the legs of a

right ___ ___ ___ _A_ ___ ___ ___ ___   ___ ___   ___ ___ ___
     4   5   7   1   8   12   9   10   4   11   4   2   10

___ ___ ___ ___ ___ ___ ___   ___ ___ ___ ___.
9   11   8   12   10   6   4   6   7   3   10

4-20 Testing for Acute, Obtuse, and Right Triangles

The following are true for triangles:

- If $a^2 + b^2 = c^2$, the triangle is a right triangle.
- If $a^2 + b^2 > c^2$, the triangle is acute.
- If $a^2 + b^2 < c^2$, the triangle is obtuse.

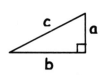

$a^2 + b^2 = c^2$
Right Triangle

$a^2 + b^2 > c^2$
Acute Triangle

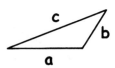

$a^2 + b^2 < c^2$
Obtuse Triangle

Directions: Classify the triangles below as acute, obtuse, or right. **Note:** c is always the longest side.

1. a = 5, b = 8, c = 10 _____
2. a = 5, b = 6, c = 7 _____
3. a = 5, b = 12, c = 13 _____
4. a = 5, b = 8, c = 12 _____
5. a = 6, b = 8, c = 10 _____
6. a = 7, b = 24, c = 25 _____
7. a = 4, b = 5, c = 6 _____
8. a = 5, b = 5, c = 9 _____
9. a = 4, b = 6, c = 9 _____
10. a = 4, b = 4, c = 5 _____
11. a = 8, b = 15, c = 17 _____
12. a = 8, b = 10, c = 14 _____

Find the square of the number of acute triangles, and add this number to the square of the number of the right triangles. If this sum equals the square of the number of obtuse triangles, your math is probably correct.

Number of acute triangles _____, squared _____

Number of right triangles _____, squared _____

Number of obtuse triangles _____, squared _____

4-21 Finding the Missing Lengths of the Sides of 45°–45°–90° and 30°–60°–90° Triangles

The diagrams below show the relationship of the length of the hypotenuse and legs of the 45°–45°–90° triangle and the 30°–60°–90° triangle.

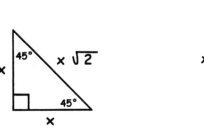

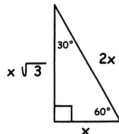

Directions: Given the length of the legs or the hypotenuse in the triangles that follow, find the missing length. Then write the corresponding letter above the answer to complete the statement at the end of the activity. The first problem is done for you.

1. The length of a leg of a 45°–45°–90° triangle is 6.

    The length of the hypotenuse is $\dfrac{6\sqrt{2}}{A}$.

2. The length of a leg of a 45°–45°–90° triangle is $6\sqrt{2}$. The length of the hypotenuse

    is $\underset{C}{\underline{\quad\quad}}$.

3. The length of the shorter leg of a 30°–60°–90° triangle is 7. The length of the longer

    leg is $\underset{E}{\underline{\quad\quad}}$ and the length of the hypotenuse is $\underset{G}{\underline{\quad\quad}}$.

4. The length of the longer leg of a 30°–60°–90° triangle is 18. The length of the short-

    er leg is $\underset{H}{\underline{\quad\quad}}$ and the length of the hypotenuse is $\underset{I}{\underline{\quad\quad}}$.

4-21 Finding the Missing Lengths of the Sides of 45°–45°–90° and 30°–60°–90° Triangles

(Continued)

---

5. The length of the hypotenuse of a 45°–45°–90° triangle is 16. The length of the leg is _____.

          L

6. The length of the hypotenuse of a 45°–45°–90° triangle is $10\sqrt{2}$. The length of the leg is _____.

      N

7. The length of the hypotenuse of a 30°–60°–90° triangle is 10. The length of the shorter leg is _____, and the length of the longer leg is _____.

        O   R

8. The length of the hypotenuse of a 30°–60°–90° triangle is $16\sqrt{3}$. The length of the shorter leg is _____ and the length of the longer leg is _____.

        S   T

All $\overline{}$ $\overline{}$ $\overline{}$ $\overline{}$ $\overline{}$ $\overline{}$ $\overline{}$ $\overline{}$ $\overset{A}{\overline{}}$ $\overline{}$ $\overline{}$ $\overline{}$ $\overline{}$ $\overline{}$

    $5\sqrt{3}$ $12\sqrt{3}$ 14 $6\sqrt{3}$ 24   24 $5\sqrt{3}$ $12\sqrt{3}$ $6\sqrt{2}$ 10 14 $8\sqrt{2}$ $7\sqrt{3}$ $8\sqrt{3}$

$\overset{A}{\overline{}}$ $\overline{}$ $\overline{}$ $\overline{}$ $\overline{}$ $\overline{}$ $\overline{}$ $\overline{}$ $\overline{}$ $\overline{}$ $\overline{}$ $\overline{}$

$6\sqrt{2}$ $5\sqrt{3}$ $7\sqrt{3}$ $12\sqrt{3}$ $8\sqrt{3}$ 5 $8\sqrt{3}$ 12 $7\sqrt{3}$ $8\sqrt{2}$ $7\sqrt{3}$ $8\sqrt{3}$ 5 $5\sqrt{3}$

$\overline{}$ $\overline{}$ $\overset{A}{\overline{}}$ $\overline{}$ $\overline{}$ $\overline{}$ $\overline{}$.

$8\sqrt{3}$ 12 $6\sqrt{2}$ $8\sqrt{2}$ $7\sqrt{3}$ 10 $7\sqrt{3}$

Name _____   Date _____

4-22 Identifying Congruent Triangles

Use a ruler and protractor to help you determine which triangles are congruent. Write a congruence statement for each group of congruent triangles. **Note:** Every triangle below is congruent to at least one other triangle.

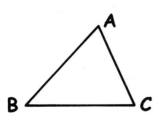 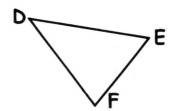 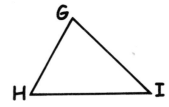

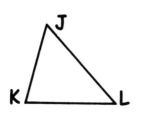 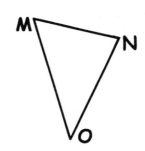 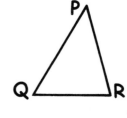

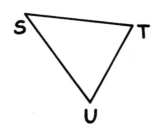 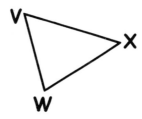

_____

_____

_____

4-23 Using SSS, SAS, ASA, AAS, and HL to Verify Congruent Triangles

Two of the triangles in each row are congruent to each other. Circle the congruent triangles and choose the postulate or theorem (SSS, SAS, ASA, AAS, or HL) that supports your answer.

Theorem

1. A.    B. 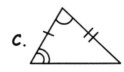   C.   _____

2. A.   B.   C.   _____

3. A.   B.   C.   _____

4. A.   B.   C.   _____

5. A.   B.   C.   _____

Name _____ **Date** _____

4-23 Using SSS, SAS, ASA, AAS, and HL to Verify Congruent Triangles

(Continued)

Theorem

6. A.   B. C. _____

7. A.   B.  C. _____

8. A.   B. C.  _____

9. A.   B. C. _____

10. A.   B. C. _____

4-24 Proving Two Triangles Are Congruent

Each pair of triangles on the left may be proven to be congruent by the accompanying theorem or postulate. Choose the information at the end of the activity that supports each postulate or theorem. Write your answers in the blanks. Each answer is used only once. The first problem is done for you.

1.

    $\triangle ABC \cong \triangle DEF$
    by SSS

    $\overline{AC} \cong \overline{DF}$

2.

    $\triangle ABC \cong \triangle EDF$
    by SAS

    _____

3.

    $\triangle ABC \cong \triangle EDF$
    by SSS

    _____

4.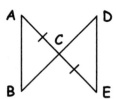

    $\triangle ABC \cong \triangle EDC$
    by SAS

    _____

5.

    $\triangle ABC \cong \triangle CAD$
    by HL

    _____

4-24 Proving Two Triangles Are Congruent (Continued)

6.   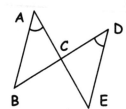 $\triangle ABC \cong \triangle DEC$
                                                      by ASA

                                                      _____

7.   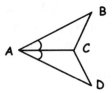 $\triangle ABC \cong \triangle ADC$
                                                      by AAS

                                                      _____

8.   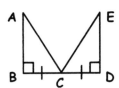 $\triangle ABC \cong \triangle EDC$
                                                      by HL

                                                      _____

9.   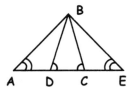 $\triangle ABC \cong \triangle EBD$
                                                      by ASA

                                                      _____

10.   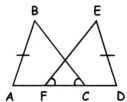 $\triangle ABC \cong \triangle DEF$
                                                      by AAS

                                                      _____

Choose your answers from among the following:				
$\angle A \cong \angle E$	$\angle B \cong \angle D$	$\angle B \cong \angle E$	$\overline{AC} \cong \overline{DF}$	$\overline{AC} \cong \overline{DC}$
$\overline{AC} \cong \overline{EC}$	$\overline{AC} \cong \overline{ED}$	$\overline{AD} \cong \overline{BC}$	$\overline{BC} \cong \overline{DC}$	$\overline{BC} \cong \overline{DF}$

© 2002 by John Wiley & Sons, Inc.

4-25 Properties of Special Quadrilaterals, 1

Quadrilaterals are four-sided polygons. Some special quadrilaterals are shown below.

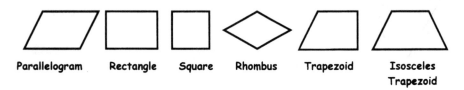

Parallelogram   Rectangle   Square   Rhombus   Trapezoid   Isosceles Trapezoid

Some of these quadrilaterals have special properties that are listed below. Write the number of the property on the line after each quadrilateral. Most will have more than one answer. Then use the information to fill in the blanks at the end of the activity.

1. Both pairs of opposite sides are parallel.
2. Only one pair of sides is parallel.
3. Only one pair of sides is congruent.
4. All angles are right angles.
5. All sides are congruent.
6. The opposite sides are congruent.
7. The opposite angles are congruent.
8. It is a special type of parallelogram.
9. It is a special type of rectangle.
10. It is a special type of rhombus.

Parallelogram: _____

Rectangle: _____

Square: _____

Rhombus: _____

Trapezoid: _____

Isosceles Trapezoid: _____

    Sum of all recorded numbers = _____

    Sum × 3 = _____

    Product − 12 = _____

The difference is the sum of the interior angles of a quadrilateral.

© 2002 by John Wiley & Sons, Inc.

Name _____   Date _____

4-26 Properties of Special Quadrilaterals, II

Study the quadrilaterals below.

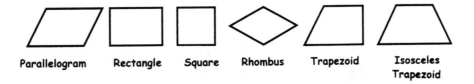

Parallelogram   Rectangle   Square   Rhombus   Trapezoid   Isosceles Trapezoid

Each of these quadrilaterals has many of the properties that follow. Write the letter of the property on the line after each quadrilateral. The number in parentheses after the quadrilateral indicates how many of the properties apply.

A. Only one pair of sides is parallel.

B. Only one pair of sides is congruent.

C. The lower base angles are congruent and the upper base angles are congruent. (These pairs of angles are not congruent to each other.)

D. The diagonals are congruent.

E. The legs are congruent.

F. Both pairs of opposite sides are parallel.

G. All pairs of consecutive angles are supplementary.

H. Only two pairs of consecutive angles are supplementary.

I. The opposite angles are congruent.

J. The opposite sides are congruent.

K. The diagonals bisect each other.

L. All angles are right angles.

M. All sides are congruent.

N. The diagonals are perpendicular to each other.

O. The diagonals bisect opposite angles.

Parallelogram (5): _____

Rectangle (7): _____

Square (10): _____

Rhombus (8): _____

Trapezoid (2): _____

Isosceles Trapezoid (6): _____

179

4-27 Identifying Quadrilaterals

Study the diagram. Find all of the rectangles, squares, rhombi, parallelograms, and trapezoids. The number in parentheses indicates the number of each type of quadrilateral. Identify them on the lines below.

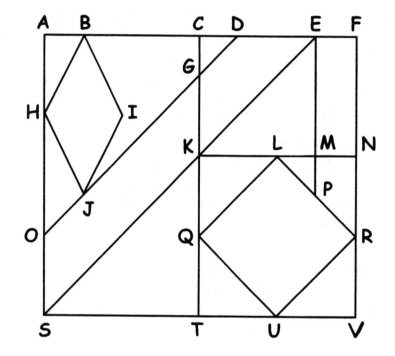

© 2002 by John Wiley & Sons, Inc.

Rectangles (5): _____

Squares (3): _____

Rhombus (1): _____

Parallelogram (1): _____

Trapezoids (10): _____

© 2002 by John Wiley & Sons, Inc.

Name _____   **Date** _____

4-28 Properties of Parallel Lines and Quadrilaterals

Study Parallelogram ABCD below. Given the following information, find the missing lengths of the segments and measures of the angles. **Note:** You may not use protractors.

$\overline{AE} \cong \overline{EG} \cong \overline{GD}$	EF = 4	$\overline{NO}$ bisects $\angle MLB$
$\overline{AF} \cong \overline{FH} \cong \overline{HB}$	AB = 15	m$\angle$ABO = 130
$\overline{IM} \perp \overline{PQ}$	AE = 4.5	m$\angle$A = 50

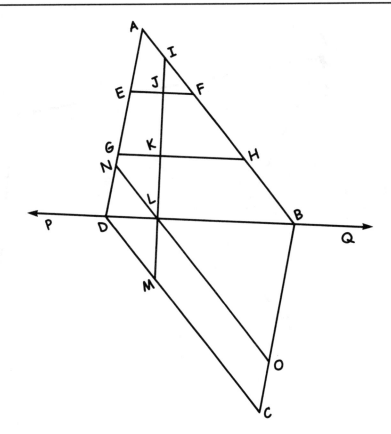

1. GH = _____
2. DB = _____
3. AD = _____
4. FH = _____
5. BC = _____

6. m$\angle$ABD = _____
7. m$\angle$AGH = _____
8. m$\angle$ADC = _____
9. m$\angle$PDA = _____
10. m$\angle$IMC = _____

11. m$\angle$LOC = _____
12. m$\angle$DNO = _____
13. m$\angle$MIB = _____
14. m$\angle$IKG = _____
15. m$\angle$BLO = _____
16. m$\angle$DGK = _____

4-29 Finding the Measures of Angles in a Quadrilateral

Study the diagram below. Given the following information, find the measure of each angle. **Note:** You may not use protractors.

$\overline{AB} \parallel \overline{DC}$ $\overline{AG} \perp \overline{DC}$ $m\angle BCD = 75$ $m\angle DIE = 120$

$\overline{EF} \parallel \overline{BC}$ $\overline{AD} \cong \overline{EF} \cong \overline{BC}$ $m\angle AJC = 130$

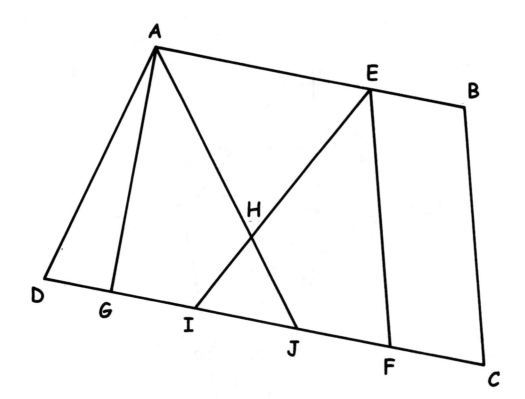

1. $m\angle BEF =$ _____
2. $m\angle EFC =$ _____
3. $m\angle AEF =$ _____
4. $m\angle ABC =$ _____
5. $m\angle EFD =$ _____

6. $m\angle AGC =$ _____
7. $m\angle GAB =$ _____
8. $m\angle ADC =$ _____
9. $m\angle DAG =$ _____
10. $m\angle AEI =$ _____

11. $m\angle IEF =$ _____
12. $m\angle EHJ =$ _____
13. $m\angle IHJ =$ _____
14. $m\angle GAJ =$ _____
15. $m\angle JAE =$ _____
16. $m\angle DAJ =$ _____

Name _____   Date _____

4-30 Dividing a Square into Pentomino Pieces

Pentominoes are figures formed by joining five congruent squares along the sides so that all sides are adjacent. There are only 12 pentominoes and they are pictured below.

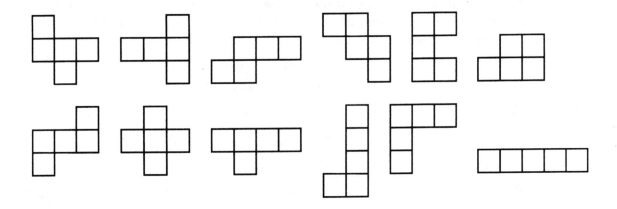

Every 5 × 5 square can be divided into five pentomino pieces. An example of such a division is shown below. Other divisions are possible. Note that each pentomino piece contains the digits 1 through 5.

1	2	3	4	5
5	4	3	5	4
2	1	2	1	3
1	2	3	3	2
5	4	5	4	1

Divide each square that follows into five pentominoes. **Note:** Your task will be easier if each pentomino piece contains the digits 1 through 5.

4	1	4	2	1
3	3	5	4	5
5	2	1	3	2
2	3	5	1	5
4	1	2	3	4

1	2	1	2	4
5	3	2	4	5
2	4	5	3	3
1	3	4	5	1
1	3	5	4	2

183

4-31 Identifying Geometric Figures in Circles

Study the diagram on the next page. Write the letter of the word or phrase on the right that matches the geometric figure on the left. **Note:** Some letters will be used more than once.

When you are finished, write the letters in order, starting with the first problem, to complete the statement at the end of the activity. Two important properties will be revealed. One applies to some circles, and the other applies to all circles.

1. _____ ∆AOC
2. _____ EF
3. _____ OD
4. _____ AB
5. _____ ∠AOC
6. _____ AB⌢
7. _____ DB
8. _____ OA
9. _____ ∆BOD
10. _____ BG
11. _____ ∠ODI
12. _____ OC
13. _____ IJ↔
14. _____ ∆AGB
15. _____ ∠CDB
16. _____ GDE⌢
17. _____ ∠BAC
18. _____ CEBD
19. _____ ∠AGB
20. _____ ∠COD
21. _____ ∠CEB
22. _____ GE⌢
23. _____ HG↔

A. a right angle
C. an isosceles triangle
D. a tangent line
E. a chord that is not the diameter
G. a diameter
I. an inscribed angle that is not a right angle
L. an inscribed quadrilateral
M. a major arc
N. a radius
O. a segment that has no special name
R. a central angle
S. a right triangle
T. a minor arc
U. a semicircle
Y. a secant line

The two properties are __.

4-31 Identifying Geometric Figures in Circles (Continued)

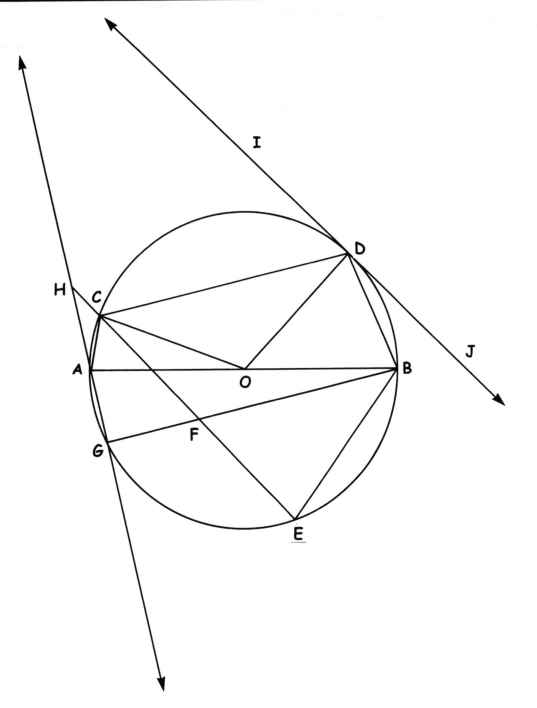

O is the center of the circle.

4-32 Finding the Measures of Missing Angles and Arcs in a Circle

Study the diagram on the next page. Given the following information, find the measures of the arcs and angles. **Note:** You may not use protractors.

$\overline{DO} \perp \overline{AB}$ $\overleftrightarrow{NQ}$ is tangent to the circle at C $m\overset{\frown}{AC}$ = 48

$m\angle GAB$ = 33 $m\angle AME$ = 104 $m\angle CHE$ = 57 $m\angle CEH$ = 58

1. $m\overset{\frown}{CD}$ = _____

2. $m\overset{\frown}{DE}$ = _____

3. $m\overset{\frown}{EB}$ = _____

4. $m\overset{\frown}{GB}$ = _____

5. $m\overset{\frown}{GH}$ = _____

6. $m\overset{\frown}{HA}$ = _____

7. $m\angle HNQ$ = _____

8. $m\angle OCQ$ = _____

9. $m\angle ECQ$ = _____

10. $m\angle AGB$ = _____

11. $m\angle ABG$ = _____

12. $m\angle ABD$ = _____

13. $m\angle ADB$ = _____

14. $m\angle HCE$ = _____

15. $m\angle BIH$ = _____

16. $m\angle CLG$ = _____

17. $m\angle AJH$ = _____

18. $m\angle ODB$ = _____

19. $m\angle OCE$ = _____

20. $m\angle OKF$ = _____

21. $m\angle AOD$ = _____

22. $m\angle AIC$ = _____

23. $m\angle GBD$ = _____

24. $m\angle HCN$ = _____

25. $m\angle CFG$ = _____

4-32 Finding the Measures of Missing Angles and Arcs in a Circle
(Continued)

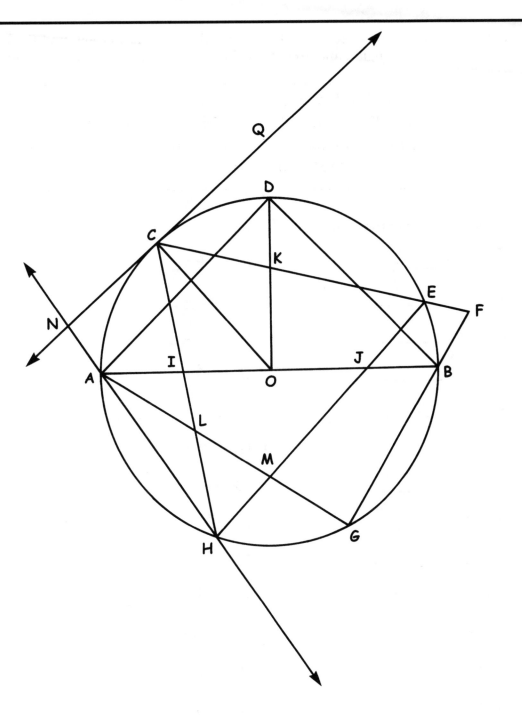

O is the center of the circle.

4-33 Measures of Segments, Angles, and Arcs

Study the diagram on the next page. Given the following information, find the measures of the segments, angles, and arcs. **Note:** You may not use protractors or rulers.

$\overline{JE}$ is the tangent to the circle at E

$m\overset{\frown}{AC} = 20$	$m\overset{\frown}{BE} = 50$	$m\overline{OE} = 7$	$m\overline{EJ} = 8$
$m\angle DOE = 88$	$m\angle CLI = 44$	$m\overline{GN} = 6.5$	$m\overline{NE} = 7.5$
	$m\angle AJI = 20$	$m\angle EJG = 78$	

Round your answers to the nearest hundredth.

1. $m\angle OEJ = $ _____

2. $m\angle EJA = $ _____

3. $m\angle ODE = $ _____

4. $m\angle EIJ = $ _____

5. $m\angle AKC = $ _____

6. $m\angle IJH = $ _____

7. $m\angle CLJ = $ _____

8. $m\angle ING = $ _____

9. $m\angle DOJ = $ _____

10. $m\overline{OD} = $ _____

11. $m\overline{AB} = $ _____

12. $m\overset{\frown}{AB} = $ _____

13. $m\overset{\frown}{DC} = $ _____

14. $m\overset{\frown}{DE} = $ _____

15. $m\overset{\frown}{EI} = $ _____

16. $m\overset{\frown}{BF} = $ _____

17. $m\overset{\frown}{FG} = $ _____

18. $m\overset{\frown}{GH} = $ _____

19. $m\overset{\frown}{HI} = $ _____

20. $m\overset{\frown}{AI} = $ _____

21. $m\overline{EI} = $ _____

22. $m\overline{JI} \approx $ _____

23. $m\overline{CN} = $ _____

24. $m\overline{IN} = $ _____

25. $m\overline{BJ} \approx $ _____

26. $m\overline{FJ} \approx $ _____

4-33 Measures of Segments, Angles, and Arcs (Continued)

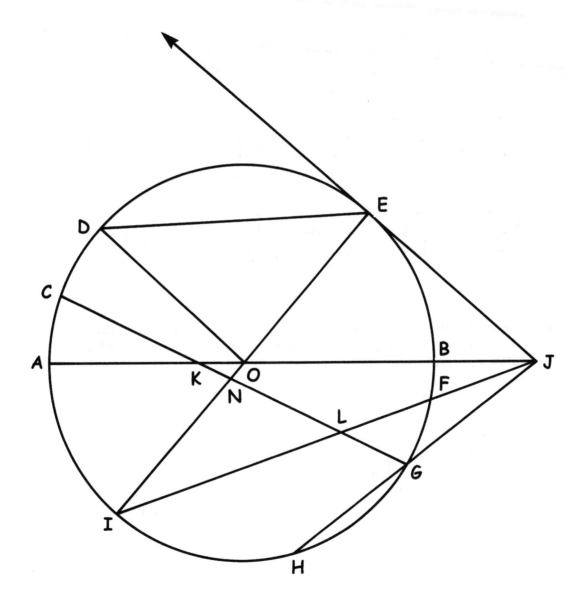

O is the center of the circle.

4-34 Determining Which Figures Form Cubes

Pentominoes are figures formed by joining five congruent squares along the sides so that all sides are adjacent. There are only 12 pentominoes, all of which are pictured below. If each pentomino was cut and folded along the adjacent edges, some would form an *open* cube. Circle those pentominoes.

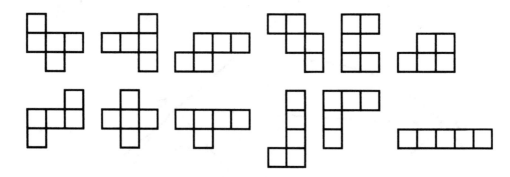

Hexominoes are figures formed by joining six congruent squares along the sides so that all sides are adjacent. There are 35 hexominoes, all of which are pictured below. If each hexomino was cut and folded along the adjacent edges, some would form a cube. Circle those hexominoes.

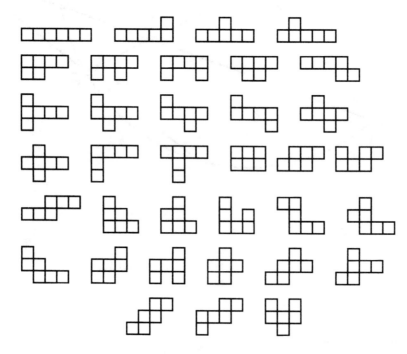

4-35 Finding Perimeters and Areas of Squares and Rectangles

Study the diagram below, which contains several squares and rectangles. Notice that some measures are given.

Identify all squares and all rectangles that are not squares. Find the perimeter and area of each. An example is done for you.

All measures are expressed in inches. (The diagram is not drawn to scale.) **Hint:** There are seven squares and six rectangles.

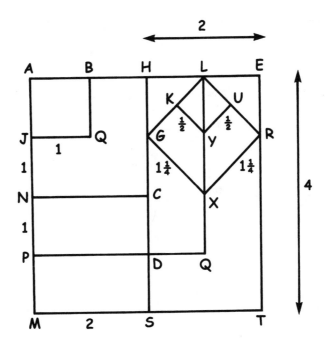

Square	Perimeter	Area
ABQJ	4 in.	1 sq.in.

Rectangle	Perimeter	Area

4-36 Finding Perimeters and Areas of Rectangles

Given the areas and perimeters of the rectangles below, find the lengths of their sides. You may find it helpful to sketch the rectangles on a separate sheet of paper.

1. **Rectangle ABCD:**   Area = 10 sq. in.   Perimeter = 22 in.

   L = _____   W = _____

2. **Rectangle RPQT:**   Area = 6 sq. ft.   Perimeter = 10 ft.

   L = _____   W = _____

3. **Rectangle GJHK:**   Area = 30 sq. ft.   Perimeter = 22 ft.

   L = _____   W = _____

4. **Rectangle HJMP:**   Area = 14 sq. cm   Perimeter = 18 cm

   L = _____   W = _____

5. **Rectangle DEGF:**   Area = 12 sq. m   Perimeter = 14 m

   L = _____   W = _____

6. **Rectangle SRVT:**   Area = 150 sq. ft.   Perimeter = 50 ft.

   L = _____   W = _____

7. **Rectangle WSNR:**   Area = 180 sq. m   Perimeter = 56 m

   L = _____   W = _____

8. **Rectangle JMRS:**   Area = 240 sq. mm   Perimeter = 64 mm

   L = _____   W = _____

Name _____   Date _____

4-37 Finding Perimeters and Areas of Quadrilaterals

Find the perimeters and areas of these quadrilaterals and write them in the spaces provided. You might find it helpful to sketch and label each figure on a separate sheet of paper. Match your numerical answer with the answer from the answer bank and write the letter of the answer on the blank beneath it. Then write the letters of your answers for each problem in order, starting with the first problem, to complete the statement at the end of the activity. The first problem is done for you.

Use the formulas that follow:

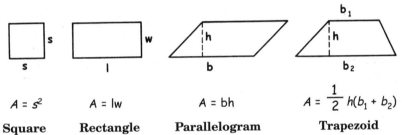

$A = s^2$	$A = lw$	$A = bh$	$A = \frac{1}{2} h(b_1 + b_2)$
Square	**Rectangle**	**Parallelogram**	**Trapezoid**

1. **Rectangle:** l = 10 in., w = 4 in.
   P = __28__ in.   A = __40__ sq. in.
   ___M___   ___A___

2. **Square:** s = 11.5 ft.
   P = _____ ft.   A = _____ sq. ft.
   _____   _____

3. **Parallelogram:** b = 9 cm, h = 6 cm, sides = 8.5 cm
   P = _____ cm   A = _____ sq. cm
   _____   _____

4. **Square:** s = 10 in.
   P = _____ in.   A = _____ sq. in.
   _____   _____

5. **Rectangle:** l = 16 m, w = 2.5 m
   P = _____ m   A = _____ sq. m
   _____   _____

6. **Trapezoid:** b_1 = 21 m, b_2 = 15 m, h = 4 m, sides = 5 m
   P = _____ m   A = _____ sq. m
   _____   _____

7. **Rectangle:** l = 8 ft., w = 5 ft.
   P = _____ ft.   A = _____ sq. ft.
   _____   _____

4-37 Finding Perimeters and Areas of Quadrilaterals (Continued)

8. **Trapezoid:** b_1 = 8 m, b_2 = 16 m, h = 3 m, sides = 5 m
   P = _____ m   A = _____ sq. m
   _____   _____

9. **Rectangle:** l = 1 cm, w = 26 cm
   P = _____ cm   A = _____ sq. cm
   _____   _____

10. **Rectangle:** l = 12 yd., w = 6 yd.
    P = _____ yd.   A = _____ sq. yd.
    _____   _____

11. **Parallelogram:** b = 14 cm, h = 2 cm, sides = 6 cm
    P = _____ cm   A = _____ sq. cm
    _____   _____

12. **Rectangle:** l = 11 ft., w = 7 ft.
    P = _____ ft.   A = _____ sq. ft.
    _____   _____

13. **Trapezoid:** b_1 = 6 m, b_2 = 14 m, h = 6 m, sides = 10 m and 6 m
    P = _____ m   A = _____ sq. m
    _____   _____

14. **Rectangle:** l = 11.2 cm, w = 2.5 cm
    P = _____ cm   A = _____ sq. cm
    _____   _____

15. **Parallelogram:** b = 12 m, h = 4.5 m, sides = 6 m
    P = _____ m   A = _____ sq. m
    _____   _____

16. **Trapezoid:** b_1 = 6 m, b_2 = 14 m, h = 6 m, sides = 8 m
    P = _____ m   A = _____ sq. m
    _____   _____

Answer Bank				
A 40	M 28	S 72	E 36	N 132.25
T 54	H 26	O 35	V 34	I 27.4
P 77	W 37	L 100	R 60	Y 46

Quadrilaterals that have the same area <u>M</u> <u>A</u> ___ ___ ___ ___

___ ___ ___ ___ ___ ___ ___ ___ ___ ___

___ ___ ___ ___ ___ ___ ___ ___ ___ .

4-38 Finding Perimeters and Areas of Triangles

Study the diagram on the next page. Find the perimeters and areas of the triangles.
  All measures are expressed in inches. The diagram is not drawn to scale. Express your answers in simplest form.

1. ΔADF   Perimeter = _____ in.   Area = _____ sq. in.

2. ΔDGF   Perimeter = _____ in.   Area = _____ sq. in.

3. ΔGFK   Perimeter = _____ in.   Area = _____ sq. in.

4. ΔBGI   Perimeter = _____ in.   Area = _____ sq. in.

5. ΔBIC   Perimeter = _____ in.   Area = _____ sq. in.

6. ΔAGF   Perimeter = _____ in.   Area = _____ sq. in.

7. ΔKFC   Perimeter = _____ in.   Area = _____ sq. in.

8. ΔBGC   Perimeter = _____ in.   Area = _____ sq. in.

4-38 Finding Perimeters and Areas of Triangles (Continued)

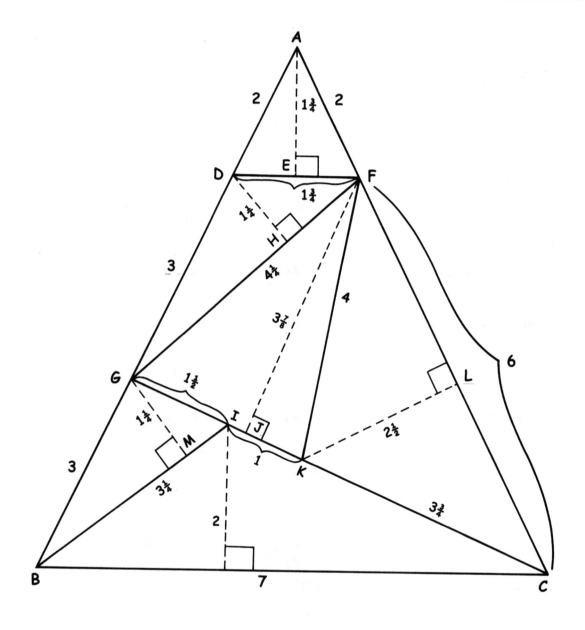

Name _____   **Date** _____

4-39 Finding Measures Associated with Circles

Given the radius or diameter of the circles below, find the indicated measures. Write the answers in the blanks that follow the problems, then write the numbers above the letters in the spaces at the end of the activity. This will reveal the value of π correct to 13 decimal places. The second problem is done for you.

Use the following formulas: $d = 2r$, $r = d \div 2$, $C = \pi d$, and $A = \pi r^2$. Use 3.14 for π.

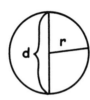

In the example of the circle above, r is the radius and d is the diameter. "C" represents the circumference (the distance around the circle), and "A" represents the area (the space inside).

1. r = 3 in.   Find d   d = ___ in.
                                            H

2. r = 4 ft.   Find r^2 $r^2 = $ _1_ _6_
                                            D

3. d = 9 cm   Find r^2 $r^2 = $ __ __ . __ __
                                                          I

4.   Find C   C ≈ __ __ . __ __ ft.
                                            A

5. r = 5 in.   Find A   A ≈ __ __ . __ __ sq. in.
                                            N

6. (10 m)   Find C   C ≈ __ __ . __ m
                                            C

197

4-39 Finding Measures Associated with Circles (Continued)

7. r = 15 yd.   Find C   C ≈ ___ ___ . ___ yd.
                                              $\overline{M}$

8.   Find r^2 r^2 = ___ ___ . ___ ___
                                              $\overline{G}$

9. d = 19 ft.   Find r   r = ___ . ___ ft.
                                            $\overline{E}$

10.   Find r^2 r^2 = ___ ___
                                                $\overline{B}$

11. d = 24 m   Find C   C ≈ ___ ___ . ___ ___ m
                                             $\overline{J}$

12. d = 36 in.   Find r   r = ___ ___ in.
                                             $\overline{L}$

13. r = 14 cm   Find r^2 r^2 = ___ ___ ___
                                                 $\overline{F}$

14. d = 10 mm   Find r^2 r^2 = ___ ___
                                                $\overline{K}$

___ . ___ ___ $\overset{1}{\_\_\_}$ ___ ___ ___ ___ ___ ___ ___ ___ ___
A   B   C   D   E   F   G   H   I   J   K   L   M   N

Name _____   **Date** _____

4-40 Finding the Circumference and Area of Circles

Find the circumference and area of each circle. Use the following formulas: $C = \pi d$ and $A = \pi r^2$. Use 3.14 for π.

1. **Swimming pool:** Diameter = 18 ft.

   C ≈ _____ ft.   A ≈ _____ sq. ft.

2. **Pizza pan:** Radius = 6 in.

   C ≈ _____ in.   A ≈ _____ sq. in.

3. **Flower bed:** Diameter = 8 ft.

   C ≈ _____ ft.   A ≈ _____ sq. ft.

4. **Tabletop:** Radius = 2 ft.

   C ≈ _____ ft.   A ≈ _____ sq. ft.

5. **Patio stepping stone:** Radius = 8 in.

   C ≈ _____ in.   A ≈ _____ sq. in.

6. **Goldfish pond:** Diameter = 6 ft.

   C ≈ _____ ft.   A ≈ _____ sq. ft.

7. **Wall clock:** Diameter = 12 in.

   C ≈ _____ in.   A ≈ _____ sq. ft.

8. **Decorative door wreath:** Diameter = 20 in.

   C ≈ _____ in.   A ≈ _____ sq. in.

9. **Dartboard:** Radius = 11 in.

   C ≈ _____ in.   A ≈ _____ sq. in.

10. **Food plate:** Radius = 5 in.

    C ≈ _____ in.   A ≈ _____ sq. in.

4-41 Finding the Areas of Plane Figures

Study the diagram. Given the following information, find the areas of the figures below.

ABCD is a rectangle
AB = 9 units
BC = 8 units
E is the midpoint of $\overline{AF}$
the circle has a radius of 2 units

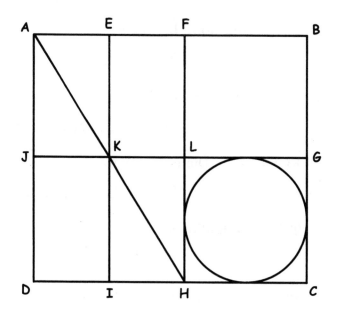

© 2002 by John Wiley & Sons, Inc.

1. Area of rectangle ABCD = _____

2. Area of the circle (rounded to the nearest whole number) ≈ _____

3. Area of △ADH = _____

4. Area of △AEK = _____

5. Area of rectangle FBCH = _____

6. Area of square FBGL = _____

7. Area of trapezoid ABGK = _____

8. Area of trapezoid EFHK = _____

9. Area of rectangle EFHI = _____

10. Area of trapezoid ABCH = _____

11. Area of trapezoid JKHD = _____

12. Area of rectangle EBCI = _____

Name _____   Date _____

4-42 Finding the Volume of Rectangular Prisms

Find the volume of the following rectangular prisms. Match the letters of the problems with their numerical answers to complete the statement at the end of the activity. Use the formula: V = lwh.

E.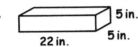

V = _____ cu. in.

H.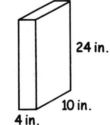

V = _____ cu. in.

D.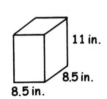

V = _____ cu. in.

S.

V = _____ cu. in.

N.

V = _____ cu. in.

L.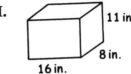

V = _____ cu. in.

T. l = 18 m
    w = 12 m
    h = 9 m

V = _____ cu. m

M. l = 6 ft.
    w = 2.5 ft.
    h = 3 ft.

V = _____ cu. ft.

4-42 Finding the Volume of Rectangular Prisms (Continued)

E. l = 16 in.
   w = 5.5 in.
   h = 12 in.
   V = _____ cu. in.

I. l = 12.5 cm
   w = 11 cm
   h = 6 cm
   V = _____ cu. cm

N. l = 14 yd.
   w = 12 yd.
   h = 6.5 yd.
   V = _____ cu. yd.

R. l = 14 ft.
   w = 6.5 ft.
   h = 6.5 ft.
   V = _____ cu. ft.

A. l = 12.5 in.
   w = 9.5 in.
   h = 3 in.
   V = _____ cu. in.

I. l = 6.5 mm
   w = 3.5 mm
   h = 2 mm
   V = _____ cu. mm

E. l = 6.5 ft.
   w = 3 ft.
   h = 4.5 ft.
   V = _____ cu. ft.

O. l = 17.5 cm
   w = 11.5 cm
   h = 4 cm
   V = _____ cu. cm

Every rectangular prism is ____ ____ ____ ____ ____

1944   1408   591.5   1056   550

____ ____ ____ ____ ____ ____ ____ ____ ____ ____ ____ .

794.75   45.5   45   87.75   1092   76   825   805   234   356.25   960

4-43 Finding Volume and Surface Area

Study the six three-dimensional figures, and the formulas for finding their volume and surface area. Each variable is also defined.

Cube

$V = e^3$

$S = 6e^2$

Rectangular Prism

$V = Bh$

$S = 2B + Ph$

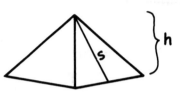

Pyramid

$V = \frac{1}{3} Bh$

$S = B + \frac{1}{2} Ps$

Cylinder

$V = Bh$

$S = 2\pi rh + 2B$

Cone

$V = \frac{1}{3} Bh$

$S = \pi rs + 2B$

Sphere

$V = \frac{4\pi r^3}{3}$

$S = 4\pi r^2$

V = volume

e = length of an edge

B = area of the base

h = height of the figure

r = radius of a circle

S = surface area

P = perimeter of the base

s = slant height of the cone or height of the faces of the pyramid

4-43 Finding Volume and Surface Area (Continued)

Directions: Find the volume and surface areas of the figures below. Use 3.14 for π. Write the letter in parentheses above the answer at the end of the activity to complete the statement.

1. **Cube:** e = 4 in.

   V = _____ cu. in. (**T**)   S = _____ sq. in. (**E**)

2. **Rectangular Prism:** l = 3 ft., w = 8 ft., h = 6 ft.

   V = _____ cu. ft. (**P**)   S = _____ sq. ft. (**E**)

3. **Pyramid:** B = 144 sq. in., h = 8 in., P = 24 in., s = 10 in.

   V = _____ cu. in. (**S**)   S = _____ sq. in. (**L**)

4. **Cylinder:** r = 5 cm, h = 4 cm

   V ≈ _____ cu. cm (**V**)   S ≈ _____ sq. cm (**E**)

5. **Cone:** r = 3 cm, h = 4 cm, s = 4 cm

   V ≈ _____ cu. cm (**Y**)   S ≈ _____ sq. cm (**I**)

6. **Sphere:** r = 6 in.

   V ≈ _____ cu. in. (**R**)   S ≈ _____ sq. in. (**C**)

Volume and surface area are measured in cubic units and square units

‗‗‗ ‗‗‗ ‗‗‗ ‗‗‗ ‗‗‗ ‗‗‗ ‗‗‗ ‗‗‗ ‗‗‗ ‗‗‗ ‗‗‗ ‗‗‗.

904.32 282.6 384   144   180 452.16 64   94.2   314   96   264 37.68

4-44 Geometry Puzzlers

Identify the geometry puzzlers. Each puzzler includes a geometric shape or concept. The first one is done for you.

1. 6 = F on a C   <u>6 faces on a cube</u> _____

2. 8 = S of a S S   _____

3. 90 = D of a R A   _____

4. 180 = D in a T   _____

5. 6 = S of a H   _____

6. 2 = S of a C   _____

7. 1 = W on a U   _____

8. 540 = D in a P   _____

9. 9 = S on a T T T B   _____

10. 360 = D in a C   _____

11. 5 = S of a P   _____

12. 9 = P in the S S   _____

13. 2 = H of a S   _____

14. 4 = A in a Q   _____

15. 4 = R A in a R   _____

16. 360 = D in a Q   _____

17. 3 = S of a T   _____

18. 5 = C on the O F   _____

19. 3 = D of a C   _____

20. 8 = S of an O   _____

4-45 Geometry Word Scramble

Unscramble the words. Each one describes a figure or concept of geometry.

1. enil   _____

2. gantenop   _____

3. trastigh nagel   _____

4. bomhurs   _____

5. aretedim   _____

6. trigh elangrit   _____

7. gohaxen   _____

8. tanirgel   _____

9. tipon   _____

10. yar   _____

11. tricalve ganles   _____

12. ip   _____

13. gelan   _____

14. trigh genal   _____

15. genahpto   _____

16. spomacs   _____

17. tonogac   _____

18. tuace laneg   _____

19. ricecl   _____

20. rentacl lange   _____

21. utace gnetrial   _____

22. ecaf   _____

23. reusaq   _____

24. gertecanl   _____

4-45 Geometry Word Scramble (Continued)

25. neterc _____

26. sotehepuyn _____

27. rindcyle _____

28. plelaral _____

29. enco _____

30. ebas _____

31. gemnest _____

32. ubec _____

33. pelan _____

34. sadiru _____

35. gopylon _____

36. uqrateelali igertanl _____

37. tosube letgrian _____

38. cendepluarirp _____

39. smirp _____

40. tozridape _____

41. crohd _____

42. mentcarompley snagel _____

43. slocisese antigrel _____

44. cadegon _____

45. soebut nagel _____

46. grocennut _____

47. texrev _____

48. plusmeptareny gansel _____

49. latadquilalrer _____

50. ramdipy _____

Section 5

ALGEBRA

Name _____   Date _____

5-1 Using the Order of Operations (Whole Numbers)

Simplify each expression and write the answer in the space provided. Then write the letter of the expression in the space above its answer at the bottom of the page to complete the statement. The first problem is done for you.

F. $3 + 2 \times 5 =$ __13__

R. $6 \cdot 4 + 1 =$ ____

O. $25 + 13 \times 5 \div 5 =$ ____

K. $9 \cdot 5 - 9 \cdot 5 =$ ____

E. $2(15 - 13) =$ ____

A. $4 + 5 \cdot (6 - 2) =$ ____

B. $3[24 \div 12 \div 2] =$ ____

S. $\dfrac{60-6 \times 2}{(8+16)\div 4} =$ _____

G. $36 \div 9 \cdot 4 =$ ____

N. $4 + 8 \times 3 =$ ____

H. $2 + 3 \cdot 5 + 4 =$ ____

I. $24 \div 3 - 2 \div 2 =$ ____

L. $(4 + 9) \times 3 =$ ____

T. $38 + 38 \div (15 + 4) =$ ____

W. $\dfrac{12+72}{6+8} =$ ____

In 1557 Robert Recorde first used the = symbol in *The Whetstone of Witte,*

__	__	__	F	__	__	__	__	__	__	__	__	__	__	__
40	21	4	13	7	25	8	40	24	39	16	4	3	25	24

__	__	__	__	__	__	__	__	__	__	__	__	__
3	38	38	0	6	25	7	40	40	4	28	7	28

__	__	__	__	__	__	__	.
4	28	16	39	7	8	21	

5-2 Using the Order of Operations (Whole Numbers and Exponents)

Every digit on the calculator display can be turned upside down to resemble a letter as shown in the chart. **Note:** Some of the letters are capitalized and some are lower case.

Numbers: 0 1 2 3 4 5 6 7 8 9
Letters: O I Z E h S g L B G

The upside-down numbers may be used to form words. Use the order of operations to find the numerical answer to each problem and write the answer in Column A. Then turn your calculator upside down and write in Column B the word the upside-down numbers spell. The first problem is done for you.

		Column A	Column B
1.	$10 + 8 + 30 \times 20 =$	618	BIG
2.	$(60 \times 50) + (70^2) - (17 \times 10 - 8) =$		
3.	$2(26 + 96 + 3 \times 15) + 360 \div 2 =$		
4.	$6^2 - 2 =$		
5.	$32 + 4 \times 96 + 3 \times 17 + 2 \times 98 =$		
6.	$7 \times 10^3 + 4 \times 10^2 - (60 + 6) =$		
7.	$95 \times 56 - 3 =$		
8.	$3 \times 15 + 50 \times 6 =$		
9.	$9(9 \times 47) =$		
10.	$6^3 + 12^2 - 2 \times 11 =$		
11.	$8^2 - 26 \div 2 =$		
12.	$(9 \times 10^2 + 5^2 + 1) \times 2^2 =$		
13.	$2(5 \times 90) - (16 \times 10 + 7) =$		
14.	$2(60)^2 + 50 \times 10 + 3^2 \times 2 =$		
15.	$5 \times 3 \times (20 \times 11 - 17) =$		
16.	$8 \times 10^3 - (3 \times 10^2 - 5 \times 7) =$		
17.	$7 + 55 \times 100 =$		
18.	$3 \times 17 + 3 \times 40 \times 6 =$		
19.	$1,284 \div 2 - 5 =$		
20.	$6 + 706 \times 10^3 =$		

© 2002 by John Wiley & Sons, Inc.

5-3 Evaluating Expressions (Whole Numbers)

Use the code provided and the clues to find the names of three great mathematicians, which will be revealed in the boxes at the end of the activity. Box 6 is completed for you.

A	B	C	D	E	F	G	H	I	J	K	L	M	N	O	P	Q	R	S	T	U	V	W	X	Y	Z
1	2	3	4	5	6	7	8	9	10	11	12	13	14	15	16	17	18	19	20	21	22	23	24	25	26

Clues:

➡ Box 6 is Z ÷ B [26 ÷ 2 = 13 so "M" is placed in Box 6]

➡ Boxes 10, 12, 38, and 39 are D + E × C

➡ Boxes 2, 24, 27, and 31 are C × K − O

➡ Box 20 is I + F

➡ Boxes 4 and 34 are B^c

➡ Box 26 is R ÷ C

➡ Box 37 is K + L − B

➡ Boxes 7, 9, 17, and 29 are O − B(A + D)

➡ Boxes 8 and 30 are (M + C) ÷ D

➡ Boxes 16 and 21 are B + R − F

➡ Boxes 1, 13, 14, 23, and 36 are $D^B − O$

➡ Box 18 is BN − E

➡ Box 25 is T − BD

➡ Boxes 5, 11, 28, and 32 are (Z + A) ÷ C

➡ Box 19 is BJ

➡ Boxes 3, 15, 22, and 33 are U ÷ G

➡ Box 35 is B(Y − V) + A

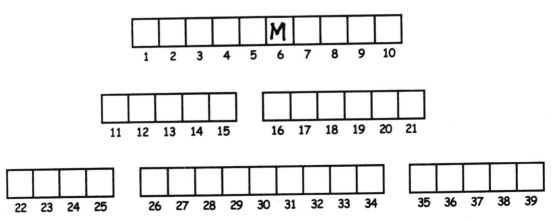

5-4   Using the Number Line

Write the letter for the points whose coordinates are given or described. Then write the letters in order, starting with the first problem, to complete the statement at the bottom. **Note:** All of the letters are used. Some may be used more than once.

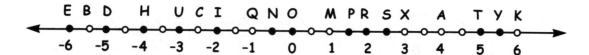

1. _____ 5

2. _____ −4

3. _____ It is the smallest integer that is graphed.

4. _____ It is the point that is the same distance from 0 as 5.

5. _____ It is 6 units to the left of 0.

6. _____ It is halfway between 0 and −1.

7. _____ It is halfway between 0 and 5.

8. _____ It has the same absolute value as 2.

9. _____ It is the largest integer that is graphed.

10. _____ It is 6 units to the right of −0.5.

11. _____ It is $\frac{3}{4}$ of the distance from 0 to 2.

12. _____ It is 6 units to the right of −4.

13. _____ It is the origin.

14. _____ It is the smallest positive number that is graphed.

15. _____ It is 4 units to the left of −2.

16. _____ It is the same distance between 0 and 4.

17. _____ 2.5 is halfway between the origin and this point.

18. _____ It is the largest number that is graphed.

Between any two real numbers there is another real number. This is called ___ ___ ___

___ ___ ___ ___ ___ ___ ___   ___ ___ ___ ___ ___ ___ ___.

5-5 Using Vectors and the Number Line

Write integers so that the vector diagrams model the addition problems. Choose the integers from the list in the box and write the corresponding letters beneath them. Write the letter of the vector closest to the number line first. Then write the letters in order, starting with the first problem, to complete the statement below. The first problem is done for you.

1.

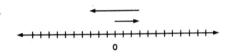

$$\underline{\quad 3 \quad} + \underline{\quad -6 \quad}$$
$$\underline{\quad S \quad} \quad \underline{\quad I \quad}$$

2.

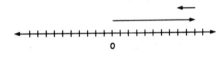

___ + ___

___   ___

3.

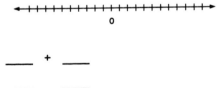

___ + ___

___   ___

4.

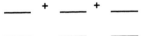

___ + ___

___   ___

5.

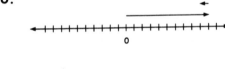

___ + ___

___   ___

6.

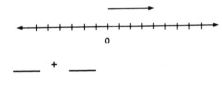

___ + ___

___   ___

7.

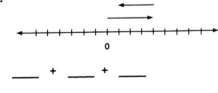

___ + ___

___   ___

8.

___ + ___ + ___

___   ___   ___

5-5 Using Vectors and the Number Line (Continued)

9.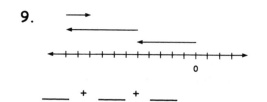

$$\underline{\quad} + \underline{\quad} + \underline{\quad}$$

$$\underline{\quad} \quad \underline{\quad} \quad \underline{\quad}$$

10.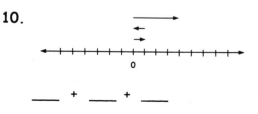

$$\underline{\quad} + \underline{\quad} + \underline{\quad}$$

$$\underline{\quad} \quad \underline{\quad} \quad \underline{\quad}$$

Choose from among these integers
–6 I   –5 M   –3 H   –2 W   –1 O   1 T
2 L   3 S   4 N   5 A   10 R

In 1845 the word *vector* was first used by an Irish mathematician named

S I __ __ __ __ __ __ __ __ __ __ __ __

__ __ __ __ __ __ __ __ __.

Name _____   Date _____

5-6   Adding Integers

Add the problems and match your answers with the answers in the box. Record both your answer and the corresponding letter in the blanks. When you are done, write the letters in order, starting with the first problem, to complete the statement below. **Note:** You will need to divide the letters to form words. The first problem is done for you.

1. $-32 + 0 =$ _−32_ _D_
2. $25 + -11 =$ _____ _____
3. $-92 + 43 + 48 + -18 =$ _____ _____
4. $16 + -2 =$ _____ _____
5. $-57 + -11 =$ _____ _____
6. $-30 + 15 + -12 + -5 =$ _____ _____
7. $-12 + -33 + -15 + 27 + -1 =$ _____ _____
8. $106 + -38 =$ _____ _____
9. $-75 + 16 + -9 =$ _____ _____
10. $-36 + 27 =$ _____ _____
11. $-8 + 39 =$ _____ _____
12. $-207 + 221 =$ _____ _____
13. $82 + -12 + -78 =$ _____ _____
14. $-15 + -34 + -19 =$ _____ _____
15. $327 + -336 =$ _____ _____
16. $-16 + -24 + 15 + 39 =$ _____ _____
17. $28 + -32 + 56 =$ _____ _____
18. $-80 + 102 + -8 =$ _____ _____
19. $21 + 23 + 46 + -54 =$ _____ _____
20. $-9 + 15 + -13 + -27 =$ _____ _____

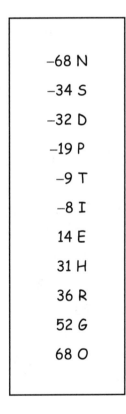

−68 N

−34 S

−32 D

−19 P

−9 T

−8 I

14 E

31 H

36 R

52 G

68 O

If you add positive and negative integers, the sum may be positive, negative, or zero.

It _D_ _____

_____.

5-7   Subtracting Integers

Subtract the problems and match your answers with the answers in the box. Record both the answer and the corresponding letter in the blanks. When you are done, write the letters in order, starting with the first problem, to complete the statement below. **Note:** You will need to divide the letters to form words. The first problem is done for you.

1. $9 - 15 =$ ___6___ ___F___
2. $-9 - 21 =$ _____ _____
3. $13 - 71 =$ _____ _____
4. $27 - 44 =$ _____ _____
5. $-12 - 15 =$ _____ _____
6. $86 - 113 =$ _____ _____
7. $-4 - 2 - 1 =$ _____ _____
8. $-6 - 19 =$ _____ _____
9. $42 - 12 =$ _____ _____
10. $135 - 160 =$ _____ _____
11. $17 - (-8) =$ _____ _____
12. $53 - 18 - (-6) =$ _____ _____
13. $89 - 9 - 23 =$ _____ _____
14. $-7 - (-20) =$ _____ _____
15. $289 - 347 =$ _____ _____
16. $12 - 89 - 16 =$ _____ _____
17. $-66 - (-49) =$ _____ _____
18. $-12 - 16 - 30 =$ _____ _____
19. $-57 - (-70) =$ _____ _____
20. $12 - (-13) =$ _____ _____
21. $-92 - 15 - (-14) =$ _____ _____
22. $-71 + 104 - 20 =$ _____ _____
23. $-37 - (-12) - 2 =$ _____ _____

-93	S
-58	R
-30	O
-27	D
-25	N
-17	A
-7	I
-6	F
13	E
25	U
30	G
41	M
57	B

Any subtraction problem can be written as an addition problem. The same rules

_F_____

_____.

Name _____   **Date** _____

5-8 Multiplying and Dividing Integers

Multiply or divide each pair of integers and place the product or quotient in the box. Then add all of the answers across each row, down each column, and along each diagonal. Write the answers in the spaces. If your math is correct, all of the sums will be equal and you will have created a magic square.

-6×-3	-23×-2	-46×1	$36 \div -2$	$120 \div 12$
-6×-7	$120 \div -4$	$-242 \div 11$	$-90 \div -15$	$-168 \div -12$
$-170 \div 5$	$-390 \div 15$	$98 \div 49$	-15×-2	-19×-2
-5×2	$76 \div -38$	$208 \div 8$	-17×-2	$190 \div -5$
$72 \div -12$	2×11	$200 \div 4$	7×-6	$252 \div -18$

Sum = _____

Sum = _____

Sum = _____

Sum = _____

Sum = _____

Sum = _____

Sum = _____ Sum = _____ Sum = _____ Sum = _____ Sum = _____ Sum = _____

Name _____   Date _____

5-9   Integer Operations

Simplify each expresssion and write the answer in the space provided. Then write the letter of the expression in the space above its answer at the bottom of the page to complete the statement. The first problem is done for you.

L. $-15 + 46 + -38 =$ __−7__

R. $-28 - (-40) =$ _____

S. $-16 \times -3 =$ _____

Y. $-8 \times 6 \times 4 \times -3 =$ _____

X. $-381 \div -3 =$ _____

H. $256 \div -4 =$ _____

W. $-4(-3 + -6 + -20) =$ _____

I. $15 - 39 - 12 - (-19) =$ _____

F. $(22 \times -4) - (-12) =$ _____

B. $34 \times 2 \times -3 =$ _____

E. $-345 + -18 + -20 + 212 =$ _____

U. $92 - (-6) + 18 - 12 =$ _____

N. $[15 + -3 - (-6)] \div (-28 + 19) =$ _____

T. $-28 - (-47) + 28 - (-54) =$ _____

O. $(25 + 2) \div (21 + -12) =$ _____

M. $(-28 \div -4) - (-52 \div -4) =$ _____

G. $(6 - 12) \times [4 - (-8)] =$ _____

P. $(-25 \times -10) \div (-5 \times -10) =$ _____

Use the following strategy for operations with integers: Simplify all

| ___ | ___ | ___ | ___ | ___ | ___ | ___ | ___ | ___ | ___ | ___ |
| -171 | 127 | 5 | 12 | -171 | 48 | 48 | -17 | 3 | -2 | 48 |

| ___ | ___ | ___ | ___ | ___ | ___ | | ___ | ___ | ___ | ___ | ___ | ___ | ___ | ___ |
| 116 | -17 | 101 | -64 | -17 | -2 | | -72 | 12 | 3 | 104 | 5 | -17 | -2 | -72 |

| ___ | ___ | ___ | ___ | ___ | L | ___ | | ___ | ___ | ___ | ___ | ___ . |
| 48 | 576 | -6 | -204 | 3 | | -7 | 48 | | -76 | -17 | 12 | 48 | 101 |

5-10   Writing and Simplifying Expressions

Using the integers −1, −2, −3, and −4, write expressions that equal the numbers at the right. You may use the four operations of addition, subtraction, multiplication, and division, as well as grouping symbols. You must use each number once in each expression. The first problem is done for you. **Note:** Several expressions are possible for some answers.

1. $-4 + -3 + -2 + -1 = -10$ _____   −10
2. _____   −9
3. _____   −8
4. _____   −7
5. _____   −6
6. _____   −5
7. _____   −4
8. _____   −3
9. _____   −2
10. _____   −1
11. _____   0
12. _____   1
13. _____   2
14. _____   3
15. _____   4
16. _____   5
17. _____   6
18. _____   7
19. _____   8
20. _____   9
21. _____   10

5-11 Evaluating Expressions (Integers and Exponents)

Evaluate each expression if a = –3, b = 3, c = 2, d = –2, e = 5, f = –5, g = 4, and h = –4. Then write the letter of the expression above its value in the blank at the bottom of the page to complete the statement. The first problem is done for you.

E. $af = \underline{\ 15\ }$

T. $b - a = \underline{\qquad}$

O. $abc = \underline{\qquad}$

Y. $ag + h = \underline{\qquad}$

H. $fg + ce = \underline{\qquad}$

A. $ab - def = \underline{\qquad}$

O. $ace - bdf = \underline{\qquad}$

M. $-(abc + d) = \underline{\qquad}$

E. $a^2 = \underline{\qquad}$

T. $-b^2 = \underline{\qquad}$

E. $c(b - c)^2 = \underline{\qquad}$

N. $-c(c - d)^2 = \underline{\qquad}$

T. $c^3 = \underline{\qquad}$

S. $d^3 = \underline{\qquad}$

S. $-6a^2 = \underline{\qquad}$

L. $abc^3 = \underline{\qquad}$

E. $(ac)^2 = \underline{\qquad}$

I. $bf - g^2 = \underline{\qquad}$

E. $e^2f^2 = \underline{\qquad}$

N. $7a^2b - 5a^3 = \underline{\qquad}$

T. $ab^2 - (ab)^2 = \underline{\qquad}$

E. $(a - bf)^2 = \underline{\qquad}$

B. $ag - e^3 = \underline{\qquad}$

P. $-a(e - h)^2 = \underline{\qquad}$

René Descartes was the first man to use a raised number for powers. However, he continued to write x^2 as xx, because the expression occupied the same amount of space as xx and it allowed the ____ ____ ____ ____   ____ ____ ____ ____
              -108 -16 243 625   -9 -60   -137 36

____ __E__ ____   ____ ____   ____ ____ ____   ____ ____ ____ ____
-54 15 8   -18 -32   6   -10 144   -8 -59 20 2

____ ____ ____ ____ .
-72 -31 324 9

5-12 Simplifying Absolute Value Expressions

Simplify each expression and write your answer in the space provided. Then write the letter of the expression in the space above its answer at the bottom of the page to complete the statement. The first problem is done for you.

P. $|3| = $ __3__

M. $|-6| = $ _____

U. $-|7| = $ _____

I. $|2 + 6| = $ _____

S. $|2 - 3| = $ _____

N. $|2| + |-3| = $ _____

E. $3|16 - 8| = $ _____

B. $3|16| - |8| = $ _____

A. $3|-16| - |2| = $ _____

Y. $-6|32 \div -4| = $ _____

T. $5 - |-6| = $ _____

W. $-|-50 + 4| = $ _____

L. $2 + |-5| = $ _____

G. $|8 + 6| = $ _____

R. $|8| - |6| = $ _____

H. $3|9 - 12| = $ _____

O. $|4 \times -4| - |6 \times 2| = $ _____

F. $|3(2 + 5)| = $ _____

V. $|3(-6 + 4)| - |15| = $ _____

The phrase *absolute value* is derived from the Latin term *absolvere,* which means "to free from." The absolute value of a number is its distance from zero on a number line.

Since any distance is ___ ___ ___ ___ ___ ___
    46 7 -46 46 -48 1

P ___ ___ ___ ___ ___ ___ ___ ___ ,   ___ ___ ___
3 4 1 8 -1 8 -9 24   -1 9 24

___ ___ ___ ___ ___ ___   ___ ___   ___ ___ ___ ___   ___ ___
5 -7 6 40 24 2   8 1   21 2 24 24   4 21

___   ___ ___ ___ ___ .
46   1 8 14 5

5-13 Simplifying Expressions (Combining Similar Terms)

Simplify each expression by filling in the blank with an integer. **Hint:** Correct answers will range from −15 to 10 and each positive or negative integer will be used only once.

1. $8x + 2x =$ _____x

2. $-2q - 5q =$ _____q

3. $-13x + x =$ _____x

4. $3ab - 6ab =$ _____ab

5. $-8 + 3x - 7 =$ _____$x +$ _____

6. $-3 + 12m - 8m + 2 =$ _____$m +$ _____

7. $2y^3 + 6y^3 + 2y - y =$ _____$y^3 +$ _____y

8. $-13g^3 - 2g - 8g^2 - 2g =$ _____$g^3 +$ _____$g^2 +$ _____g

9. $5(x - 1) + 2x =$ _____$x +$ _____

10. $-(3x + 14) - 7x =$ _____$x +$ _____

11. $-3(b^2 - 3b) - 6b^2 =$ _____$b^2 +$ _____b

12. $-9 - (2 - 5c) =$ _____$c +$ _____

13. $4 - 2(5 - b) =$ _____$b +$ _____

14. $x - 3(x - 2) =$ _____$x +$ _____

© 2002 by John Wiley & Sons, Inc.

© 2002 by John Wiley & Sons, Inc.

5-14 Matching and Evaluating Expressions

Match each phrase with its algebraic expression in the box. Record the letter of the expression in the blank before the phrase. Next, write the letters in order, starting with the first problem, to complete the statement at the end of the activity. Follow the directions revealed in the statement and write your answer in the blank at the end of each phrase. **Hint:** n represents "number."

1. _____ 2 less than a number _____

2. _____ a number squared _____

3. _____ the absolute value of twice a number _____

4. _____ the average of 2 and a number _____

5. _____ a number decreased by 2 _____

6. _____ 2 increased by a number _____

7. _____ 2 more than a number _____

8. _____ the product of a number and 2 _____

9. _____ twice a number squared _____

10. _____ half of a number _____

11. _____ twice a number _____

12. _____ 2 decreased by a number _____

5-14 Matching and Evaluating Expressions (Continued)

---

13. _____ a number divided by 2 _____

14. _____ the difference of a number and 2 _____

15. _____ twice the sum of a number and 2 _____

16. _____ 2 divided by a number _____

17. _____ 2 times the absolute value of a number _____

18. _____ the sum of a number and twice the number _____

19. _____ a number increased by 2 _____

20. _____ the product of 2 and a number squared _____

21. _____ a number minus 2 _____

22. _____ a number divided by 2 _____

© 2002 by John Wiley & Sons, Inc.

Choose from these Expressions				
S. $n + 2$	**A.** $2\,|n|$	**E.** $n - 2$	**F.** $2 - n$	**I.** $2n$
L. $n + 2n$	**N.** $\frac{n}{2}$	**O.** $(2n)^2$	**P.** $|2n|$	**Q.** $2(n + 2)$
R. $(n + 2) \div 2$	**T.** $2n^2$	**U.** $\frac{2}{n}$	**X.** n^2	

Evaluate each __ __ __ __ __ __ __ __ __ __ __ __ __ __ __

__ __ __ __ __ __ __ __ __ __ __ .

5-15 Solving One-step Equations

Solve each equation. Write the letter of the problem above its solution to find the message below. A famous group of mathematicians and their motto will be revealed. The first problem is done for you.

A. $x + 7 = 28$, $x = \underline{\ 19\ }$

B. $x - 11 = -3.8$, $x = \underline{\hspace{1cm}}$

E. $-27 = x + 5$, $x = \underline{\hspace{1cm}}$

G. $3.1 = -5.9 + x$, $x = \underline{\hspace{1cm}}$

H. $9x = 45$, $x = \underline{\hspace{1cm}}$

I. $\frac{1}{3}x = -15$, $x = \underline{\hspace{1cm}}$

L. $-20 = -\frac{5}{2}x$, $x = \underline{\hspace{1cm}}$

M. $-11x = -121$, $x = \underline{\hspace{1cm}}$

N. $x - 2.7 = 2.5$, $x = \underline{\hspace{1cm}}$

O. $x - 9 = 3.7$, $x = \underline{\hspace{1cm}}$

P. $7 = x + 3.4$, $x = \underline{\hspace{1cm}}$

R. $-\frac{5}{7}x = 35$, $x = \underline{\hspace{1cm}}$

S. $-11 = x + 2$, $x = \underline{\hspace{1cm}}$

T. $-0.6 = 1.4 + x$, $x = \underline{\hspace{1cm}}$

U. $\frac{x}{8} = -3$, $x = \underline{\hspace{1cm}}$

Y. $\frac{1}{2}x = 8$, $x = \underline{\hspace{1cm}}$

```
___  ___  ___   ___  ___  ___  ___  _A_  ___  ___  ___  ___  _A_  ___  ___ :
-2    5   -32   3.6  16   -2    5   19    9  12.7  -49  -32   19  5.2  -13
```

```
" _A_  ___  ___    ___  ___  ___  ___  ___  ___    _A_  ___  ___
  19    8    8     -2   5   -45  5.2   9   -13      19  -49  -32
```

```
___  ___  ___  ___  ___  ___  ___ . "
5.2  -24   11  7.2  -32  -49  -13
```

5-16 Solving Linear Equations with Variables on One Side

Solve each equation and place the solution in the space provided to create a magic square. When you add your answers in each row, each column, and each diagonal, the sum should be the same.

$3e - e - 2 = 0$ $e =$ _____	$4m - 7m = -24$ $m =$ _____	$-2 = -15 + p$ $p =$ _____	$-\dfrac{1}{2}r = -6$ $r =$ _____
$a + 4 + 2 = 20$ $a =$ _____	$c - 30 = -19$ $c =$ _____	$t - 3 = -1$ $t =$ _____	$14 = -7 + 3h$ $h =$ _____
$7(y-1) - 2y = 13$ $y =$ _____	$7 - (1-q) = 11$ $q =$ _____	$(x-3) + 17 = 30$ $x =$ _____	$d - 24 = -15$ $d =$ _____
$8(f-7) = 64$ $f =$ _____	$2 = -10 + y + 2$ $y =$ _____	$-27w = -81$ $w =$ _____	$-2 + (1+z) = 5$ $z =$ _____

What is the sum of each row, column, and diagonal of this magic square? _____

Name _____   Date _____

5-17 Solving Multi-step Equations with Variables on One Side

Solve each equation. Write the letter of the problem in the blank above its solution to complete the statement below. The first problem is done for you.

A. $4n - 20 = 36$, n = __14__

R. $2n - 18 = 44$, n = _____

D. $8n + 12 = -84$, n = _____

I. $3n - 1 = 17$, n = _____

T. $8 = 5n - 12$, n = _____

E. $49n - 186 = 5{,}351$, n = _____

M. $15.8 = 16 + 0.2n$, n = _____

Y. $-\frac{3}{4} = 3 - \frac{1}{2}n$, n = _____

O. $6n + \frac{3}{4} = -\frac{3}{4}$, n = _____

B. $0 = 1\frac{3}{5} - \frac{1}{5}n$, n = _____

S. $\frac{2}{9} = \frac{1}{3} - \frac{4}{9}n$, n = _____

H. $4(n - 3) = -24$, n = _____

U. $2(n - 4) = 26$, n = _____

N. $-5(n + 7) = -25$, n = _____

Z. $\frac{1}{4}(n - 24) = 13$, n = _____

To make an equivalent equation, you must add or subtract the same number from both sides of the equation and multiply or divide ___ ___ ___ ___
8   -0.25   4   -3

___ ___ ___ ___ ___   ___ ___   ___ ___ ___   ___ A ___ ___
0.25 6 -12 113 0.25   8   7.5   4   -3   113   0.25 14 -1 113

___ ___ ___ ___ ___ ___ ___   ___ ___ ___ ___ ___ ___ .
-2 -0.25 -2 76 113 31 -0.25   -2 17 -1 8 113 31

5-18 Solving Equations with Variables on Both Sides

Solve each equation. Then write the variable of each problem above its value to complete a quote from Karl Friedrich Gauss. (Gauss was an insightful mathematician who was able to "know" the solution to a problem before he was able to do the mathematics.)

1. $8 - 5a = 3a$, $a =$ ___1___
2. $-16 + 2b = 6b$, $b =$ _____
3. $18 - d = 2d$, $d =$ _____
4. $6e = 4e + 20$, $e =$ _____
5. $2g + 5 = -g - 4$, $g =$ _____
6. $4 - 7h = h + 4$, $h =$ _____
7. $4i + 6 = -i - 4$, $i =$ _____
8. $5k - 20 = -2 + 8k$, $k =$ _____
9. $3l + 2 = -l - 2$, $l =$ _____
10. $2n - 11 = -6 + n$, $n =$ _____
11. $-7o = 3(5 - 3o)$, $o =$ _____
12. $4(r + 7) = 7 + r$, $r =$ _____
13. $8s + 2 = 3(s + 4)$, $s =$ _____
14. $-36 + 2t = -3t - 4t$, $t =$ _____
15. $2 - 3u = -2u - 20$, $u =$ _____
16. $4v - 2(v + 5) = -(2v + 15)$, $v =$ _____
17. $6w + 3(w + 2) = -(2w + 7) + w$, $w =$ _____
18. $4(y - 3) + 3y = -(5y - 21) + y$, $y =$ _____

"___ ___ $\overset{a}{\_\_\_}$ ___ ___ ___ ___ ___ ___ ___ ___ ___ ___ ___'
  -2   0   1 -1.25 10   4   0   10   -7   10   2   22   -1   4

___ ___ ___ ___ ___ ___ ___ ___ ___ ___ ___ ___
 -4   22   4   -2   6   7.5   5 7.5   4   3   10   4

___ ___ ___ ___ ___ ___ ___ ___ ___ ___ ___ ___ ___."
 -6   5   7.5 -1.3   0 7.5 -1.3   4 7.5   -3   10   4   -2   4

5-19 Evaluating Formulas

Evaluate each formula and solve for the variable. Write your answer in the blank. Then write the letter of the problem above its answer to complete the statement. The first problem is done for you.

Use the distance formula, $d = rt$, where d = distance, r = rate, and t = time.

W. If $r = 60$ mph and $t = 2$ hr., $d =$ __120__ mi.

N. If $d = 20$ mi. and $t = 0.5$ hr., $r =$ _____ mph.

L. If $r = 45$ mph and $d = 60$ mi., $t =$ _____ hr.

Use the formula for finding the circumference of a circle, $C = \pi d$, where C = the circumference, $\pi \approx 3.14$, and d = the diameter.

E. If $d = 3.5$ in., $C \approx$ _____ in.

H. If $C \approx 25.12$ in., $d =$ _____ in.

Use the formula for finding simple interest, $I = prt$, where I = the amount of interest, p = the principal, r = the rate of interest, and t = the time.

O. If $p = \$200$, $r = 6\%$, and $t = 2$ yr., $I = \$$_____

A. If $I = \$36$, $r = 5\%$, and $t = 3$ yr., $p = \$$_____

V. If $I = \$360$, $p = \$1,200$, and $t = 5$ yr., $r =$ _____%

T. If $I = \$1,050$, $p = \$10,000$, and $r = 6\%$, $t =$ _____ yr.

Name _____   Date _____

5-19 Evaluating Formulas (Continued)

Use the formula for finding the perimeter of a rectangle, $P = 2l + 2w$, where P = perimeter, l = the length, and w = the width.

P.   If $l = 3$ in. and $w = 5$ in., $P =$ _____ in.

B.   If $P = 17$ in. and $w = 7.5$ in., $l =$ _____ in.

U.   If $P = 20.5$ in. and $l = 7$ in., $w =$ _____ in.

Use the formula for finding the volume of a rectangular prism, $V = lwh$, where V = the volume of the prism, l = the length of the base, w = the width of the base, and h = the height of the prism.

S.   If $l = 5.5$ in., $w = 2.5$ in., and $h = 7$ in., $V =$ _____ cu. in.

K.   If $V = 30$ cu. in., $w = 7.5$ in., and $h = 1$ in., $l =$ _____ in.

R.   If $V = 27$ cu. in., $l = 2$ in., and $h = 9$ in., $w =$ _____ in.

F.   If $V = 11.25$ cu. in., $l = 1.5$ in., and $w = 1.5$ in., $h =$ _____ in.

Francois Viète was the first mathematician to use letters of the

___	___	___	___	___	___	___	___		___	___	___
240	1.$\overline{3}$	16	8	240	1	10.99	1.75		5	24	1.5

___	___	___	___	___	**W**	___		___	___	___	___	___	___ .
3.25	40	4	40	24	120	40		6	240	1.$\overline{3}$	3.25	10.99	96.25

© 2002 by John Wiley & Sons, Inc.

Name _____   Date _____

5-20 Solving Inequalities

Match each inequality on the left with its solution on the right. Record the letter of the answer in the blank before each problem. Then write the letter of the inequality above its problem number to complete the statement below. The first problem is done for you.

1. __D__ $n + 9 > 12$

2. _____ $n - 4 \geq 6$

3. _____ $-2 < n - 4$

4. _____ $-6 < 3 - 3n$

5. _____ $n - 5 < -4$

6. _____ $-3 \geq n - 4$

7. _____ $-n - 3 \geq 5$

8. _____ $3n < 0$

9. _____ $-7n > 21$

10. _____ $-5n \geq -40$

11. _____ $4n > -16$

12. _____ $7 - 2n \leq 19$

13. _____ $4n + 6 \leq 2n - 6$

14. _____ $2n - 5 < n + 2$

15. _____ $5n - 4 - 6n \geq -10$

16. _____ $3(n + 4) > 15$

17. _____ $3n - 2(n - 4) > 7$

18. _____ $-5n + 2(n + 15) < 51$

19. _____ $7n - 9(n + 1) \geq -5$

G.	$n \leq -8$
E.	$n < -3$
U.	$n \geq 10$
B.	$n \leq -6$
M.	$n > -1$
H.	$n > 2$
T.	$n \leq -2$
Y.	$n > 1$
O.	$n > -7$
D.	$n > 3$
F.	$n \leq 6$
R.	$n < 1$
C.	$n > -4$
A.	$n < 7$
N.	$n \leq 1$
L.	$n \geq -6$
Q.	$n \leq 8$
I.	$n < 0$
S.	$n < 3$

If you multiply or divide both sides of an inequality by a negative number, you must

___ ___ ___ ___ ___ ___   ___ ___ ___
11 3 14 6 7 9   19 3 9

_D_ ___ ___ ___ ___ ___ ___ ___ ___   ___ ___   ___ ___ ___
1 8 5 9 11 19 8 18 6   18 15   19 3 9

___ ___ ___ ___ ___ ___ ___ ___ ___ ___   ___ ___ ___ ___ ___ ___.
8 6 9 10 2 14 12 8 19 16   4 16 17 13 18 12

233

5-21 Graphing Inequalities and Combined Inequalities

Write the letter of the graph (shown on the next page) in the blank before the inequality or combined inequality. Then write the letter of the graph above the problem number below to find a message. The first problem is done for you.

1. __R__ x < –3

2. _____ x ≥ 2

3. _____ x ≤ 0

4. _____ –3 < x

5. _____ x > 0

6. _____ –3 ≥ x

7. _____ x ≠ 0

8. _____ –3 < x < 2

9. _____ x > 2 or x ≤ –3

10. _____ x > –3 and x ≤ 2

11. _____ x ≥ 2 or x < –3

12. _____ x < –3 or x > 2

13. _____ x > 2 and x ≤ 2

14. _____ –3 ≤ x < 2

© 2002 by John Wiley & Sons, Inc.

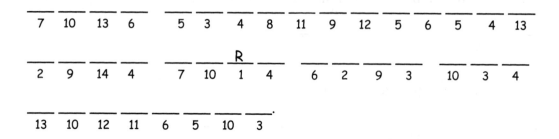

```
___ ___ ___ ___    ___ ___ ___ ___ ___ ___ ___ ___ ___ ___ ___ ___
 7  10  13   6      5   3   4   8  11   9  12   5   6   5   4  13

___ ___ ___ ___    ___ ___  R  ___   ___ ___ ___ ___   ___ ___ ___
 2   9  14   4      7  10   1   4     6   2   9   3    10   3   4

___ ___ ___ ___ ___ ___ ___ ___ .
13  10  12  11   6   5  10   3
```

Name ______________________ Date __________

5-21 Graphing Inequalities and Combined Inequalities *(Continued)*

I. 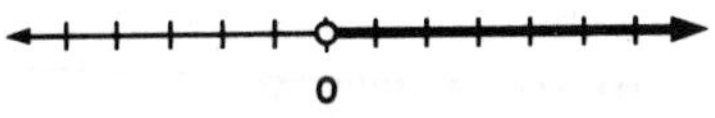

T. 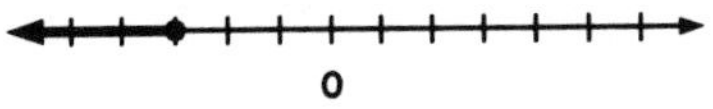

H. 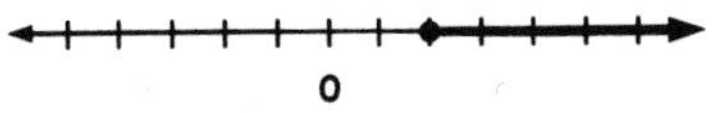

Q. 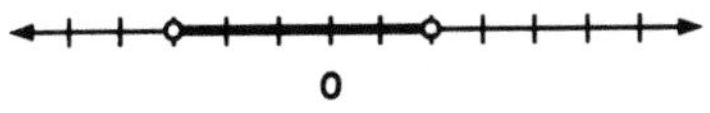

R. 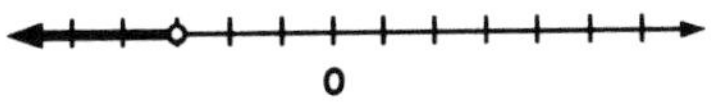

N. 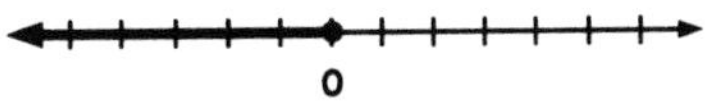

U. 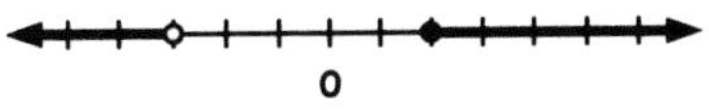

A. 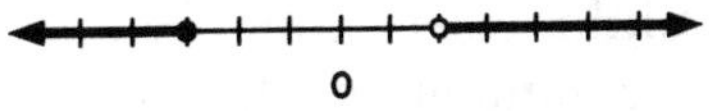

M. 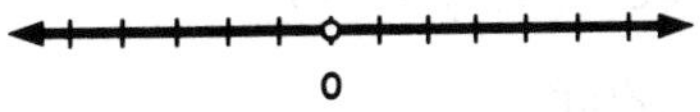

E. 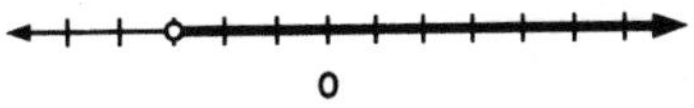

V. 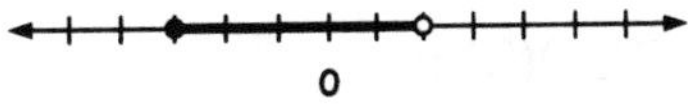

L. 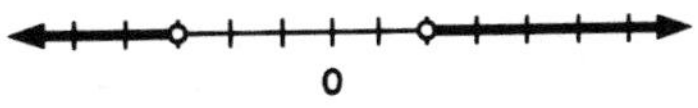

O. 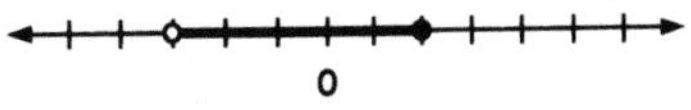

S. 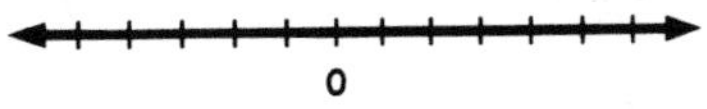

5-22 Multiplying and Dividing Monomials

One monomial is missing in each problem. The missing monomial appears in the box. Write the monomials and the letters of the monomials in the corresponding blanks. Write the letters you placed in the problems in order, starting with the first problem, to complete the statement below. **Note:** You will need to divide the letters to form words. The first problem is done for you.

1. __W__ $(3a)(3a^4)$ = __$9a^5$__

2. ____ $\dfrac{25a^2}{5a}$ = ____

3. ____ $\dfrac{9a^4}{3a}$ = ____

4. ____ $\dfrac{-24ab}{-6b}$ = ____

5. ____ $-4a^3b^3 = (-2ab^3)($____$)$

6. ____ $8a^5b = (2ab)($ ____$)$

7. ____ $(3a^3)(5)$ = ____

8. ____ $(4a)(3a) + ($ ____$)(7a) = 26a^2$

9. ____ $($ ____$)(a) + (3a^3)(2a^5) = 10a^8$

10. ____ $(3a^2)($ ____$)(7ab) = 84a^6b$

11. ____ $\dfrac{8a^2b^3}{ab^3}$ = ____

12. ____ $\dfrac{(3a^5)(2a^4)}{3a}$ = ____

13. ____ $\dfrac{(6a^7)(2a^5)}{4a^3}$ = ____

14. ____ $\dfrac{(2a^2b)(3a^2b)}{b^2}$ = ____

15. ____ $36a^9b^5 = (4a^3b^2)($ ____$)(3ab^3)$

O.	$2a$
I.	$2a^2$
T.	$2a^8$
U.	$4a^7$
W.	$9a^5$
H.	$8a$
G.	$4a^3$
A.	$4a^4$
D.	$3a^5$
M.	$15a^3$
E.	$6a^4$
L.	$4a$
L.	$3a^3$
R.	$3a^9$
I.	$5a$

In 1631, __W_____

was the first mathematician to use "×" as a symbol for multiplication.

5-23 Adding and Subtracting Polynomials

Add or subtract each polynomial. Write the result in descending order with respect to x, placing one term in each blank. Some terms will have letters beneath them. Find these terms at the bottom of the page and write the corresponding letters above them to complete the statement.

1. $(3x^3 + x^2 - 2x - 5) + (x^2 - 5x + 7) =$ ___ + ___ + ___ + ___
$\qquad\qquad\qquad\qquad\qquad\qquad\qquad\qquad\quad$ R $\quad$ M

2. $(5x^3 + x^2 - 3x + 7) + (3x^2 + 8x + 2) =$ ___ + ___ + ___ + ___
$\qquad\qquad\qquad\qquad\qquad\qquad\qquad\qquad\qquad\quad$ P

3. $(3x^3 + 7x - 12) + (3x^3 + 7x^2 - x + 15) =$ ___ + ___ + ___ + ___
$\qquad\qquad\qquad\qquad\qquad\qquad\qquad\qquad\quad$ E $\qquad$ L

4. $(9x^2 + 6x - 3) + (2x^2 + 3x - 1) =$ ___ + ___ + ___
$\qquad\qquad\qquad\qquad\qquad\qquad\qquad\quad$ A $\quad$ D

5. $(8x^3 + 3x^2 - 5x - 11) + (2x^2 - 8x + 11) =$ ___ + ___ + ___
$\qquad\qquad\qquad\qquad\qquad\qquad\qquad\qquad\qquad\quad$ O

6. $(2x^3 + 6x^2 + x) + (2x^2 - 10x + 1) =$ ___ + ___ + ___ + ___
$\qquad\qquad\qquad\qquad\qquad\qquad\qquad\quad$ Y $\qquad\qquad$ H

7. $(4x^3 - x - 5) - (x^2 - 5x + 7) =$ ___ + ___ + ___ + ___
$\qquad\qquad\qquad\qquad\qquad\qquad\qquad\quad$ W $\quad$ S

8. $(5x^3 - x^2 - 2) - (4x^3 - x^2 - 9) =$ ___ + ___
$\qquad\qquad\qquad\qquad\qquad\qquad\quad$ T

9. $(x^3 + x^2 - 3x - 8) - (3x^3 - 2x^2 - 3x + 9) =$ ___ + ___ + ___
$\qquad\qquad\qquad\qquad\qquad\qquad\qquad\qquad\quad$ C

10. $(-2x^3 - 2x) - (2x^3 - 2x) =$ ___
$\qquad\qquad\qquad\qquad\qquad\qquad\quad$ U

11. $(11x^2 + 3x + 8) - (x^2 + 3x - 10) =$ ___ + ___
$\qquad\qquad\qquad\qquad\qquad\qquad\qquad\qquad\quad$ N

12. $(5x^2 - 11x - 3) - (7x^2 - 11x + 7) =$ ___ + ___
$\qquad\qquad\qquad\qquad\qquad\qquad\qquad\quad$ I

Polynomial comes from two Greek words:

___ ___ ___ ___ ___   ___ ___ ___   ___ ___ ___ ___ ___
5x −13x 6x −4x³ 4x   9x 18 −4   18 −13x 2 −13x 4x

___ ___ ___ ___ ___   ___ ___ ___ ___   ___ ___ ___ ___
−x² 1 −2x² −2x³ 1   2 6x³ 9x 18   2 9x 18 2x³

___ ___ ___ ___ ___ .
5x 9x 2x² x³ 4x

5-24 Multiplying Polynomials by Monomials and Polynomials

Solve the following and express your answers in simplest form. Fill in each blank with a number or variable. Then write the letter of each answer above the answer to complete the statement at the end of the activity. The first problem is done for you.

1. $6x(-x^2 - 3x - 8) = \underset{D}{\underline{-6}}x^3 - 18x^2 - \underset{I}{\underline{48}}x$

2. $-5x^2(x^3 - 6x^2 + 8x - 5) = -5x^5 + \underset{N}{\underline{\quad}}x^4 - 40x^3 + \underset{A}{\underline{\quad}}x^2$

3. $2x(-x + 1) = -2x^2 + 2\underset{B}{\underline{\quad}}$

4. $3x(-3x + 2) + 4(3x - 1) = -9x^2 + \underset{M}{\underline{\quad}}x - 4$

5. $3xy^2(4x + 6y - 10) = \underset{I}{\underline{\quad}}x^2y^2 + 18xy^3 - 30\underset{M}{\underline{\quad}}$

6. $-9x^2(y^3 - 4) + 3x(xy^3 + x) = -6x^2y^3 + 39\underset{I}{\underline{\quad}}$

7. $(x + 5)(x - 8) = x^2 + \underset{E}{\underline{\quad}}x + \underset{W}{\underline{\quad}}$

8. $(x + 5)(3x + 4) = 3x^2 + \underset{O}{\underline{\quad}}x + \underset{L}{\underline{\quad}}$

9. $(x + 3)(x - 3) = x^2 + \underset{C}{\underline{\quad}}$

10. $(x + 4)(3x - 2) = \underset{S}{\underline{\quad}}x^2 + 10x - \underset{R}{\underline{\quad}}$

© 2002 by John Wiley & Sons, Inc.

Name _____   **Date** _____

5-24 Multiplying Polynomials by Monomials and Polynomials
(Continued)

---

11. $(4x - 3)(x + 6) = 4x^2 + \underset{M}{\underline{\quad}}x - 18$

12. $(2x - 5)(7x - 3) = 14x^2 - \underset{N}{\underline{\quad}}x + 15$

13. $(4x + 5)(2 - 4x) = \underset{A}{\underline{\quad}}x^2 + \underset{C}{\underline{\quad}}x + \underset{I}{\underline{\quad}}$

14. $(7x - 3)(x - 5) = 7x^2 - \underset{T}{\underline{\quad}}x + 15$

15. $(4x + y)(x - 2y) = 4x^2 - 7\underset{E}{\underline{\quad}} - \underset{S}{\underline{\quad}}y^2$

16. $(x - y)(2x + 3y) = 2x^2 + \underset{T}{\underline{\quad}}xy - 3y^2$

17. $(x + 4y)(x - 4y) = x^2 - \underset{E}{\underline{\quad}}y^2$

18. $(x - y)(x + 5y) = x^2 + \underset{R}{\underline{\quad}}xy - 5y^2$

To multiply a binomial by a monomial, use the Distributive Property. To multiply two binomials, use FOIL or use the Distributive Property ___ ___ ___ ___ ___

1	-40	x^2	-9	xy

___ ___ ___D   ___ ___ ___ ___ ___ ___ ___   ___ ___I ___ ___ ___ ___ ___

25	41	-6		-12	19	18	x	10	30	-3		2	48	xy^2	12	20	-16	4

___ ___ ___ ___ ___ .

38	16	8	21	3

5-25 Factoring Binomials and Trinomials

Factor each binomial and trinomial below. Following the problems, the factors are written below points in what appears to be a random fashion. Use a ruler to connect the circles joining the factors of each problem. The first problem is done for you. **Note:** Some factors will be used more than once. If you connect factors correctly, you will create a symmetric figure.

1. $x^2 - 6x - 27 =$ _____ $(x - 9)(x + 3)$ _____

2. $3x^2 - 9x =$ _____

3. $x^2 - 4 =$ _____

4. $x^2 - 14x + 45 =$ _____

5. $x^2 + 3x - 18 =$ _____

6. $2x^2 + 3x - 2 =$ _____

7. $x^2 - 3x - 40 =$ _____

8. $2x^2 + 5x + 3 =$ _____

9. $x^2 - 6x + 5 =$ _____

10. $4x^2 + 44x =$ _____

11. $3x^2 - 7x + 2 =$ _____

12. $2x^2 + 9x + 4 =$ _____

13. $x^2 + 2x - 3 =$ _____

14. $x^2 + 11x + 30 =$ _____

5-25 Factoring Binomials and Trinomials (Continued)

15. $3x^2 + 30x = $ _____

16. $x^2 - 11x + 24 = $ _____

17. $2x^2 + 8x = $ _____

18. $x^2 - 49 = $ _____

19. $6x^5 - 24x^4 = $ _____

20. $8x^2 + 10x - 3 = $ _____

21. $x^2 - 10x = $ _____

22. $x^2 - 10x - 11 = $ _____

23. $x^2 + 2x - 63 = $ _____

24. $x^2 + 4x - 32 = $ _____

25. $4x^2 + 51x - 13 = $ _____

26. $2x^2 - 19x - 10 = $ _____

27. $x^2 - 3x - 88 = $ _____

28. $2x^2 + 26x = $ _____

29. $x^2 + 9x = $ _____

30. $6x^2 - 5x + 1 = $ _____

31. $x^2 + 18x + 77 = $ _____

32. $4x^2 + 40x = $ _____

33. $6x^5 - 18x^4 = $ _____

5-25 Factoring Binomials and Trinomials (Continued)

Use a ruler to connect each pair of factors by drawing a line between the circles above them.

2x + 1   x   x - 7

x + 5   x - 10   x - 5   x + 9   x + 6

x + 4   x + 7

             3x - 1   x - 2

2x   x + 11

x + 13   x - 9   x - 1   4x

4x-1   x + 10

2x - 1   x + 2

2x + 3   3x

x - 8   x - 11   x + 3   x - 4   x - 3

x + 1   x + 8   6x⁴

5-26 Factoring Trinomials

Each binomial in the Binomial Bank is a factor of at least one of the trinomial problems that follow. Write the letters of each pair of binomials that are factors of each trinomial in the boxes at the bottom of the page to find a message. **Hint:** Since multiplication is commutative, you may have to change the order in which you have written the letters in some problems.

Binomial Bank

A. $(x + 3)$	**B.** $(x - 2)$	**C.** $(x + 8)$	**D.** $(x + 9)$
E. $(x - 6)$	**F.** $(x + 5)$	**H.** $(x - 5)$	**I.** $(x - 1)$
L. $(x - 8)$	**M.** $(x - 3)$	**N.** $(x + 4)$	**O.** $(x + 2)$
R. $(x - 20)$	**S.** $(x + 7)$	**T.** $(x - 4)$	

1. $x^2 - 3x - 18$

2. $x^2 + 3x - 40$

3. $x^2 + 7x + 10$

4. $x^2 - 9x + 20$

5. $x^2 + x - 42$

6. $x^2 - 10x + 24$

7. $x^2 - 21x + 20$

8. $x^2 + 6x + 8$

9. $x^2 - 4x + 3$

10. $x^2 - 5x - 24$

11. $x^2 + 15x + 56$

12. $x^2 + 7x + 12$

13. $x^2 - 8x + 12$

14. $x^2 + 8x + 15$

15. $x^2 + 4x - 32$

16. $x^2 - 18x - 40$

17. $x^2 + 3x - 54$

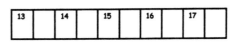

5-27 Solving Equations by Using the Zero Product Property

Solve each equation for x. Each equation has two answers. Place one answer in each column. Then locate each pair of answers on the diagram and use a ruler to draw a line to connect each pair. The result will be a rebus that should remind you of quadratic equations. The first problem is done for you.

		Column A	Column B
1.	$x(x - 3) = 0$	0	3
2.	$(x + 3)(x + 7) = 0$	_____	_____
3.	$(x + 4)(x - 5) = 0$	_____	_____
4.	$x^2 - 5x = 0$	_____	_____
5.	$x^2 = 1$	_____	_____
6.	$x^2 + 8x + 7 = 0$	_____	_____
7.	$x^2 + 6x = 16$	_____	_____
8.	$x^2 - 4x = 60$	_____	_____
9.	$x^2 = 10x - 24$	_____	_____
10.	$x^2 = 36$	_____	_____
11.	$x^2 = 3x + 40$	_____	_____
12.	$x^2 + x = 12$	_____	_____
13.	$x^2 = -5x - 6$	_____	_____
14.	$x^2 + 2x = 63$	_____	_____

-9 •   8 •   0 •| 5 •   -6 •   10 •   1 •

‑8 • 2 •   -3 • -2 •

-5 •   7 •   3 •| -4 •   6 •   4 •   -7 • -1 •

© 2002 by John Wiley & Sons, Inc.

5-28 Simplifying Rational Expressions

Simplify each rational expression and match your answers with the answers in the box. Place the letter of the answer in the space before the expression. When you are done, write the letters in order, starting with the first problem, to complete the statement at the end of the activity. **Note:** Some letters will be used more than once. You will need to divide the letters to form words. The first problem is done for you.

1. __D__ $\dfrac{x^2-4}{x+2}$ = ____ $x-2$ ____

2. ____ $\dfrac{x+5}{2x+10}$ = ____

3. ____ $\dfrac{3x+15}{x^2+7x+10}$ = ____

4. ____ $\dfrac{x-3}{7x-21}$ = ____

5. ____ $\dfrac{x^2+4x}{x^2+9x}$ = ____

6. ____ $\dfrac{x^2+4x-21}{2x^2-18}$ = ____

7. ____ $\dfrac{3x-6}{x^2-4}$ = ____

8. ____ $\dfrac{4x^2}{10x^2}$ = ____

9. ____ $\dfrac{x^2-25}{3x-15}$ = ____

10. ____ $\dfrac{x-2}{7x-14}$ = ____

11. ____ $\dfrac{x-1}{x^2-3x+2}$ = ____

12. ____ $\dfrac{x^2+7x+10}{x^2+2x+15}$ = ____

13. ____ $\dfrac{2x^2-6x}{5x^2-15x}$ = ____

Answer box:

N. $\dfrac{3}{x+2}$

I. $\dfrac{x+7}{2x+6}$

A. $\dfrac{2}{5}$

D. $x-2$

U. $\dfrac{6x^2}{x+5}$

O. $\dfrac{1}{7}$

Z. $\dfrac{4}{x-1}$

M. $\dfrac{x+4}{x+9}$

R. $\dfrac{1}{x-2}$

C. $\dfrac{x+2}{x-3}$

Q. $\dfrac{3}{2x-10}$

L. $\dfrac{x+9}{x+2}$

E. $\dfrac{1}{2}$

T. $\dfrac{x+5}{3}$

5-28 Simplifying Rational Expressions
(Continued)

14. _____ $\dfrac{3x+9}{x^2+5x+6}$ = _____

15. _____ $\dfrac{9}{3x+6}$ = _____

16. _____ $\dfrac{2x-2}{14x-14}$ = _____

17. _____ $\dfrac{x^2+4x-5}{3x-3}$ = _____

18. _____ $\dfrac{x^2-9x-8}{2x^2-18x-16}$ = _____

19. _____ $\dfrac{3x^2+15x}{2x^3-50x}$ = _____

20. _____ $\dfrac{6x^3-24x^2}{x^2+x-20}$ = _____

21. _____ $\dfrac{2x^2-8}{5x^2-20}$ = _____

22. _____ $\dfrac{x^2+7x-18}{x^2-4}$ = _____

23. _____ $\dfrac{4x+28}{x^2+6x-7}$ = _____

24. _____ $\dfrac{x-2}{2x-4}$ = _____

25. _____ $\dfrac{x-3}{x^2-5x+6}$ = _____

26. _____ $\dfrac{x^2+7}{7x^2+49}$ = _____

Since division by zero is undefined, the

D _____

_____.

5-29 Multiplying and Dividing Rational Expressions

Multiply or divide each rational expression, then match your answer with the answers in the box. Place the letter of the answer in the space before the expression. When you are done, write the letters in order, starting with the first problem, to complete the statement at the end of the activity. **Note:** Some letters will be used more than once. You will need to divide the letters to form words.

1. _____ $\dfrac{4}{xy} \cdot \dfrac{y}{2x} =$ _____

2. _____ $\dfrac{6x^2y}{7} \cdot \dfrac{14xy}{3x} =$ _____

3. _____ $\dfrac{x+4}{x-3} \cdot \dfrac{x-3}{x+4} =$ _____

4. _____ $\dfrac{x+4}{x-2} \cdot \dfrac{x-2}{2x+8} =$ _____

5. _____ $\dfrac{x^2}{x+5} \cdot \dfrac{x^2+7x+10}{x} =$ _____

6. _____ $\dfrac{x}{x-7} \cdot \dfrac{x^2-49}{x} =$ _____

7. _____ $\dfrac{2x^2-8}{x+2} \cdot \dfrac{1}{x-2} =$ _____

8. _____ $\dfrac{x^2+3xy+2y^2}{x+2y} \cdot (x+y) =$ _____

9. _____ $\dfrac{4}{xy} \div \dfrac{x}{2y} =$ _____

L. $x+7$

T. $\dfrac{1}{x+3}$

U. $\dfrac{3}{2}$

S. $\dfrac{2}{x^2}$

I. -1

O. $x^2 + 2x$

B. $\dfrac{1}{2}$

N. $x^2 + 2xy + y^2$

Y. $4x^2y^2$

D. $\dfrac{8}{x^2}$

P. $\dfrac{x-4}{x+4}$

M. 1

A. 2

5-29 Multiplying and Dividing Rational Expressions (Continued)

10. _____ $\dfrac{x^2y}{3} \div \dfrac{x^2y}{3} =$ _____

11. _____ $\dfrac{3x+12}{x+2} \div \dfrac{6x+24}{3x+6} =$ _____

12. _____ $\dfrac{x^2+5x-14}{x} \div \dfrac{3x-6}{3x} =$ _____

13. _____ $\dfrac{x-3}{x+3} \div (x-3) =$ _____

14. _____ $\dfrac{x-2}{2x+1} \div \dfrac{2-x}{2x+1} =$ _____

15. _____ $\dfrac{(x-4)^3}{(x+4)^3} \div \dfrac{(x-4)^2}{(x+4)^2} =$ _____

16. _____ $\dfrac{x^2+4x-21}{x+3} \cdot \dfrac{x+3}{x^2-4x+3} \div \dfrac{1}{x-1} =$ _____

17. _____ $\dfrac{2x^3}{3y^3} \cdot 6y^5 \div x =$ _____

Multiplication and division are inverse operations. To divide rational expressions, you must find the reciprocal of the expression to the right of the division

_____

_____.

5-30 Adding and Subtracting Rational Expressions

Simplify and write your answers in the spaces provided. Find each numerator and denominator on the diagram on the next page. Use a ruler to connect each pair to complete the design.

1. $\dfrac{4}{3x} + \dfrac{2}{3x} =$ _____

2. $\dfrac{6}{4x} - \dfrac{9}{4x} =$ _____

3. $\dfrac{5}{4x} - \dfrac{3}{4x} =$ _____

4. $\dfrac{8x}{x-4} + \dfrac{3x}{x-4} =$ _____

5. $\dfrac{3x}{x+2} + \dfrac{x+4}{x+2} =$ _____

6. $\dfrac{x}{5} - \dfrac{2x+3}{5} =$ _____

7. $\dfrac{x-3}{8} - \dfrac{3x-5}{8} =$ _____

8. $\dfrac{3}{5x-15} - \dfrac{2}{15-5x} =$ _____

9. $\dfrac{5}{x} + \dfrac{2}{x^2} =$ _____

10. $\dfrac{4}{3x} - \dfrac{1}{6x^2} =$ _____

11. $\dfrac{3x-2}{6} - \dfrac{x-3}{9} =$ _____

12. $\dfrac{x+1}{x} - \dfrac{x}{x+1} =$ _____

13. $\dfrac{3x}{4x-20} + \dfrac{15}{20-4x} =$ _____

14. $\dfrac{-3}{x+1} - \dfrac{5}{-x-1} =$ _____

5-30 Adding and Subtracting Rational Expressions (Continued)

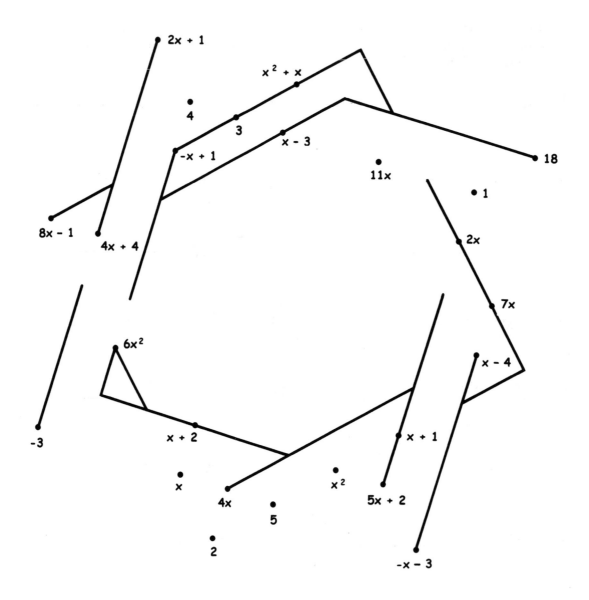

2x + 1

x² + x

4

3

x − 3

-x + 1

18

11x

1

8x − 1

4x + 4

2x

7x

6x²

x − 4

-3

x + 2

x + 1

x

4x

x²

5x + 2

5

2

-x − 3

Name _____   **Date** _____

5-31 Dividing Polynomials

Divide each polynomial. Write your answers in descending order with respect to x to fill in the blank of each problem. Match the letter beneath each answer with its answer at the end of the activity to complete the statement.

1. $(18x^2 - 51x) \div 3x = 6x - \underline{\hspace{1.5cm}}$
O

2. $(x^3 - 18x^2 + 3x - 7) \div x = x^2 - \underline{\hspace{1.5cm}} x + 3 - \underline{\hspace{1.5cm}}$
$I E$

3. $(4x^3 + 6x^2 - 20x - 4) \div 2x = 2x^2 + 3x - 10 - \underline{\hspace{1.5cm}}$
R

4. $(9x^2 - 3x - 12) \div 3x^2 = 3 - \underline{\hspace{1.5cm}} - \dfrac{4}{x^2}$
C

5. $(x^2 + x - 30) \div (x + 6) = x - \underline{\hspace{1.5cm}}$
S

6. $(x^2 - 2x - 24) \div (x + 4) = \underline{\hspace{1.5cm}} x - 6$
H

7. $(2x^2 - 11x + 12) \div (2x - 3) = x - \underline{\hspace{1.5cm}}$
A

8. $(3x^2 + 7x + 4) \div (x - 3) = 3x + 16 - \underline{\hspace{1.5cm}}$
T

9. $(2x^2 + 3x + 5) \div (x - 3) = 2x + 9 + \underline{\hspace{1.5cm}}$
J

10. $(2x^2 - 23x + 36) \div (2x - 3) = x - 10 + \underline{\hspace{1.5cm}}$
W

11. $(x^2 - 8) \div (x - 3) = x + 3 + \underline{\hspace{1.5cm}}$
M

12. $(x^2 - 10x - 2) \div (x + 4) = x - \underline{\hspace{1.5cm}} + \dfrac{54}{x+4}$
N

The division symbol was first used in 1659 by ___ ___ ___ ___ ___
$5 \quad \dfrac{6}{2x-3} \quad 18 \quad 5 \quad 5$

___ ___ ___ ___ ___ ___ ___ ___ ___ ___ ___ ___
$\dfrac{1}{x-3} \quad 4 \quad \dfrac{52}{x-3} \quad 1 \quad \dfrac{7}{x} \quad \dfrac{1}{x-3} \quad 4 \quad \dfrac{52}{x-3} \quad 18 \quad \dfrac{1}{x} \quad 18 \quad 4 \quad 14$

___ ___ ___ ___ ___ ___ ___ ___ ___ ___ .
$\dfrac{32}{x-3} \quad 17 \quad 1 \quad 4 \quad 14 \quad 14 \quad \dfrac{2}{x} \quad 4 \quad 1 \quad 14$

5-32 Solving Rational Equations

Solve for x. Write the letter of the problem above its answer to complete the statement below. **Note:** For some problems, x has more than one answer.

O. $\dfrac{7x}{3} - \dfrac{8x}{15} = -9$, x = _____

P. $\dfrac{x+1}{x} + \dfrac{1}{2x} = 4$, x = _____

H. $3x - \dfrac{3}{4} = \dfrac{2x}{3}$, x = _____

N. $\dfrac{4x+5}{x-4} = \dfrac{5x}{x-4}$, x = _____

A. $5x - \dfrac{2}{3} = \dfrac{-5x}{6}$, x = _____

L. $\dfrac{x}{x+2} - \dfrac{2}{2-x} = \dfrac{x+6}{x^2-4}$, x = _____

U. $\dfrac{x}{x+2} = 4 - \dfrac{2}{x+2}$, x = _____

R. $\dfrac{2x}{x-4} - 2 = \dfrac{4}{x+5}$, x = _____

E. $\dfrac{2x}{x-4} = 5 - \dfrac{1}{x-4}$, x = _____

I. $\dfrac{5}{x} + \dfrac{3}{x+1} = \dfrac{10}{x}$, x = _____

S. $2 - \dfrac{8}{x} = \dfrac{2}{3}$, x = _____

M. $\dfrac{x}{x+6} = \dfrac{1}{x+2}$, x = _____

B. $\dfrac{2}{x} - \dfrac{8}{x} = -15$, x = _____

V. $\dfrac{2}{x-2} = 2 - \dfrac{4}{x}$, x = _____

T. $\dfrac{5}{2x} + \dfrac{3}{4} = \dfrac{9}{4x}$, x = _____

X. $\dfrac{4}{x-4} = \dfrac{3x}{x+3}$, x = _____

Some ___ ___ ___ ___ ___ ___ ___ ___   ___ ___ ___ ___
$\frac{1}{2}$ −14 −5 $\frac{2}{5}$ −1 7 −3,2 6 $\frac{9}{28}$ $\frac{4}{35}$ 1,4 7

___ ___ ___ ___ ___ ___ ___ ___ ___ ___
7 6,−$\frac{1}{2}$ −$\frac{1}{3}$ −14 $\frac{4}{35}$ 5 7 −5 $\varnothing$ 6

___ ___ ___ ___ ___ ___ ___ ___ ___.
6 −5 −1 $\varnothing$ −$\frac{1}{3}$ −2$\frac{1}{2}$ −5 5 6

Name _____   Date _____

5-33 Finding the Slope and Y-intercept of a Line

Find the slope and y-intercept of the line for the given equation. Match your answers with the answers shown in the box. Record the corresponding letter of the slope and the corresponding letter of the y-intercept in the spaces provided. When you are done, write the letters for each problem in order, starting with the first problem, to complete the statement below. The first problem is done for you.

	Slope	Y-intercept
1. $y = 3x - 1$	L	I
2. $y = 2x + 1$	_____	_____
3. $y = -x - 10$	_____	_____
4. $x - 2y = 4$	_____	_____
5. $y = -3x + 1$	_____	_____
6. $2x - y = -8$	_____	_____
7. $y = -6x$	_____	_____
8. $8x + 2y = 1$	_____	_____
9. $3x - 4y = -4$	_____	_____
10. $y = 3x - 2$	_____	_____
11. $x - 2y = 2$	_____	_____
12. $4x - 2y = -1$	_____	_____

A. -2

C. $\frac{1}{3}$

D. $\frac{1}{6}$

E. 1

F. 8

G. $\frac{1}{4}$

H. $\frac{3}{4}$

I. -1

K. -3

L. 3

M. -4

N. 2

O. 0

R. -6

S. -10

T. $\frac{1}{2}$

U. 6

X. $\frac{2}{3}$

5-33 Finding the Slope and Y-intercept of a Line (Continued)

13. $y = x - 6$ _____   _____

14. $y = -4x + 3$ _____   _____

15. $x + y = 2$ _____   _____

16. $y = 6x - 4$ _____   _____

17. $4x + y = 1$ _____   _____

18. $2x + y = 2$ _____   _____

19. $x + y = 2$ _____   _____

20. $x - 4y = -32$ _____   _____

21. $2y = 6x - 4$ _____   _____

22. $2x - 3y = -3$ _____   _____

23. $6x - 3y = -1$ _____   _____

24. $3x - 4y = 0$ _____   _____

25. $36x + 6y = 1$ _____   _____

The word L I __ __   __ __   __ __ __ __ __

__ __ __ __   __ __   __ __ __ __ __

__ __ __ __   "__ __ __ __ __"

__ __ __ __ __ __ __   __ __ __ __ __

__ __ __ __ __ .

5-34 Identifying Points and Lines

Study the accompanying graphs of lines and points. Each line is referred to by an "*l*" with a subscript and also by an upper-case letter. Points are labeled by upper-case letters.

Several clues follow. Place the letter of the line or point in the blank before each clue. When you are done, write the letters in order, starting with the first problem, to complete the phrase on the next page. The phrase reveals a geometric concept, named for Rene Descartes.

1. _____ The point $(-4, -1)$.

2. _____ The y-axis.

3. _____ The only line that lies entirely in quadrants I and II.

4. _____ The line parallel to l_4.

5. _____ The line perpendicular to l_4.

6. _____ The only vertical line except for the y-axis.

7. _____ The line that intersects l_4 at $(1, -1)$.

8. _____ The only vertical line that contains the origin.

9. _____ This line has a slope of -1 and contains $(0, 0)$.

10. _____ This point is not on any line and is in quadrant III.

11. _____ The origin.

12. _____ The point where the y-axis and x-axis intersect.

13. _____ The only line other than the x-axis that has a slope equal to 0.

14. _____ The point $(-7, 2)$.

15. _____ The y-intercept of this line is $(0, -3)$.

16. _____ The only line that lies entirely in quadrants II and IV.

17. _____ All lines except vertical lines intersect this line.

18. _____ The y-intercept of this line is $(0, 5)$.

19. _____ The slope of this line equals 1.

20. _____ The x-intercept of this line is $(-6, 0)$.

21. _____ The point $(2,6)$.

22. _____ This line is contained in quadrants II and III.

23. _____ This line intersects l_7 at $(-2, 7)$.

24. _____ This line intersects l_5 at $(-6, -6)$.

25. _____ The point $(0, 7)$.

5-34 Identifying Points and Lines
(Continued)

The ___ __ __ __ __ __ __ __ __ __

__ __ __ __ __ __ __ __ __

__ __ __ __ __ __.

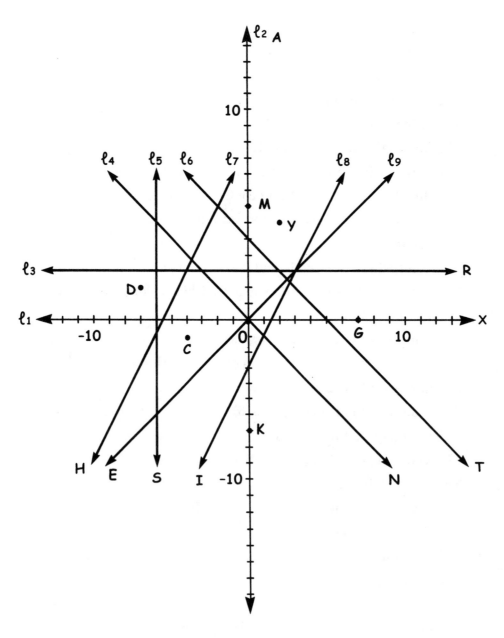

5-35 Evaluating Functions

Evaluate each function in the top box at the given value. Write your answer in the blank after the equal sign for each problem, then match your answer with the corresponding letter in the bottom box. Write the letter in the blank before the problem. When you are done, write the letters in order, starting with the first problem, to complete the statement below. **Note:** Some answers will be used more than once.

$$f(x) = x^2 + 1 \qquad g(x) = |x| + 2 \qquad h(x) = 3$$
$$j(x) = x \qquad k(x) = -x$$

1. _____ k(2) = _____

2. _____ j(2) = _____

3. _____ h(2) = _____

4. _____ g(2) = _____

5. _____ f(2) = _____

6. _____ g(−4) = _____

7. _____ f(−4) = _____

8. _____ g(−1) = _____

9. _____ f(3) = _____

10. _____ k(3) = _____

11. _____ k(4) = _____

12. _____ f[g(4)] = _____

13. _____ j[k(7)] = _____

14. _____ g(−2) = _____

15. _____ h(7) = _____

16. _____ g[f(4)] = _____

17. _____ g[j(15)] = _____

18. _____ g[k(1)] = _____

19. _____ k[g(5)] = _____

E 3	B 5	U −2	R −7	U 19	N −3	H −4
Y 6	A 37	O 10	L 17	D 4	S 2	

The expression f(x) to represent a function was first

—— —— —— —— ——   —— ——   —— —— —— —— —— —— ——

—— —— —— —— —— .

5-36 Solving Systems of Equations

Solve each system of equations. Write the values for x and y in the blank spaces after each problem. Then use a ruler to connect the values for x to the values for y on the figure that follows. If you are correct, a figure that appears to change in depth will result.

1. $x - y = 2$, $x =$ _____
   $x + y = 8$, $y =$ _____

2. $x - y = 6$, $x =$ _____
   $2x + y = 3$, $y =$ _____

3. , $y = -x + 2$, $x =$ _____
   $y = x - 2$, $y =$ _____

4. $3x - y = 17$, $x =$ _____
   $y + 2x = 8$, $y =$ _____

5. $x - y = -8$, $x =$ _____
   $x + y = 12$, $y =$ _____

6. $2y - 3x = 4$, $x =$ _____
   $x = -2$, $y =$ _____

7. $2x - 3y = 19$, $x =$ _____
   $5y - 2x = -37$, $y =$ _____

8. $25x - 10y = 100$, $x =$ _____
   $5y + 15x = 60$, $y =$ _____

9. $x + y = -3$, $x =$ _____
   $y = -3$, $y =$ _____

10. $-x - y = -8$, $x =$ _____
    $-x + y = 12$, $y =$ _____

11. $-x + y = 2$, $x =$ _____
    $x + y = 0$, $y =$ _____

12. $x + y = 14$, $x =$ _____
    $-4x + 3y = 14$, $y =$ _____

13. $x - 4y = -16$, $x =$ _____
    $x - 2y = -4$, $y =$ _____

14. $3x - y = -10$, $x =$ _____
    $-5x - y = 14$, $y =$ _____

© 2002 by John Wiley & Sons, Inc.

Name _____   Date _____

5-37 Simplifying Radical Expressions

Solve each problem and write the value of each letter in the spaces after the problem. To complete the statement below, write the letter above its corresponding number. The first problem is done for you.

1. $\sqrt{48} = N\sqrt{S}$ N = __4__   S = __3__
2. $\sqrt{56} = D\sqrt{H}$ D = _____   H = _____
3. $\sqrt{49} = R$ R = _____
4. $\sqrt{75} = A\sqrt{S}$ A = _____   S = _____
5. $\sqrt{I} = I$ I = _____
6. $\sqrt{250} = A\sqrt{C}$ A = _____   C = _____
7. $\sqrt{27} = S\sqrt{S}$ S = _____
8. $\sqrt{81} = T$ T = _____
9. $\sqrt{135} = S\sqrt{Y}$ S = _____   Y = _____
10. $\sqrt{50} = A\sqrt{D}$ A = _____   D = _____
11. $\sqrt{M} = S\sqrt{D}$ M = _____   S = _____   D = _____
12. $\sqrt{52} = D\sqrt{F}$ D = _____   F = _____
13. $\sqrt{121} = G$ G = _____
14. $\sqrt{384} = O\sqrt{E}$ O = _____   E = _____
15. $\sqrt{144} = L$ L = _____
16. $\sqrt{68} = D\sqrt{W}$ D = _____   W = _____
17. $\sqrt{171} = S\sqrt{B}$ S = _____   B = _____
18. $\sqrt{U} = N$ U = _____   N = _____
19. $\sqrt{72} = E\sqrt{D}$ E = _____   D = _____
20. $\sqrt{T} = S$ T = _____   S = _____

```
___  ___  N   ___    ___  ___  S   ___  ___  ___  ___  ___  S
 7    6    4    6      2    6    3   10    5    7    9    6    3

___  ___  ___  S   ___    ___  S   ___  ___    ___  ___  ___
13    1    7    3    9     16    3    6    2      9   14    6

___  ___  ___  ___  ___  ___  ___    S   ___  ___  ___  ___  ___
 7    5    2    1   10    5   12      3   15   18   19    8   12

___  ___  ___  ___    ___  ___    S   ___  ___  ___  ___
 9   14    5    9     17    6      3    9    1   12   12

___   S   ___    ___  ___  ___  ___  ___ .
16    3    6      9    8    2    5   15
```

5-38 Adding, Subtracting, Multiplying, and Dividing Radical Expressions

Evaluate each expression. The answers for the expressions are in the box. Write the answer in the space provided. **Note:** Each answer is the solution to at least one problem.

1. $3\sqrt{5}\,\sqrt{3}$ = _____

2. $\sqrt{81} - \sqrt{16}$ = _____

3. $\dfrac{\sqrt{300}}{2}$ = _____

4. $\dfrac{\sqrt{72}}{3}$ = _____

5. $\sqrt{27} + \sqrt{12}$ = _____

6. $\dfrac{\sqrt{75}}{\sqrt{3}}$ = _____

7. $\sqrt{3}\,\sqrt{9}$ = _____

8. $\sqrt{54} - \sqrt{24}$ = _____

9. $\dfrac{9\sqrt{5}}{\sqrt{3}}$ = _____

10. $\sqrt{15} + \sqrt{60}$ = _____

11. $\sqrt{2}\,\sqrt{3}$ = _____

12. $\sqrt{15}\sqrt{5}$ = _____

13. $\sqrt{90} + \sqrt{250}$ = _____

14. $\sqrt{9} + \sqrt{16}$ = _____

15. $\dfrac{6\sqrt{6}}{\sqrt{8}}$ = _____

16. $\sqrt{9+16}$ = _____

17. $\left(\sqrt{7}\right)^2$ = _____

18. $4\sqrt{2} - \sqrt{8}$ = _____

19. $2\sqrt{40} + \sqrt{160}$ = _____

20. $\dfrac{8}{\sqrt{8}}$ = _____

$\sqrt{6}$	5	$5\sqrt{3}$	$3\sqrt{15}$
$2\sqrt{2}$	$3\sqrt{3}$	7	$8\sqrt{10}$

5-39 Solving Radical Equations

Solve each radical equation. Write your answers in the spaces provided. Then write the letter of the problem above its solution to complete the statement at the bottom of the page. **Note:** Solutions must be real numbers.

L. $\sqrt{x} = 7$ x = _____   **V.** $3 + \sqrt{x} = 5$ x = _____

N. $\sqrt{x} = \frac{1}{2}$ x = _____   **H.** $8 + 2\sqrt{x} = 0$ x = _____

T. $\sqrt{2x} = 6$ x = _____   **I.** $5 - 2\sqrt{x} = 0$ x = _____

A. $2\sqrt{5x} = 4$ x = _____   **S.** $6 - \sqrt{x} = 1$ x = _____

D. $\sqrt{\frac{x}{5}} = 2$ x = _____   **E.** $5 - 2\sqrt{x} = 2$ x = _____

C. $\sqrt{x-2} = 3$ x = _____   **B.** $\sqrt{3x+4} - 1 = 4$ x = _____

R. $\sqrt{9x} - 9 = 0$ x = _____

A radical equation is an equation with

___ ___ ___ ___ ___ ___ ___ ___ ___   ___ ___   ___ ___ ___
4   0.8   9   6.25   0.8   7   49   2.25   25   6.25 0.25   18 $\varnothing$ 2.25

___ ___ ___ ___ ___ ___ ___ ___ .
9   0.8   20   6.25   11   0.8   0.25   20

5-40 Solving Quadratic Equations

Solve each quadratic equation. Write the roots in the blanks provided at the end of the problem. Be sure to write the smaller root first. Match your answers with the answers on the right, then write the corresponding letters below each answer. When you are done, write the letters in order from left to right, starting with the first problem, in the spaces to complete the statement below. The first problem is done for you.

1. $x^2 - 3x = 0$ ___0___ ___3___
     ___M___ ___A___

2. $x^2 = 100$ _____ _____
     _____ _____

3. $x^2 - 9x + 18 = 0$ _____ _____
     _____ _____

4. $6x^2 = 54$ _____ _____
     _____ _____

5. $x^2 + 12x + 35 = 0$ _____ _____
     _____ _____

6. $x^2 + 4x - 2 = 0$ _____ _____
     _____ _____

7. $2x^2 + 24x + 54 = 0$ _____ _____
     _____ _____

8. $x^2 + 11x = -30$ _____ _____
     _____ _____

9. $x^2 - 25 = 0$ _____ _____
     _____ _____

E	−3
D	−7
M	0
B	−2 + √6
R	−6
V	6
L	−9
H	10
T	5
A	3
U	−2 − √6
O	−5
Y	−10

© 2002 by John Wiley & Sons, Inc.

Some quadratic equations may have two real roots, some may have two conjugate imaginary roots, and some _M_ _A_ ___   ___ ___ ___ ___   ___

___ ___ ___ ___ ___ ___   ___ ___ ___ ___.

Section 6

DATA ANALYSIS

6-1 Constructing a Bar Graph

A *bar graph* shows information by the use of bars. Use the data below to complete the accompanying bar graph.

Restaurants and Food	Calories
Wendy's	
Hamburger	280
French Fries	270
Cola	130
White Castle	
Hamburger	135
French Fries	115
Cola	120
Burger King	
Hamburger	340
French Fries	230
Cola	280
McDonald's	
Hamburger	280
French Fries	210
Cola	150

(**Note:** Portion sizes are not necessarily the same.)

6-1 Constructing a Bar Graph (Continued)

Complete the bar graph to show the amount of calories in foods served at popular fast-food restaurants.

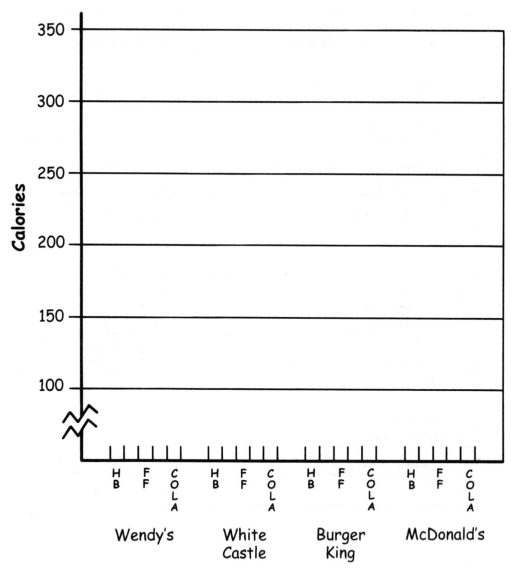

Calories in Foods at Fast-Food Restaurants

6-2 Constructing a Pictogram

A *pictogram* is a special type of bar graph in which a picture, or symbol, is used to show information. Use the data below to complete the accompanying pictogram and show some of the biggest money-making movies of the 20th century in the United States. (**Note:** This only includes movie ticket sales. Also, the totals have been rounded to the nearest ten million dollars.)

Movie	Ticket Sales (in millions)
E.T.	$400
Forrest Gump	$330
Independence Day	$310
Home Alone	$290
Star Wars	$460
Star Wars: The Phantom Menace	$430
Return of the Jedi	$310
The Empire Strikes Back	$290
Titanic	$600
Jurassic Park	$360

6-2   Constructing a Pictogram (Continued)

Complete the pictogram to show the total ticket sales for the movies listed on the chart. To represent the ticket sales amount, choose a symbol equal to $100 million dollars. Good symbols to use might be a ticket stub or movie reel. Use your imagination.

Big Money-Making Movies of the 20th Century

Movie	Ticket Sales (in millions)

Name _____   Date _____

6-3   Constructing a Histogram

A *histogram* is a special type of bar graph. It displays the frequency of data that has been organized into equal distributions.

For example, some teachers might count the number of grades on a test and make a frequency table and histogram. The histogram at the right shows the results of a test for a class that received 10 A's, 5 B's, 4 C's, 1 D, and 1 F.

Use the table of classic TV shows to complete the accompanying histogram and show the number of these programs that premiered during each decade.

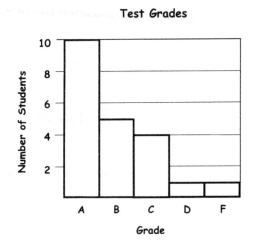

Classic TV Shows	Original Years Televised
"I Love Lucy"	1951–1957
"The Andy Griffith Show"	1960–1968
"M*A*S*H"	1972–1983
"The Dick Van Dyke Show"	1961–1966
"Cheers"	1982–1993
"The Mary Tyler Moore Show"	1970–1977
"Happy Days"	1974–1984
"Bewitched"	1964–1972
"Star Trek"	1966–1969
"The Carol Burnett Show"	1967–1978
"Seinfeld"	1990–1998
"The Twilight Zone"	1959–1964
"The Cosby Show"	1984–1992
"All in the Family"	1971–1983
"Mission: Impossible"	1966–1973

6-3 Constructing a Histogram (Continued)

Complete the histogram from the information you were given about classic TV shows. Set up your histogram according to decades, showing when each TV show premiered. **Hint:** Make a frequency table to organize your data.

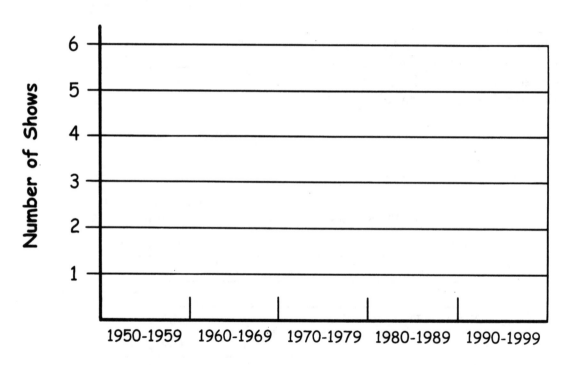

Classic TV Shows and First Broadcast Dates

Name _____   Date _____

6-4 Constructing a Line Graph

A *line graph* displays information as points that are connected with line segments. Line graphs are often used to show trends, or how things change over a period of time. Use the data below to construct a line graph on a separate sheet of paper.

Average Daily Temperatures for January 1 through 7 (in degrees Fahrenheit)	
Monday:	37°
Tuesday:	39°
Wednesday:	41°
Thursday:	43°
Friday:	35°
Saturday:	30°
Sunday:	29°

Follow these steps to construct your graph:

1. Make a grid. Label the lines so that the days are along the bottom and the temperatures are along the left side.

2. Mark the dots for the data.

3. Connect the dots.

4. Put the title on the top of the graph.

Answer these questions when you are done with your graph.

1. Describe the trend of temperatures for the first week of January. _____

_____

2. What was the average temperature of the week? Round your answer to the nearest degree. _____

6-5   Constructing a Conversion Chart

A graph can be a useful way to convert from one set of measurements to another. Use the following data of the weights of common foods to complete the accompanying conversion chart for ounces and grams.

Item	Weight (in ounces)	Weight (in grams)
candy bar	1.45	41.1
6 hot dog rolls	9	255
soup mix	2	56.7
1 box of cookies	7	198
100 tea bags	8	226
1 jar of jelly	10	283
1 can of gravy	10.25	291
1 brownie	2.5	71
small bag of M&Ms®	1.95	55
1 package of chocolate candy	1.3	37.5

Use the accompanying grid to plot the weights of the foods. When you are done with your chart, use the chart to estimate the following:

3 ounces ≈ _____ grams   600 grams ≈ _____ ounces

4 ounces ≈ _____ grams   250 grams ≈ _____ ounces

Name _____

6-5 Constructing a Conversion Chart
(Continued)

Using the data you were given, complete the conversion chart for ounces and grams.
Note: The scales are provided. The ounces are graphed along the horizontal line and
the grams are graphed along the vertical line. Then create a line of best fit.

Conversion Chart for Ounces and Grams

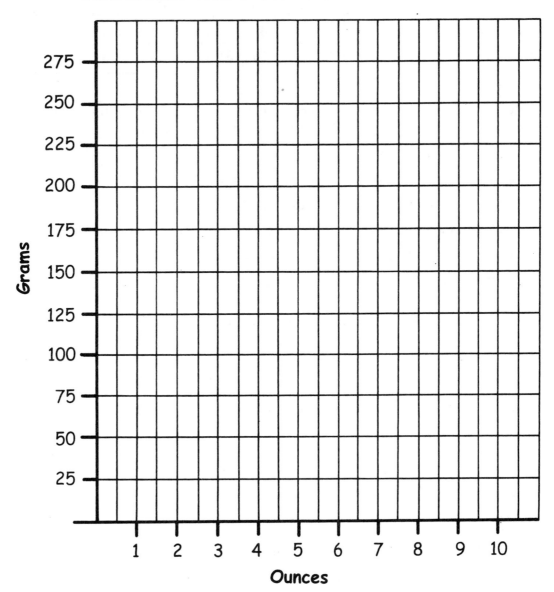

6-6   Creating Multiple Line Graphs

The table below shows the normal average monthly temperatures of Caribou, Maine; Washington, D.C.; and Miami, Florida.

Normal Average Monthly Temperature (in degrees F)

	J	F	M	A	M	J	J	A	S	O	N	D
Caribou	11	13	24	37	50	60	65	63	54	43	31	16
Washington, D.C.	31	34	42	53	62	71	76	74	67	55	45	35
Miami	67	68	72	75	79	81	83	83	82	78	73	69

Study the table and, on a separate sheet of paper, create a multiple line graph showing the normal average monthly temperatures of the cities. Follow these steps.

1. Draw the vertical and horizontal axes.

2. Choose an appropriate scale and list the temperature along the vertical axis.

3. List the months along the horizontal axis.

4. Plot the temperatures on the graph, using a different color for each city.

5. Connect the points, using these same colors for each city.

6. Be sure to include a title and legend for your graph.

When you are done with your graph, answer the following questions.

1. For which city is the average temperature in May twice the average temperature in January? _____

2. What month is the coldest in all three cities? _____

3. What two months are always the warmest?

   _____

4. What city has the greatest range in average temperature?

   _____

5. What city has the smallest range in average temperature?

   _____

© 2002 by John Wiley & Sons, Inc.

Name _____   Date _____

6-7   Understanding Circle Graphs, I

Circle graphs, also called pie graphs, can be used to compare information. They often display information in percents.

Use the following data to label the circle graph below. Then answer the questions. Europe is placed on the graph for you as an example.

Percent of the World's Land Area

North America:	16%
South America:	12%
Europe:	7%
Africa:	20%
Asia:	30%
Oceania:	5%
Antarctica:	10%

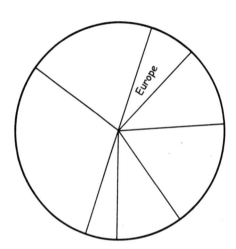

Note: Oceania includes Australia, New Zealand, and the Pacific Islands. Percentages have been rounded to the nearest whole.

1. Which two continents account for half of the Earth's land area?

   _____

2. What is the combined percent of the land area of the three smallest continents?

   _____

3. What percent of the Earth's land area does North and South America cover?

   _____

6-8 Understanding Circle Graphs, II

A *circle graph,* or pie graph, represents data as a part of a whole. The entire circle represents 100%. Each part of the graph is called a sector.

The table below summarizes the way a high school student spends a typical day. Calculate the length of time spent on each activity and use this information to complete the accompanying chart. **Note:** Miscellaneous activities include many activities that require short amounts of time, such as showering, brushing teeth, getting dressed, walking the dog, etc. After you complete the chart, write the name of the activity in the appropriate sector of the circle graph.

Time	Activity
6:15 A.M.	Alarm rings
6:15–7:00	Miscellaneous activities
7:00–7:20	Eating breakfast
7:20–7:45	Traveling to school on the bus
7:45–8:00	Miscellaneous activities
8:00–11:15	Classes
11:15–11:45	Lunch
11:45 A.M.–2:15 P.M.	Classes
2:15–4:15	Soccer game
4:15–4:30	Traveling home
4:30–4:45	Miscellaneous activities
4:45–6:15	Homework
6:15–6:45	Eating dinner
6:45–7:45	Homework
7:45–8:00	Miscellaneous activities
8:00–10:30	Watching TV
10:30–10:45	Miscellaneous activities
10:45 P.M.–6:15 A.M.	Sleep

Name _____   Date _____

6-8 Understanding Circle Graphs, II
(Continued)

Time Spent on Activities in Hours and Minutes

Eating _____

Attending Classes _____

Traveling _____

Playing Soccer _____

Doing Homework _____

Watching TV _____

Sleeping _____

Miscellaneous Activities _____

Label the circle graph below.

Daily Activities

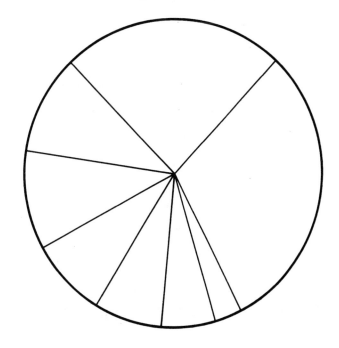

6-9   Creating a Stem-and-Leaf Plot

A *stem-and-leaf plot* displays all data in a given set of information. Each number is represented by a stem and a leaf. The *leaf* is the last digit of the number. The *stem* is the digit (or sometimes digits) remaining when the leaf is dropped.

Make a stem-and-leaf plot for the ages of the U.S. presidents at their inauguration. Use a separate sheet of paper for your plots. Use your display to find the range, mean, median, and mode of the ages. **Note:** If a president served consecutive terms, the age is his age at the inauguration of his first term.

Name	Age at Inauguration	Name	Age at Inauguration
Washington	57	Harrison, B.	55
Adams, J.	61	Cleveland	55
Jefferson	57	McKinley	54
Madison	57	Roosevelt, T.	42
Monroe	58	Taft	51
Adams, J.Q.	57	Wilson	56
Jackson	61	Harding	55
Van Buren	54	Coolidge	51
Harrison, W.	68	Hoover	54
Tyler	51	Roosevelt, F.D.	51
Polk	49	Truman	60
Taylor	64	Eisenhower	62
Fillmore	50	Kennedy	43
Pierce	48	Johnson, L.B.	55
Buchanan	65	Nixon	56
Lincoln	52	Ford	61
Johnson, A.	56	Carter	52
Grant	46	Reagan	69
Hayes	54	Bush, G.H.	64
Garfield	49	Clinton	46
Arthur	51	Bush, G.W.	54
Cleveland	47		

6-10 Creating a Box-and-Whisker Plot

A *box-and-whisker plot* displays the median of a set of data, the median of each half of the data, and the least and greatest values of the data. Box-and-whisker plots are used to compare sets of data.

In this activity you will construct a box-and-whisker plot of the posttest scores of Mr. Mendez's fifth-period math class. The steps to construct the plot will be explained and illustrated by the pretest scores. Following are the pretest and posttest scores of Mr. Mendez's students.

Student Number	Pretest Score	Posttest Score
1	40	81
2	44	76
3	50	80
4	50	91
5	34	55
6	40	85
7	43	83
8	55	93
9	57	99
10	38	82
11	54	91
12	40	85
13	44	87
14	40	80
15	42	78
16	32	78
17	30	76
18	20	66
19	48	83
20	39	92

279

6-10 Creating a Box-and-Whisker Plot
(Continued)

To construct a box-and-whisker plot:

1. First arrange the data in order from least to greatest. In the case of the pretest, this is:

   20, 30, 32, 34, 38, 39, 40, 40, 40, 40, 42, 43, 44, 44, 48, 50, 50, 54, 55, 57

2. Find the median. In this case, it is the average of 40 and 42, which is 41.

3. Find the median of the first half of the data. In this case, the median of 20 to 40 is 38.5.

4. Find the median of the second half of the data. In this case, the median of 42 to 57 is 49.

5. Identify the highest and lowest scores. These are called the *outlier scores*. In this case, 20 is the least score and 57 is the greatest.

6. Draw a number line ranging from the smallest to the largest numbers and graph these numbers on the number line.

7. Graph the median of the set of data, the median of the first half of the set of data, the median of the second half of the set of the data, and "box" them in. Draw "whiskers" to the smallest and largest value as illustrated below.

Pretest Scores

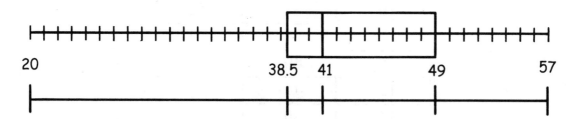

Each section contains 25% of the data.

Construct a box-and-whisker plot of the posttest scores on a separate sheet of paper. Follow the same procedure as shown above.

6-11 Finding the Mean, Median, Mode, and Range

Given the following information, answer the questions below. Then write the letter of the correct answer in the space above its answer to complete the statement at the end of the activity.

1. The scores of nine golfers finishing 18 holes of golf are 67, 68, 68, 68, 70, 71, 72, 77, and 78.

   F. The range is _____.   **E.** The mode is _____.

   S. The median is _____.   **H.** The mean is _____.

2. The weights (in kilograms) of the starting players of the basketball team are 93, 84, 79, 82, and 87.

   W. The range is _____.

   U. The median is _____.

   I. The mean is _____.

3. Manny's history test scores for this marking period are 90, 84, 90, and 68.

   R. The range is _____.   **N.** The mode is _____.

   T. The median is _____.   **A.** The mean is _____.

   O. Suppose that one more test is given. What score would Manny need to have an average of 85? _____

4. Suppose the lowest of Manny's four scores is dropped.

   Y. The new mean of his scores is _____.

   M. The new range is _____.

Sixty-two and two-sevenths   __ __   __ __ __   __ __ __ __   __ __
                             85 70   87 71 68   6 68 83 90   93 11

__ __ __ __   __ __ __ __ __ __ __ .
88 93 84 22   83 90 70 14 68 22 70

6-12 Using the Mean, Median, Mode, and Range

A part of Ms. Smith's gradebook is shown below. Find the mean test scores of each student and record the scores in the last column.

Student	Test 1	Test 2	Test 3	Test 4	Test 5	Mean
One	90	100	92	87	96	
Two	83	86	86	75	85	
Three	86	88	85	83	83	
Four	100	90	87	88	85	

Now try to find the first names of the students by using the following clues.

- The mode of John's scores is 86.
- The median of Maria's scores is 88.
- Joe's scores have a 13-point range.
- The median of John's scores is the same as the mean of Sally's scores.

Student One's first name is _____.

Student Two's first name is _____.

Student Three's first name is _____.

Student Four's first name is _____.

Section 7

POTPOURRI

Name _____   Date _____

7-1   Knowing Your Math Facts

Read each statement below. If a statement is true, follow its instructions. If a statement is false, skip it and go to the next one. If you complete the activity correctly, you will find a special number.

Write the number of the day of your birthday. _____

1. If a square is a rectangle, add 5 to the number of your birthday. The new number is _____.

2. If a circle has 360°, add 7. The new number is _____.

3. If a hexagon has seven sides, subtract 6. The new number is _____.

4. If 11 is a prime number, add 103. The new number is _____.

5. If 100 millimeters equal 1 meter, subtract 53. The new number is _____.

6. If 29 is a composite number, add 28. The new number is _____.

7. If $\frac{2}{3}$ is an example of a repeating decimal, subtract 63. The new number is _____.

8. If 8 is a factor of 12, subtract 17. The new number is _____.

9. If equivalent fractions represent equal value, add 8. The new number is _____.

10. If $\frac{4}{3}$ is an example of a proper fraction, subtract 10. The new number is _____.

11. If a triangle has 3 sides, add 6. The new number is _____.

12. If 38 inches equal 1 yard, subtract 14. The new number is _____.

13. If a right angle equals 90°, subtract 12. The new number is _____.

14. If 100% equals 1, subtract 14. The new number is _____.

15. If a simple fraction multiplied by its reciprocal equals 1, subtract 40. The new number is _____.

16. If all prime numbers are odd, add 32. The new number is _____.

17. If 32 is a multiple of 8, add 8. The new number is _____.

18. If the word "fathom" is a term most used to measure weight, add 18. The new number is _____.

19. If the ratio of 5 to 4 can also be written as 5:4, subtract 4. The new number is _____.

20. If 0° on the Celsius scale and 32° on the Fahrenheit scale equal the freezing point of water, subtract 4. The new number is _____. This should be your special number.

7-2   Equivalent Values

Write the letter of the numbers or expressions on the right in the blank before their equivalent value on the left. When you are done, write the letters in order, starting with the first problem, to complete the statement. The first problem is done for you.

1. __E__ 4,592

2. _____ 12

3. _____ 5 × 5

4. _____ 3.8

5. _____ 0.40

6. _____ $0.75

7. _____ 0.6000

8. _____ $\frac{4}{9}$

9. _____ 414.0

10. _____ 3^2

11. _____ 8^2

12. _____ 86

13. _____ 1

I.   81 ÷ 9

W. 38%

S. $4^1 - 2^2$

I. $\frac{18}{18}$

F.   4

T.   16

D.   258/3

F.   27

E.   2 out of 5

N. $39 \times \frac{2}{2}$

R. $24 \div \frac{1}{2}$

E.   56 × 82

E.   150%

7-2   Equivalent Values (Continued)

14. _____ 3 cubed

        D. 45×9.2

15. _____ square root of 16

        S. $\frac{3}{5}$

16. _____ 1.5

        N. $192 \div 3$

17. _____ 48

        P. $5(2 + 3)$

18. _____ 2^8

        X. $\frac{36}{3}$

19. _____ 39

        Y. 40 to 50

20. _____ $4 \times 2 \div 4 \times 2 \times 4$

        R. $3\frac{4}{5}$

21. _____ 0.38

        S. 3 quarters

22. _____ 64×0.5

        E. $\frac{12}{27}$

23. _____ 4/5

        E. 256

24. _____ 0

        A. 32

Numbers can be E __ __ __ __ __ __ __ __   __ __ __
__ __ __ __ __ __ __ __ __   __ __ __ __ .

7-3   Identifying Math Words

Use the clues on the left to write the math words on the right.

1. from the Latin word "addere"   _ _ _ I _ I _ _

2. GCF (last word)   _ A _ _ _ R

3. lines that meet at right angles   _ _ _ _ _ N _ _ _ _ _ A _

4. four-sided figure   _ _ A _ _ _ _ _ T _ _ _ _ _

5. comparison of two numbers   _ A _ _ _

6. meaning equal   _ _ _ I _ _ _ E _ _

7. the study that includes points, lines, angles   _ E _ M _ _ _ _ _

8. having no limit   _ _ _ _ _ N _ _ E

9. unit of measure of electrical power   _ _ _ O _ A _ _

10. from the Latin word "fractus"   _ _ _ _ C _ _ O _

11. likelihood of an event happening   _ _ _ _ _ A _ _ _ I _ _

12. three-dimensional surface, all points of which are equidistant from a fixed point   _ _ _ E _ _

13. having all angles of the same measure   _ _ _ _ _ A _ _ U _ _ _

14. word meaning the number of parts in a hundred   _ E _ _ _ _ N _

15. closed plane figure bounded by straight line segments   _ _ L _ _ O _

16. lines that never meet   _ _ _ _ A _ L _ _ _

17. mirror-like images   _ _ _ M _ T _ _ _

18. temperature is measured in these   _ _ _ R _ E _

19. device that makes computation easier   _ _ _ _ C _ _ _ _ _ _ R

20. operation in which the difference of two numbers is found

    _ _ _ _ _ _ _ C _ I _ _

Name _____   Date _____

7-4   Facts and Mystery Numbers

Find the mystery number to find the missing fact.

1. The dragonfly is the fastest insect. To find how fast it can fly in miles per hour, find this number:
    - It is an even, two-digit number.
    - The difference between the digits is 3.
    - The one's digit is twice the ten's digit.

    The number is _____.

2. The number of primary teeth of the average child is less than the number of teeth of an average adult, who has 32. To find the number of primary teeth of an average child, find this number:
    - It is an even, two-digit number.
    - The ten's digit is two more than the one's digit.
    - The square of the ten's digit is four more than the one's digit .

    The number is _____.

3. The normal human heart beats a remarkable number of times per minute. To find the normal number of beats of the average human heart per minute, find this number:
    - It is an even, two-digit number.
    - The sum of the digits is 9.
    - The sum of the squares of the digits is 53.

    The number is _____.

4. The giraffe is the world's tallest animal. To find the height of the giraffe in feet, find this number:
    - It is an odd two-digit number.
    - The ten's digit is less than the one's digit.
    - The product of the digits is 9.

    The number is _____.

5. The fastest fish is the sailfish. To find how fast the sailfish swims in miles per hour, find this number:
    - It is an even two-digit number.
    - The ten's digit is two less than the one's digit.
    - The square of the ten's digit is 36.

    The number is _____.

7-4 Facts and Mystery Numbers
(Continued)

---

6. The Portuguese man-of-war is a jellyfish found in many warm ocean waters. It is known for its painful sting (which can be fatal in some cases) and also for its long tentacles. To find the length of its tentacles in feet, find this number:
   - It is an even two-digit number.
   - The difference between the digits is 7.
   - The square of the one's digit is itself.

   The number is _____.

7. There are many distinctive breeds of cats. To find the number of breeds of cats, find this number:
   - It is an odd two-digit number.
   - The sum of the digits is 9.
   - The square of the one's digit is 49.

   The number is _____.

8. The average American uses a lot of water each day in drinking, cooking, bathing, and cleaning. To find the amount of water in gallons the average American uses each day, find this number:
   - It is an odd three-digit number.
   - The sum of the numbers is 12.
   - The ten's digit is twice the sum of the one's and hundred's digits.

   The number is _____.

9. The world is a big place with many countries. To find how many countries there are in the world, find this number:
   - It is an even three-digit number.
   - The hundred's digit is one less than the one's digit.
   - The square of the middle number is 27 times the sum of the other two digits.

   The number is _____.

10. Each year the average American uses a great amount of wood and wood products. In fact, if this amount was added up, it would equal the height of a tall tree. To find how tall in feet this tree would be, find this number:
    - It is an even three-digit number.
    - The hundred's digit plus the one's digit equals 1.
    - The square of the hundred's digit is one more than the sum of the other two digits.

    The number is _____.

© 2002 by John Wiley & Sons, Inc.

7-5   Mathematicians and Their Achievements

Match each problem with its answer (found in the answer box) to find the major achievements of each mathematician. The first problem is done for you. **Note:** Mathematicians come from all parts of the world, as shown by the nationalities of the men and women below.

1. **Sir Isaac Newton** (ENGLISH)

    89 + 56 = __145__

    _____algebra, calculus_____

2. **Sophie Germain** (FRENCH)

    7,045 − 3,902 = _____

    _____

3. **Diophantus** (GREEK)

    27.4 × 86 = _____

    _____

4. **Bonaventura Cavalieri** (ITALIAN)

    $\frac{1}{2}$ of 88 = _____

    _____

5. **Omar Khayyam** (PERSIAN)

    96 ÷ $\frac{1}{2}$ = _____

    _____

6. **Lady Murasaki** (JAPANESE)

    983 − 5.73 = _____

    _____

7. **Pythagoras** (GREEK)

    $7\frac{1}{2} - 3\frac{3}{4}$ = _____

    _____

8. **Leonhard Euler** (SWISS)

    4.8 ÷ 0.12 = _____

    _____

9. **Ahmes** (EGYPTIAN)

    6.2 + 9.7 = _____

    _____

10. **Emmy Noether** (GERMAN)

    $5 - \frac{3}{4}$ = _____

    _____

11. **Tsu Chung-chi** (CHINESE)

    45.09 ÷ 0.03 = _____

    _____

12. **Aryabhata** (HINDU)

    9.6 − 0.042 = _____

    _____

7-5   Mathematicians and Their Achievements (Continued)

13. Euclid (GREEK)

$0.048 \times 5.4 =$ _____

_____

14. John Napier (SCOTTISH)

$2\frac{1}{2} \times 3\frac{1}{5} =$ _____

_____

15. Carl Friedrich Gauss (GERMAN)

$17.5 + 3.46 =$ _____

_____

16. Jamshid al-Kashi (ARABIAN)

$16 \div \frac{4}{5} =$ _____

_____

17. George Joachim (AUSTRIAN)

$5\frac{7}{8} + 4\frac{1}{4} =$ _____

_____

18. Gottfried Wilhelm von Leibniz (GERMAN)

$92.3 - 1.69 =$ _____

_____

19. Sonya Kovalevsky (RUSSIAN)

$34 + 5.71 - 23.45 =$ _____

_____

20. Srinivasa Ramanujan (HINDU)

$1.2 \times 0.34 \div 0.25 =$ _____

_____

44: geometry	1,503: pi	20.96: number theory, geometry
977.27: permutations, combinations	20: coordinates, pi	$3\frac{3}{4}$: geometry, trigonometry
3,143: symmetry	9.558: pi	$10\frac{1}{8}$: trigonometry, algebra
40: polyhedra, functions	8: decimals, logarithms	15.9: circles, fractions
145: algebra, calculus	90.61: calculus, functions, infinity	16.26: sequences, series
$4\frac{1}{4}$: algebra	192: geometry	0.2592: geometry
2,356.4: algebra	1.632: algebra	

Name _____   **Date** _____

7-6 Math and Interesting Facts

Read the facts below, then study the equations that follow them. Write whether each equation is true or false on the line. If the equation is true, the fact is true. If the equation is false, the fact is false.

1. The amount of water that pours over Niagara Falls every second could fill about 20,000 bathtubs.

   $4.8 = 480\%$ _____

2. Niagara Falls is the highest waterfall in the world at nearly 1,000 feet in height.

   $\frac{2}{9} = \frac{14}{64}$ _____

3. The largest exposed rock in the world is Ayers Rock in Australia. It is about 1.5 miles long.

   $50\% = $ one half _____

4. If all the insects in the world were weighed, ants would make up $\frac{1}{10}$ of the total weight.

   $8\frac{1}{2} = 85$ out of 100 _____

5. About 83% of the Earth's surface is covered with sea water.

   $0.03\overline{3} = \frac{1}{3}$ _____

6. To stay healthy, the average person needs about $2\frac{1}{2}$ quarts of water per day.

   18 inches = 1.5 feet _____

7. The lowest point in North America is Death Valley in California at 382 feet below sea level.

   $3{,}704 - 0.0683 = 3.6457$ _____

7-6   Math and Interesting Facts
(Continued)

_____

8. The longest river in the world is the Nile in Egypt at 4,160 miles.

   $28 \div 0.070 = 400$ _____

9. With about 290,000 different species, there are more beetles than any other kind of animal on Earth.

   $45 = 25\%$ of 180 _____

10. The world's biggest island is Madagascar, off the coast of Africa, with an area of 226,658 square miles.

    56% of $320 = 169.2$ _____

11. Hawaii is the smallest state in the United States.

    $11 - 9\frac{2}{3} = 2\frac{1}{3}$ _____

12. The first modern Olympic games were held in New York City in 1896. Only thirteen countries and 311 athletes participated.

    $0.25 = \frac{1}{4} = 0.25\%$ _____

13. Each day the average person's heart beats about 100,000 times and pumps about 2,000 gallons of blood.

    3 to $2 = 3/2 = 1.5$ _____

14. Oregon's Crater Lake is the deepest lake in the world at 1,932 feet.

    $\frac{1}{2}$ of $40 = 40 \div \frac{1}{2}$ _____

15. The world's biggest lake is Lake Superior with an area of 31,820 square miles.

    0.75 of $120 = 0.5$ of 240 _____

7-7 Following Math Directions

Follow the directions to find an important message.

1. Add 34 to 4.2. If the answer is 7.6, place an E in the first blank below and an R in the second blank. If the answer is 38.2, write an S in the first blank and an N in the second.

2. Add 13 and 18. If the answer is a composite number, write an L in the third blank and an S in the fourth. If the answer is a prime number, write an O and an I in the blanks.

3. Multiply 84 by 28. If the answer can be rounded to 2,350, place a T and a C in the next two blanks. If the answer cannot be rounded to 2,350, place an R and a U.

4. Multiply $9 \times 8 \times 0 \times 7 \times 3$. If the answer is greater than 1,510, write an O and a W in the next two blanks. If the answer is less than 1,510, write an E and an R in the blanks.

5. Divide 2 by 2. Divide $\frac{1}{2}$ by $\frac{1}{2}$. If the answer is the same, write an I and a D in the next two blanks. If the answers are different, write a T and an S in the two blanks.

6. Subtract 0.64 from 100. If the answer is 99.36, write a D and an E in the next two blanks. If the answer is 0.36, write an A and an H in the blanks.

7. Divide 721 by 7. If the answer is 13, write a V and an M in the next two blanks. If the answer is 103, write a W and an O in the blanks.

8. Find 50% of 200. If the answer equals the number of pennies in a dollar, write an L and an L in the next two blanks. If the answer equals 40, write a T and a J in the next two blanks.

9. Subtract 867 from 1,001. If the sum of the three digits that make up the answer is 8, place an O and an F in the next two blanks. If the sum of the digits is 9, place a U and a K in the blanks.

10. Add 45 and 19. If the answer is a multiple of 12, write an M and an R in the next two blanks. If the answer is a multiple of 8, write an E and a V in the blanks.

11. Divide $3\frac{3}{4}$ by $\frac{3}{4}$. If the answer is a factor of 25, write an A and an H in the next two blanks. If the answer is a mixed number, write a T and a D in the blanks.

12. Find 25% of 84. If 7 is a factor of the answer, write a U and an O in the blanks. If 11 is a factor, write a W and an A in the blanks.

13. Subtract 13 from 26. If the answer equals $\frac{1}{3}$ of 26, write an R in the final blank. If the answer equals $\frac{1}{2}$ of 26, write a Y.

__ __

Reverse the letters and break them into words. If you did your work correctly, you will find a message.

7-8 Math Is Everywhere

Work with a partner and use the letters that make up the statement below to form as many words as you can that are related to math. Consult your text and reference books.

Great examples of mathematics are to be found everywhere in the world.

_____

_____

_____

_____

_____

_____

_____

_____

_____

_____

_____

Name _____   **Date** _____

7-9 Math and Me

Think about all the ways mathematics affects your life. Make a list of these ways.

_____

_____

_____

_____

_____

_____

_____

_____

_____

_____

_____

_____

_____

7-10   Find the Pattern

Study and describe the patterns below. The first problem is done for you.

1. $15 \rightarrow 7, 21 \rightarrow 9, 27 \rightarrow 11$
    <u>divide by 3, add 2</u>_____

2. $8 \rightarrow 27, 7 \rightarrow 24, 10 \rightarrow 33$

    _____

3. $18 \rightarrow 57, 21 \rightarrow 66, 25 \rightarrow 78$

    _____

4. $7 \rightarrow 27, 10 \rightarrow 36, 13 \rightarrow 45$

    _____

5. $3 \rightarrow 12, 2 \rightarrow 10, 9 \rightarrow 24$

    _____

6. $12 \rightarrow 5, 16 \rightarrow 7, 24 \rightarrow 11$

    _____

7. $11 \rightarrow 4.5, 20 \rightarrow 9, 8 \rightarrow 3$

    _____

8. $9 \rightarrow 8.5, 15 \rightarrow 11.5, 18 \rightarrow 13$

    _____

9. $8 \rightarrow 1, 10 \rightarrow 1.5, 12 \rightarrow 2$

    _____

10. $14 \rightarrow 8.5, 16 \rightarrow 9.5, 18 \rightarrow 10.5$

    _____

11. $8 \rightarrow 21, 12 \rightarrow 31, 16 \rightarrow 41$

    _____

12. $11 \rightarrow 13.5, 12 \rightarrow 15, 13 \rightarrow 16.5$

    _____

Create and describe three patterns of your own on the back of this sheet.

7-11   Scrambled Math

Unscramble the following phrases to find a common expression based on mathematics.

1. xtsih esens

_____

2. ngigo ni rceslci

_____

3. melpis sa neo, wto, rhete

_____

4. noe ni a lmniloi

_____

5. yroft nkiws

_____

6. ndbhei het hgiet labl

_____

7. cabk ot urqeas oen

_____

8. alpy ndecso ldedif

_____

9. venseht aevhne

_____

10. a tpcriue si rothw a uhstndao rsdwo

_____

11. tow daehs ear tbrete anht noe

_____

12. upt otw nda wto teghotre

_____

13. fhla a flao si tterbe htan onne

_____

14. a rbdi ni ndha si rothw otw ni hte hubs

_____

15. otw si pcmonya tub hrtee si a dcorw

_____

7-12 Working with Variables

Use the clues to find the values of the variables, then use the values to evaluate each equation.

- The variable **a** is 2 less than the Cardinal Directions. It is also the first prime number.

  a = _____

- The variable **b** is a number that symbolized wisdom and knowledge to ancient mystics. It is 1 more than the cube of 2.

  b = _____

- The variable **c** is a common number in history. In mythology it is the number of Fates, the number of Graces, and the number of Furies. It is also symbolic of the triangle.

  c = _____

- The variable **d** is the number of the Wonders of the Ancient World. It is also the square root of 49.

  d = _____

- The variable **e** is the number of signs of the Zodiac. The square of this number equals 144.

  e = _____

1. $15a =$ _____

2. $8,181 \div b =$ _____

3. $3(b + e) =$ _____

4. $(7 + c)(e - d) =$ _____

5. $ab(8 + c) =$ _____

6. $(e - c) + b(5 + c) =$ _____

7. $(140 - b) - (de) =$ _____

8. $(bc + 18)(e \div 2) =$ _____

9. $(a + c)^2 (8 + e) =$ _____

10. $(d^2 + 32) \div (e - c) =$ _____

11. $ab^2c(15 - d) =$ _____

12. $b^2(10 - d) + [4c(7 + 8)] =$ _____

13. $6(c^3 - e) - \left(\frac{1}{2} a + b \right) =$ _____

14. $[5b(a^2 + 5) - 5(c + d)] =$ _____

15. $\left[7a^2(d + 8) + \frac{1}{2}(b - c) \right] =$ _____

7-13 Deciphering Dates in Roman Numerals

Although at its height the Roman Empire stretched from England to the Middle East, and Roman law was the law of many lands, the Romans never created an efficient number system. Numbers were written in symbols, read from left to right. When a symbol of lesser value came *before* a symbol of greater value, the lesser was subtracted from the greater. For example, IX = 9, or 1 subtracted from 10. When a symbol of lesser value came *after* a symbol of greater value, the two were added. For example, XI = 11, or 10 plus 1.

Following are the major symbols of Roman Numerals:

I = 1	**V** = 5	**X** = 10	**L** = 50
C = 100	**D** = 500	**M** = 1,000	

Directions: Match the Roman numeral date with the modern date found in the box on the next page. Matching the dates correctly will reveal the date of some of the world's major inventions.

Write the letter and the modern date in the blank before the Roman date. The first one is done for you. When you are done, write the letters in order, starting with the first problem, to complete the statement.

1. __N__ _1879_ MDCCCLXXIX
   electric light bulb
   (THOMAS A. EDISON)

2. ____ ____ MDCCCLXXXVIII
   ballpoint pen
   (JOHN LOUD)

3. ____ ____ CV
   paper
   (TS'AU LUN)

4. ____ ____ MDCCCXCII
   automobile
   (CHARLES E. and J. FRANK DURYEA)

5. ____ ____ MDCCC
   electric battery
   (ALESSANDRO VOLTA)

6. ____ ____ MDCCCLXXVI
   telephone
   (ALEXANDER G. BELL)

7-13 Deciphering Dates in Roman Numerals (Continued)

7. ____ ____ MDCCXIV

mercury thermometer

(Gabriel Fahrenheit)

8. ____ ____ MCMXLVII

microwave oven

(Percy L. Spencer)

9. ____ ____ MCCL

magnifying glass

(Roger Bacon)

10. ____ ____ MDCCIX

piano

(Bartolomeo Cristofori)

11. ____ ____ MCMIII

propeller airplane

(Orville and Wilbur Wright)

12. ____ ____ MCMXI

air-conditioning

(Willis H. Carrier)

13. ____ ____ MCMXLII

electronic computer

(John V. Atanasoff, Clifford Berry)

14. ____ ____ MCMLXXII

video game—Pong

(Norman Buschnel)

15. ____ ____ MDCVIII

telescope

(Hans Lippershey)

© 2002 by John Wiley & Sons, Inc.

Z. 1911	R. 1903	O. 1608
F. 1250	S. 105	O. 1714
E. 1942	L. 1947	N. 1879
R. 1972	O. 1888	O. 1709
B. 1876	Y. 1892	M. 1800

In Roman numerals, there is N ___   ___ ___ ___ ___ ___ ___

___ ___ ___ ___ ___ ___ ___ .

7-14 Using a Number-box Cipher

A *number-box cipher* consists of five rows and five columns that make 25 boxes. See the example to the right.

Because there are 26 letters of the alphabet, one box must contain two letters. Since X is not used very often, X and Y may be placed in the same box.

The boxes are numbered 1 to 5 across and down. The numbers obtained from the rows and columns represent letters. For example, 11 (row 1, column 1) represents A; 32 (row 3, column 2) stands for L, and 43 (row 4, column 3) stands for R.

Directions: Number-box ciphers can be used for both deciphering and writing codes. Use the number-box cipher to find the name of the man whose portrait is on the front of each monetary bill listed below. Write his name above his code.

	1	2	3	4	5
1	A	B	C	D	E
2	F	G	H	I	J
3	K	L	M	N	O
4	P	Q	R	S	T
5	U	V	W	XY	Z

Denomination	Portrait
$1	_____ 53–11–44–23–24–34–22–45–35–34
$2	_____ 25–15–21–21–15–43–44–35–34
$5	_____ 32–24–34–13–35–32–34
$10	_____ 23–11–33–24–32–45–35–34
$20	_____ 25–11–13–31–44–35–34
$50	_____ 22–43–11–34–45
$100	_____ 21–43–11–34–31–32–24–34

Use the number-box cipher to write the official motto of the United States, "In God We Trust," which has appeared on all U.S. currency since 1955.

_____

_____

7-15 Lines of Symmetry and Braille

In 1824, Louis Braille, a 15-year-old blind French boy, developed a coded alphabet that today bears his name. The Braille alphabet is illustrated below.

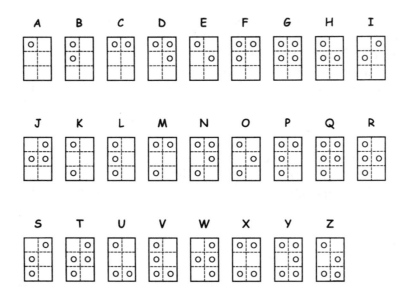

Each letter is represented by a raised dot or dots on an imaginary 2×3 grid. For example, the letter A is represented by a raised dot in the upper left-hand corner of the grid. The other parts of the grid are not raised.

Just as some letters of our alphabet have horizontal and/or vertical lines of symmetry, so does Braille. For example, the letter C in Braille has one vertical line of symmetry (see above). A vertical line placed halfway between the two raised dots divides the grid into two parts, each of which is a mirror image of the other. The letter L has one horizontal line of symmetry. A horizontal line placed halfway between the top of the grid and the bottom of the grid divides the grid into two parts, which are mirror images.

Directions: Use the Braille alphabet to answer the following questions.

1. Which two letters, other than C, have a vertical line of symmetry?

   _____

2. Which five letters, other than L, have a horizontal line of symmetry?

   _____

3. Which seven pairs of letters are mirror images of each other?

   _____

7-16 A Puzzle of Numbers and Languages

The words for the numbers one to ten are written below in German, French, Spanish, and Italian. Place each word in the proper place on the puzzle. Be certain that the word is the only one that can be written in the space. Some letters are provided for you. **Note:** Write "uno" on the grid only once.

German	French	Spanish	Italian
eins	un	uno	uno
zwei	deux	dos	due
drei	trois	tres	tre
vier	quatre	cuatro	quattro
funf	cinq	cinco	cinque
sechs	six	seis	sei
sieben	sept	siete	sette
acht	huit	ocho	otto
neun	neuf	nueve	nove
zehn	dix	diez	dieci

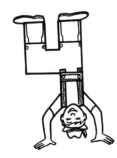

7-16 A Puzzle of Numbers and Languages (Continued)

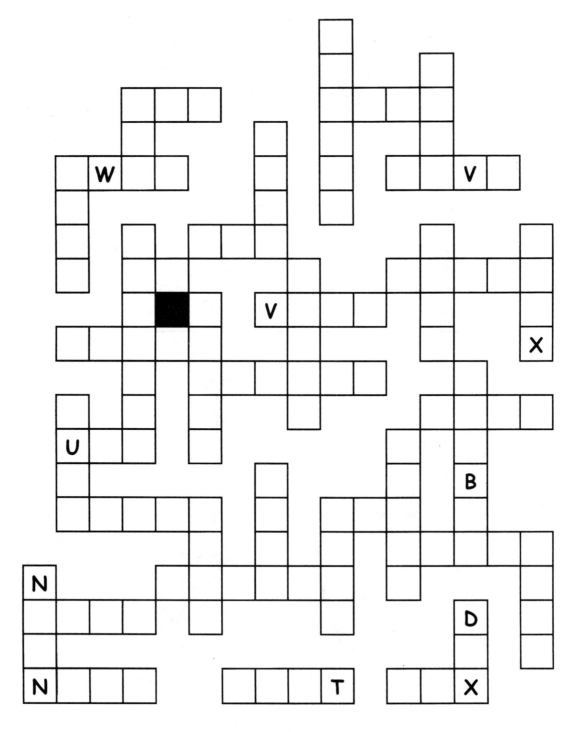

7-17   Math Words Used Every Day

Twenty-five words that have a mathematical meaning as well as an everyday meaning are hidden in the word search below. The words are written backwards, forwards, vertically, horizontally, and diagonally. The first letter of each word and the total number of letters it has are listed beneath the puzzle. Use these clues to find and circle the math words in the puzzle.

```
M  A  E  S  I  T  I  E  M  I  R  P  E  X  E  Y
E  E  V  E  N  U  C  N  R  B  A  V  D  E  B  S
T  P  D  T  L  P  R  O  D  U  C  T  D  S  S  D
I  O  K  I  J  O  V  C  W  X  D  R  O  H  C  P
S  W  N  N  A  I  H  R  F  O  R  M  U  L  A  F
O  E  M  D  C  N  Q  G  U  O  E  A  F  R  L  A
P  R  K  E  U  T  E  B  D  Q  B  M  R  A  E  C
M  W  M  G  E  Z  L  L  I  N  T  E  R  E  S  T
O  C  U  R  V  E  B  U  C  R  R  A  Y  T  A  O
C  T  J  E  N  A  S  E  G  M  E  N  T  F  H  R
L  Z  I  E  V  I  T  I  S  O  P  A  P  S  G  O
```

A_____ (4)   F_____ (6)   P_____ (5)
C_____ (5)   F_____ (7)   P_____ (5)
C_____ (9)   I_____ (8)   P_____ (8)
C_____ (4)   L_____ (4)   P_____ (7)
C_____ (4)   M_____ (4)   R_____ (3)
C_____ (5)   M_____ (6)   S_____ (5)
D_____ (6)   O_____ (3)   S_____ (3)
D_____ (6)   P_____ (5)   S_____ (7)
E_____ (4)

7-18 Mathematical Palindromes

In language, palindromes are words that are spelled the same forwards and backwards. Two common examples are "dad" and "mom."

Numbers can also be palindromes. The year 2002 is a palindrome because it reads the same front to back and back to front. Any number can lead you to a mathematical palindrome. All you need to do is reverse the digits and add them to the original number.

Here is an example. Start with 18. Reverse the digits so that you have 81. Now add: $18 + 81 = 99$, which is a palindrome. Some numbers can lead you to a palindrome in a few steps, but others may require several.

Try 372. $372 + 273 = 645$. $645 + 546 = 1,191$. $1,191 + 1,911 = 3,102$. $3,102 + 2,013 = 5,115$, which is a palindrome. The palindrome was reached in four steps.

Directions: Find the palindromic sums for the following numbers.

1. 38   _____
2. 87   _____
3. 206   _____
4. 658   _____
5. 864   _____
6. 752   _____
7. 279   _____
8. 1,426 _____

9. 8,694 _____
         _____
10. 485 _____
         _____
11. 5,372 _____
         _____
12. 1,845 _____
         _____

Find three palindromic numbers of your own, showing the steps to achieve them. Use the back of this sheet.

7-19   Codebreaking

Use the partially completed translation key to help you decode the statement about mathematics. Then complete the translation key.

"π + ∠ ⊥ □ π + ∠ # > ↔   # ↔   ∠ ⊥ □ $ □ ~

∅ # ∠ ⊥   ∅ ⊥ # > ⊥   ∞ ÷ ≈   ⊥ + ↔   ∅ ± # ∠ ∠ □ ~

∠ ⊥ □   – ~ # ≠ □ ± ↔ □ . "   ∞ + % # % □ ÷

Translation Key

A	B	C	D	E	F	G	H	I	J	K	L	M
+	Δ				( )	∞			×	‹		π

N	O	P	Q	R	S	T	U	V	W	X	Y	Z
~		/		↔	∠					→	||	°

Name ______________________________ Date __________

7-20 A Personal Statement About Mathematics

Mathematics is fundamental to our lives. Without math we could not perform the simplest calculations, measure distances, weights, or temperature, or even tell time accurately. We would find it impossible to accomplish routine tasks and understand our world.

Directions: Think about the many ways mathematics affects your world and write a personal statement about math. To help you clarify your thoughts, consider the following questions:

- How do you use mathematics?
- When do you use math?
- Where do you use math?
- What would the world be like without math?
- Why do we need math?
- Who, besides yourself, uses math in their work or responsibilities?

Notes:

© 2002 by John Wiley & Sons, Inc.

ANSWER KEY

Section 1
Whole Numbers: Theory and Operations

1-1. **R.** 90; **G.** correct; **P.** 1,380; **T.** 1,286; **I.** 1,071; **I.** 9,776; **R.** 12,228; **A.** 10,079; **E.** 6,635; **O.** 18,114; **O.** 18; **N.** 212; **E.** 69; **H.** correct; **V.** 319; **S.** 1,861; **S.** 619; **C.** correct; **E.** 3,452; **N.** 4,354
Addition and subtraction are INVERSE OPERATIONS.

1-2.

1.
```
    8 4
  × 3 9
  7 5 6
2 5 2
3,2 7 6
```

2.
```
    7 6
  × 8 2
  1 5 2
6 0 8
6,2 3 2
```

3.
```
    4 7
  × 6 8
  3 7 6
2 8 2
3,1 9 6
```

4.
```
    5 6
  × 7 5
  2 8 0
3 9 2
4,2 0 0
```

13.
```
    7 9 4
  ×    6 8
  6 3 5 2
4 7 6 4
5 3,9 9 2
```

14.
```
    8 2 6
  ×  7 6 3
  2 4 7 8
4 9 5 6
5 7 8 2
6 3 0,2 3 8
```

15.
```
      7 3 8
  ×   6 0 4
    2 9 5 2
  0 0 0
4 4 2 8
4 4 5,7 5 2
```

5.
```
    6 3
  × 4 5
  3 1 5
2 5 2
2,8 3 5
```

6.
```
    4 9 6
  ×    5 7
  3 4 7 2
2 4 8 0
2 8,2 7 2
```

7.
```
    6 0 7
  ×    3 8
  4 8 5 6
1 8 2 1
2 3,0 6 6
```

8.
```
    2 7 8
  ×    5 4
  1 1 1 2
1 3 9 0
1 5,0 1 2
```

16.
```
    6 7 3 2
  ×      5 4
  2 6 9 2 8
3 3 6 6 0
3 6 3,5 2 8
```

17.
```
    4 0 7 8
  ×      8 6
  2 4 4 6 8
3 2 6 2 4
3 5 0,7 0 8
```

18.
```
    9 6 7 8
  ×      4 7
  6 7 7 4 6
3 8 7 1 2
4 5 4,8 6 6
```

9.
```
    4 3 0
  ×    7 6
  2 5 8 0
3 0 1 0
3 2,6 8 0
```

10.
```
    9 4 7
  ×    6 4
  3 7 8 8
5 6 8 2
6 0,6 0 8
```

11.
```
    6 8 7
  ×    8 0
5 4,9 6 0
```

12.
```
    4 3 9
  ×    1 9
  3 9 5 1
  4 3 9
8,3 4 1
```

19.
```
      7 0 0 9
  ×     3 6 2
    1 4 0 1 8
  4 2 0 5 4
2 1 0 2 7
2,5 3 7,2 5 8
```

20.
```
      6 3 7 4
  ×     5 8 6
    3 8 2 4 4
  5 0 9 9 2
3 1 8 7 0
3,7 3 5,1 6 4
```

1-3. **1.** 4,332; **2.** 2,584; **3.** 5,208; **4.** 1,656; **5.** 2,419; **6.** 32,760; **7.** 48,675; **8.** 63,080; **9.** 13,906; **10.** 25,143; **11.** 8,760; **12.** 84,994; **13.** 12,272; **14.** 230,476; **15.** 339,822; **16.** 123,120; **17.** 642,246; **18.** 571,676; **19.** 2,368,052; **20.** 2,104,378
Column A

1-4. **1.** 483 × 12 = 5,796; **2.** 297 × 18 = 5,346; **3.** 1,738 × 4 = 6,952; **4.** 1,963 × 4 = 7,852; **5.** 198 × 27 = 5,346; **6.** 157 × 28 = 4,396; **7.** 186 × 39 = 7,254; **8.** 159 × 48 = 7,632
Challenge: 32,547,891 × 6 = 195,287,346

1-5. **1.** 16R10; **2.** 75R9; **3.** 89R8; **4.** 18R7; **5.** 36R6; **6.** 23R5; **7.** 41R4; **8.** 69R3; **9.** 52R2; **10.** 98R1
The remainders decrease by one from ten to one.

1-6.

1.
```
        3 8 R 2
  2 3 ) 8 7 6
        6 9
        1 8 6
        1 8 4
            2
```

2.
```
        1 2 R 28
  7 5 ) 9 2 8
        7 5
        1 7 8
        1 5 0
          2 8
```

3.
```
        2 0 R 33
  4 8 ) 9 9 3
        9 6
          3 3
```

4.
```
          7 R 13
  6 7 ) 4 8 2
        4 6 9
          1 3
```

5.
```
        5 9 R 20
  6 4 ) 3 7 9 6
        3 2 0
          5 9 6
          5 7 6
            2 0
```

6.
```
          7 8 R 56
  8 7 ) 6 8 4 2
        6 0 9
          7 5 2
          6 9 6
            5 6
```

7.
```
        4 3 9 R 5
  1 9 ) 8 3 4 6
        7 6
        7 4
        5 7
        1 7 6
        1 7 1
            5
```

8.
```
        1 7 9 R 17
  3 4 ) 6 1 0 3
        3 4
        2 7 0
        2 3 8
          3 2 3
          3 0 6
            1 7
```

9.
```
          1 3 3 R 25
  5 6 ) 7 4 7 3
        5 6
        1 8 7
        1 6 8
          1 9 3
          1 6 8
            2 5
```

10.
```
        1 9 6 R 14
  4 6 ) 9 0 3 0
        4 6
        4 4 3
        4 1 4
          2 9 0
          2 7 6
            1 4
```

11.
```
          4 4 R 74
  8 8 ) 3 9 4 6
        3 5 2
          4 2 6
          3 5 2
            7 4
```

12.
```
          3 0 R 8
  7 3 ) 2 1 9 8
        2 1 9
            8
```

13.
```
        4 0 1 R 15
  6 7 ) 2 6 8 8 2
        2 6 8
            8 2
            6 7
            1 5
```

14.
```
        8 2 0 R 40
  9 0 ) 7 3 8 4 0
        7 2 0
          1 8 4
          1 8 0
            4 0
```

15.
```
          7 8 R 350
  6 1 5 ) 4 8 3 2 0
        4 3 0 5
          5 2 7 0
          4 9 2 0
            3 5 0
```

16.
```
          1 0 8 5 R 188
  8 7 2 ) 9 4 6 3 0 8
        8 7 2
          7 4 3 0
          6 9 7 6
            4 5 4 8
            4 3 6 0
              1 8 8
```

1-7.

Q.
```
      48
    x 76
    ─────
     288
    3360
    ─────
    3,648
```

C.
```
      90
    x 47
    ─────
     630
    3600
    ─────
    4,230
```

P.
```
      86
    x 54
    ─────
     344
    4300
    ─────
    4,644
```

O.
```
      63
    x 70
    ─────
    4,410
```

A.

Correct

E.
```
      638
    x  68
    ──────
     5104
    38280
    ──────
    43,384
```

B.
```
      409
    x  74
    ──────
     1636
    28630
    ──────
    30,266
```

I.

Correct

F.
```
      746
    x  87
    ──────
     5222
    59680
    ──────
    64,902
```

P.
```
      489
    x 706
    ──────
     2934
    3423
    ──────
    345,234
```

A.
```
        24 R 10
    34 )826
        68
        ───
        146
        136
        ───
         10
```

S.

Correct

S.

Correct

N.
```
        92 R 11
    86 )7923
        774
        ───
        183
        172
        ───
         11
```

M.
```
        104
    57 )5928
        57
        ───
        228
        228
        ───
```

T.
```
        80 R 88
    96 )7768
        768
        ───
         88
          0
        ───
         88
```

O.
```
        1563 R 39
    43 )67248
        43
        ───
        242
        215
        ───
        274
        258
        ───
        168
        129
        ───
         39
```

R.

Correct

I.
```
        750 R 4
    84 )63004
        588
        ───
        420
        420
        ───
          4
          0
        ───
          4
```

Along with addition and subtraction, multiplication and division are BASIC OPERATIONS in mathematics.

1-8.

¹1	³3		⁴9	⁵5		⁵4	2
	2			3	2		8
⁶4	⁷2		⁸5	7	6
	0			5
	5			6
	¹⁰3	2	¹¹3		¹²9	¹³6
	1		¹⁴7	¹⁵6		7
¹⁶7	1		¹⁷5	8		¹⁸9	8

1-9.

¹1	0	1	²8	6
	3		8
³2	⁴8	8		⁵2		⁶2	⁷1	9
	6		⁸5	3	1	2		7
	4				2
⁹8	9	¹⁰3		9		¹¹3	7	8
	7		¹²3	¹³2	3	1
	¹⁴6	7	5	5		0
¹⁵7	¹⁶9	1		8		¹⁷6	3	8
	1		5
	6		¹⁸3	9	9	0		¹⁹5
²⁰6	3	5		4		²¹1	4	9
		²²3		0
²³6	1	6	1	7

1-10. Various arrangements are possible. Following are possible answers.

1.
```
  7 1
+ 5 2
-----
1 2 3
```

2.
```
  7 5
- 1 2
-----
  6 3
```

3.
```
    7 1
  x 5 2
-------
 3,6 9 2
```

4.
```
      7 5 2
  1 ) 7 5 2
```

5.
```
  3 6 9
+   4 8
-------
  4 1 7
```

6.
```
  3 4 6
-   9 8
-------
  2 4 8
```

7.
```
    3 6 9
  x   4 8
---------
 17,7 1 2
```

8.
```
      4 3 7
  8 ) 3 4 9 6
```

1-11. Answers will vary.

1-12. Answers will vary.

1-13. **2.** 771—ill; **3.** 5,663—eggs; **4.** 514—his; **5.** 883—ebb; **6.** 808—Bob; **7.** 51—is; **8.** 337—Lee; **9.** 14—hi; **10.** 4,614—high; **11.** 663—egg; **12.** 3,807—lobe; **13.** 3,705—sole; **14.** 7,735—sell; **15.** 7,334—heel; **16.** 3,704—hole

1-14. Following are possible answers. **1.** $2 \times (1 + 3) = 8$; **2.** $(2 \times 3) - 1 = 5$; **3.** $(3 + 1) \div 2 = 2$; **4.** $(2 - 1) \times 3 = 3$; **5.** $3 \times (2 + 1) = 9$; **6.** $(2 \times 3) + 1 = 7$; **7.** $(2 \times 3) \div 1 = 6$; **8.** $1 \times (3 - 2) = 1$; **9.** $(3 \times 4) \times (1 + 2) = 36$; **10.** $(4 + 2) \div (3 - 1) = 3$; **11.** $(2 \div 1) \times (4 - 3) = 2$; **12.** $(2 \times 3) - (4 + 1) = 1$
Student equations will vary.

1-15.   Some equations may have more than one answer. Following are possible answers.

1. $5 + (3 - 2) + 1 = 7$;   **2.** $(5 \times 3) - (2 + 1) = 12$;   **3.** $(5 - 3) - (2 - 1) = 1$;

4. $(5 \times 1) \div (3 - 2) = 5$;   **5.** $(3 + 5) \div (2 - 1) = 8$;   **6.** $(3 \times 2) \times (5 + 1) = 36$;

7. $(5 - 3) \times 2 - 1 = 3$;   **8.** $(2 \times 3) - (5 + 1) = 0$;   **9.** $5 + [(3 - 1) \times 2] = 9$;   **10.** $(5 + 1) \div 3 + 2 = 4$;

11. $5 \times [(3 \times 2) + 1] = 35$;   **12.** $[(2 - 1) \times 5] \times 3 = 15$

Student equations may vary.

1-16.   Accept all reasonable explanations. Following are possible answers.

2. The answer is 20. Add the numbers in the first row, multiply the sum by the number in the lower right-hand box.

3. The answer is 2. The product of the numbers in the upper half of the circle is placed in the bottom half of the circle.

4. The answer is 41. Square each number in the top half of the circle, add the sum of the squares, and place the sum in the bottom half of the circle.

5. The answer is 8. The number in the upper left-hand box is doubled and placed in the lower right-hand box. Also, the number in the upper right-hand box is doubled and placed in the lower left-hand box.

6. The answer is 28. The number in the upper left-hand box is multiplied by 2, the number in the upper right-hand box is multiplied by 3, and the number in the lower right-hand box is multiplied by 4. The sum of these numbers is recorded in the lower left-hand box.

7. The answer is 7. The smaller number in the top half of the circle is subtracted from the larger. The difference is placed in the lower part of the circle.

8. The answer is 15. The numbers in the diagonal from the upper left to the bottom right are added. The sum is multiplied by the number in the upper right-hand box. This product is placed in the lower left-hand box.

9. The answer is 3. The numbers are subtracted from each other, starting with the number in the upper right-hand box, moving in either a clockwise or counterclockwise direction.

10. The answer is 2. The numbers in the upper left-hand box are divided by the number in the lower right-hand box. The quotient is subtracted from the number in the upper right-hand box. The difference is placed in the lower left-hand box.

1-17.   **1.** 72,483 and 8;   **2.** 45,900 and 5;   **3.** 256,310 and 2;   **4.** 38,384,601 and 3;

5. 345,206,321 and 4;   **6.** 468,222,715 and 1;   **7.** 515,763 and 7;   **8.** 7,980,345,602 and 9;

9. 30,000,690,210 and 0;   **10.** 246,987,000,023 and 6

It's important to know your PLACE IN MATH.   Ninety-six billion, two hundred eighty-seven million, forty-five thousand, two hundred thirty-one

1-18.

1-19.   **1.** 1,400; **2.** 6,010; **3.** 70; **4.** 9,000; **5.** 60,000; **6.** 1,700; **7.** 78,650;
8. 1,400,000; **9.** 79,000; **10.** 80; **11.** 3,400; **12.** 51,800; **13.** 1,000; **14.** 30,000;
15. 5,000,000; **16.** 17,500,000; **17.** 2,000; **18.** 21,410; **19.** 60,000; **20.** 200,000;
Sum: 24,505,520

1-20.   **2.** 51; **3.** 100; **4.** 9; **5.** 15; **6.** 24; **7.** 39; **8.** 30; **9.** 18; **10.** 63;
11. 45; **12.** 60; **13.** 36; **14.** 57; **15.** 54; **16.** 12; **17.** 42; **18.** 27; **19.** 21; **20.** 48

1-21.

	Number	2	3	4	5	6	8	9	10	12	Sum
1	75		X		X						8
2	80	X		X	X		X		X		29
3	156	X	X	X		X				X	27
4	237		X								3
5	256	X		X			X				14
6	1,020	X	X	X	X	X			X	X	42
7	1,326	X	X			X					11
8	1,340	X		X	X				X		21
9	1,755		X		X			X			17
10	2,223		X					X			12
11	7,368	X	X	X		X	X			X	35
12	46,440	X	X	X	X	X	X	X	X	X	59

Take any number having two or more digits. Rearrange the digits in any order. Of the two numbers you now have, subtract the smaller from the larger. The difference will always be divisible by nine.

1-22.

	Number	Divisible by 7	Divisible by 11	neither
1	121		X	
2	237			X
3	256			X
4	455	X		
5	616	X	X	
6	623	X		
7	3,080	X	X	
8	3,386			X
9	3,682	X		
10	4,087			X
11	4,477		X	
12	8,784			X
Sum		8,456	8,294	16,750

Answers may vary. One possibility follows. The sum of the numbers checked in Column 2 plus the sum of the numbers checked in Column 3 equals the sum of the numbers checked in Column 4.

1-23.   **2.** {1, 2, 4, 8, 16};   **3.** {1, 2, 3, 4, 6, 8, 12, 24};   **4.** {1, 3, 9, 27};   **5.** {1, 2, 4, 7, 14, 28};
6. {1, 2, 3, 5, 6, 10, 15, 30};   **7.** {1, 3, 11, 33};   **8.** {1, 2, 3, 4, 6, 9, 12, 18, 36};   **9.** {1, 2, 19, 38};
10. {1, 3, 13, 39};   **11.** {1, 2, 4, 5, 8, 10, 20, 40};   **12.** {1, 2, 4, 11, 22, 44};   **13.** {1, 3, 5, 9, 15, 45};
14. {1, 2, 23, 46};   **15.** {1, 2, 5, 10, 25, 50}
ONE IS A FACTOR OF EVERY NUMBER.

1-24.   **1.** 3;   **2.** 6;   **3.** 4;   **4.** 13;   **5.** 13;   **6.** 4;   **7.** 2;   **8.** 1;   **9.** 3;   **10.** 6;   **11.** 8;   **12.** 4;
13. 7;   **14.** 13;   **15.** 3;   **16.** 18;   **17.** 24;   **18.** 9;   **19.** 8;   **20.** 5;   **21.** 9;   **22.** 12;   **23.** 6;
24. 1
A COMMON FACTOR MAY BE THE GCF.

1-25.   **1.** 24;   **2.** 16;   **3.** 9;   **4.** 80;   **5.** 15;   **6.** 5;   **7.** 21;   **8.** 3
The sum is 173. It is the GCF of 519 and 865.

1-26.   **1.** A;   **2.** L;   **3.** W;   **4.** A;   **5.** Y;   **6.** S;   **7.** D;   **8.** E;   **9.** F;   **10.** I;   **11.** C;
12. I;   **13.** E;   **14.** N;   **15.** T
Prime numbers are ALWAYS DEFICIENT.

1-27.   **1.** T;   **2.** H;   **3.** E;   **4.** P;   **5.** R;   **6.** I;   **7.** N;   **8.** C;   **9.** E;   **10.** O;   **11.** F;   **12.** A;
13. M;   **14.** A;   **15.** T;   **16.** E;   **17.** U;   **18.** R;   **19.** S
THE PRINCE OF AMATEURS.

1-28.   **2.** $2 \times 3 \times 3$;   **3.** $2 \times 2 \times 5$;   **4.** 2×11;   **5.** $2 \times 2 \times 2 \times 3$;   **6.** $2 \times 3 \times 17$;   **7.** 5×31;
8. 13×13;   **9.** 5×41;   **10.** $3 \times 3 \times 23$;   **11.** 7×37;   **12.** $3 \times 5 \times 19$;   **13.** $2 \times 2 \times 5 \times 43$;
14. $2 \times 3 \times 5 \times 29$
THE FUNDAMENTAL THEOREM OF ARITHMETIC.

1-29.   **1.** EM;   **2.** IR;   **3.** PI;   **4.** SP;   **5.** RI;   **6.** ME;   **7.** SP;   **8.** EL;   **9.** LE;   **10.** DB;
11. AC;   **12.** KW   **13.** AR;   **14.** DS
EMIRP IS PRIME SPELLED BACKWARDS.

1-30.   **2.** 3 + 5;   **3.** 5 + 5 or 3 + 7;   **4.** 5 + 7;   **5.** 7 + 7 or 3 + 11;   **6.** 5 + 11 or 3 + 13;
7. 5 + 13 or 7 + 11;   **8.** 3 + 17 or 7 + 13;   **9.** 11 + 11 or 5 + 17 or 3 + 19;   **10.** 5 + 23 or 11 + 17;
11. 5 + 31 or 7 + 29 or 13 + 23 or 17 + 19;   **12.** 5 + 43 or 7 + 41 or 11 + 37 or 17 + 31 or 19 + 29;
13. 3 + 47 or 7 + 43 or 13 + 37 or 19 + 31;   **14.** 7 + 47 or 11 + 43 or 13 + 41 or 17 + 37 or 23 +
31;   **15.** 3 + 59 or 19 + 43 or 31 + 31;   **16.** 3 + 67 or 11 + 59 or 23 + 47 or 17 + 53 or 29 + 41

1-31.   **1.** 15, 4;   **2.** 36, 24;   **3.** 18, 144;   **4.** 30, 60;   **5.** 105, 63;   **6.** 120, 56
Sum (column 1) = 324;   Sum (column 2) = 351;   LCM of the sums = 4,212

1-32.   **1.** 9, 27;   **2.** 100, 1,000;   **3.** 144, 1,728;   **4.** 36, 216;   **5.** 49, 343;   **6.** 4, 8;
7. 81, 729;   **8.** 64, 512;   **9.** 169, 2,197;   **10.** 16, 64;   **11.** 196, 2,744;   **12.** 121, 1,331;
13. 25, 125
RENE DESCARTES WAS THE FIRST TO USE RAISED NUMBERS FOR POWERS.

1-33.   **2.** 24, N;   **3.** 125, Y;   **4.** 24, N;   **5.** 81, U;   **6.** 343, M;   **7.** 512, B;   **8.** 16, E;   **9.** 8, R;
10. 32, T;   **11.** 1, O;   **12.** 32, T;   **13.** 216, H;   **14.** 16, E;   **15.** 121, Z;   **16.** 16, E;   **17.** 8, R;
18. 1, O;   **19.** 64, P;   **20.** 1, O;   **21.** 100, W;   **22.** 16, E;   **23.** 8, R;   **24.** 65, I;   **25.** 243, S;
26. 16, E;   **27.** 144, Q;   **28.** 81, U;   **29.** 20, A;   **30.** 169, L;   **31.** 32, T;   **32.** 1, O;   **33.** 1, O;
34. 24, N;   **35.** 16, E
ANY NUMBER TO THE ZERO POWER IS EQUAL TO ONE.

1-34.   **2.** 1.1×10^4; 3.5×10^7;   **3.** 8.9×10^4;   **4.** 1.4×10^3;   **5.** 8.0×10^3;   **6.** 3.6×10^7;
7. 1.07×10^5;   **8.** 1.06×10^4 **9.** 2.389×10^5; 2.16×10^3;   **10.** 6.0×10^2;   **11.** 5.0×10^{10};
12. 2.0×10^{11}

1-35.   **1.** 170,000;   **2.** 60,000;   **3.** 350,000,000;   **4.** 7,340,000;   **5.** 8,700,000,000,000;
6. 9,450;   **7.** 68,000,000,000;   **8.** 458,000;   **9.** 621,700,000   **10.** 5,704,000,000;
11. 20,400,000;   **12.** 70
Accept any reasonable problems.

1-36.   **2.** 10, 12, 14;   **3.** 32, 64, 128;   **4.** 11, 13, 17;   **5.** 40, 48, 56;   **6.** 18, 21, 24;   **7.** 3, 8, 4;
8. 125, 216, 343;   **9.** 8, 13, 21;   **10.** 91, 140, 204;   **11.** 21, 22, 23;   **12.** 36, 40, 42
THESE NUMBERS ARE SPELLED WITHOUT AN E.

1-37.   Accept reasonable articles.

1-38.   In some cases, answers may vary. Possible answers include the following. **1.** $3^2 = 9$;
2. 11×11;   **3.** 1×10^2;   **4.** $5 - 4$;   **5.** 5^2;   **6.** 3^3;   **7.** 4^0 **8.** V (Roman Numeral)   **9.** $12^0 = 1$;
10. $4^0 - 4^0 + 4^0 - 4^0 = 0$

1-39.   **1.** add;   **2.** sum;   **3.** zero;   **4.** one;   **5.** subtract;   **6.** quotient;   **7.** product;
8. multiply;   **9.** difference;   **10.** divide;   **11.** factor;   **12.** divisor;   **13.** plus;   **14.** multiple;
15. exponent;   **16.** prime;   **17.** composite;   **18.** double;   **19.** round;   **20.** square

1-40.   **2.** F;   **3.** H;   **4.** S;   **5.** T;   **6.** I;   **7.** Y;   **8.** L;   **9.** R;   **10.** P;   **11.** U;   **12.** G;
13. E;   **14.** B;   **15.** A;   **16.** M;   **17.** O;   **18.** C
THE ESSENCE OF ALL THINGS IS NUMBERS—PYTHAGORAS.

Section 2
Fractions, Decimals, and Percents

2-1. **1.** $\frac{8}{16}$ F; **2.** $\frac{21}{24}$ R; **3.** $\frac{6}{9}$ A; **4.** $\frac{15}{25}$ C; **5.** $\frac{25}{100}$ T; **6.** $\frac{6}{27}$ I; **7.** $\frac{18}{21}$ O; **8.** $\frac{12}{33}$ N;

9. $\frac{75}{100}$ S; **10.** $\frac{12}{40}$ A; **11.** $\frac{30}{48}$ R; **12.** $\frac{3}{27}$ E; **13.** $\frac{54}{60}$ P; **14.** $\frac{32}{36}$ A; **15.** $\frac{28}{35}$ R; **16.** $\frac{28}{60}$ T;

17. $\frac{40}{96}$ S; **18.** $\frac{2}{12}$ O; **19.** $\frac{18}{33}$ F; **20.** $\frac{20}{45}$ W; **21.** $\frac{35}{42}$ H; **22.** $\frac{27}{72}$ O; **23.** $\frac{4}{14}$ L; **24.** $\frac{60}{84}$ E;

25. $\frac{28}{52}$ S

FRACTIONS ARE PARTS OF WHOLES.

2-2. A simplified fraction IS IN LOWEST TERMS.

2-3. Improper fractions should always be expressed as MIXED OR WHOLE NUMBERS.

2-4. **1.** >; **2.** <; **3.** <; **4.** =; **5.** <; **6.** =; **7.** <; **8.** >; **9.** <; **10.** >; **11.** >; **12.** >;
13. <; **14.** =; **15.** >; **16.** <; **17.** <; **18.** <; **19.** >; **20.** <; **21.** >; **22.** >
A good strategy for comparing fractions is to FIND COMMON DENOMINATORS.

2-5. **1.** $\frac{1}{2}, \frac{13}{24}, \frac{5}{8}, \frac{3}{4}$; **2.** $\frac{2}{3}, \frac{3}{4}, \frac{5}{6}, \frac{11}{12}$; **3.** $\frac{1}{3}, \frac{3}{5}, \frac{11}{15}, \frac{23}{30}$;

4. $\frac{1}{3}, \frac{3}{5}, \frac{7}{10}, \frac{5}{6}$; **5.** $\frac{9}{16}, \frac{7}{12}, \frac{5}{8}, \frac{3}{4}$; **6.** $\frac{5}{8}, \frac{2}{3}, \frac{3}{4}, \frac{7}{9}$

A good strategy for ordering fractions is to find common denominators and WRITE EQUIVA-
LENT FRACTIONS.

2-6. **2.** three sevenths H; **3.** five sixths E; **4.** one half L; **5.** four and six sevenths A;
6. seven eighths T; **7.** ten thirteenths I; **8.** three tenths N; **9.** five and two thirds W;
10. three fourths O; **11.** nine and three fifths R; **12.** one third D; **13.** five eighths F;
14. eight and three sevenths R; **15.** two and one ninth A; **16.** nine twenty seconds C;
17. three T; **18.** five fourteenths U; **19.** seventeen twentieths S
The word fraction is derived from THE LATIN WORD FRACTUS, which means "to break."

2-7. Accept any reasonable answers.

2-8.

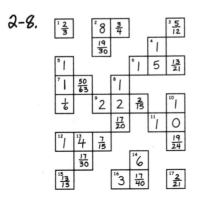

2-9.

1. $5\frac{1}{3} = 5\frac{5}{15} = \boxed{4}\boxed{\frac{20}{15}}$
   $- 3\frac{4}{5} = 3\frac{12}{15} = 3\frac{12}{15}$
   $\boxed{1}\frac{8}{15}$

2. $7\frac{2}{5} = 7\frac{8}{20} = 6\boxed{\frac{28}{20}}$
   $- 2\frac{3}{4} = 2\frac{15}{20} = 2\frac{15}{20}$
   $4\frac{13}{20}$

3. $11\frac{2}{9} = 11\frac{4}{18} = \boxed{10}\frac{22}{18}$
   $- 6\frac{5}{6} = 6\boxed{\frac{15}{18}} = 6\frac{15}{18}$
   $4\frac{7}{18}$

4. $8\frac{3}{7} = 8\frac{6}{14} = 7\boxed{\frac{20}{14}}$
   $- 7\frac{9}{14} = 7\boxed{\frac{9}{14}} = 7\frac{9}{14}$
   $\frac{11}{14}$

5. $\boxed{9}\frac{1}{8} = \boxed{9}\boxed{\frac{7}{56}} = 8\boxed{\frac{63}{56}}$
   $- 6\frac{2}{7} = 6\boxed{\frac{16}{56}} = 6\frac{16}{56}$
   $\boxed{2}\boxed{\frac{47}{56}}$

6. $21\frac{3}{8} = 21\boxed{\frac{9}{24}} = \boxed{20}\frac{33}{24}$
   $- \boxed{10}\frac{5}{6} = \boxed{10}\boxed{\frac{20}{24}} = \boxed{10}\boxed{\frac{20}{24}}$
   $10\frac{13}{24}$

7. $\boxed{8} = 7\boxed{\frac{3}{3}}$
   $- 3\frac{2}{3} = 3\frac{2}{3}$
   $\boxed{4}\boxed{\frac{1}{3}}$

8. $12\frac{2}{9} = 12\boxed{\frac{4}{18}} = \boxed{11}\boxed{\frac{22}{18}}$
   $- \boxed{8}\frac{13}{18} = \boxed{8}\frac{13}{18} = \boxed{8}\frac{13}{18}$
   $3\boxed{\frac{9}{18}} = 3\frac{1}{2}$

9. $8\frac{3}{16} = 8\frac{3}{16} = \boxed{7}\boxed{\frac{19}{16}}$
   $- \boxed{3}\frac{1}{4} = \boxed{3}\frac{4}{16} = \boxed{3}\frac{4}{16}$
   $4\boxed{\frac{15}{16}}$

10. $19\frac{5}{12} = 19\frac{5}{12} = 18\boxed{\frac{17}{12}}$
    $- 11\frac{3}{4} = 11\boxed{\frac{9}{12}} = 11\boxed{\frac{9}{12}}$
    $7\boxed{\frac{8}{12}} = 7\boxed{\frac{2}{3}}$

11. $13\frac{2}{15} = 13\boxed{\frac{4}{30}} = 12\frac{34}{30}$
    $- 8\frac{5}{6} = 8\boxed{\frac{25}{30}} = 8\boxed{\frac{25}{30}}$
    $\boxed{4}\frac{9}{30} = \boxed{4}\boxed{\frac{3}{10}}$

12. $10\boxed{\frac{3}{10}} = 10\boxed{\frac{3}{10}} = 9\boxed{\frac{13}{10}}$
    $- 7\frac{1}{2} = 7\frac{5}{10} = 7\frac{5}{10}$
    $2\boxed{\frac{8}{10}} = 2\boxed{\frac{4}{5}}$

2-10.

$1\frac{1}{3}$	$\frac{1}{2}$	$1\frac{5}{12}$
$1\frac{5}{6}$	$1\frac{1}{12}$	1
$\frac{3}{4}$	$1\frac{2}{3}$	$\frac{5}{6}$

$\frac{7}{8}$	$\frac{3}{4}$	$1\frac{3}{8}$	$1\frac{1}{4}$
$1\frac{3}{4}$	$1\frac{1}{8}$	1	$\frac{3}{8}$
$1\frac{1}{2}$	$1\frac{7}{8}$	$\frac{1}{4}$	$\frac{5}{8}$
$\frac{1}{8}$	$\frac{1}{2}$	$1\frac{5}{8}$	2

$\frac{1}{2}$	$2\frac{2}{3}$	$1\frac{1}{2}$	$3\frac{2}{3}$	$2\frac{1}{2}$
$3\frac{1}{3}$	$1\frac{1}{3}$	$3\frac{1}{2}$	$2\frac{1}{3}$	$\frac{1}{3}$
$1\frac{1}{6}$	$4\frac{1}{6}$	$2\frac{1}{6}$	$\frac{1}{6}$	$3\frac{1}{6}$
4	2	$\frac{5}{6}$	3	1
$1\frac{5}{6}$	$\frac{2}{3}$	$2\frac{5}{6}$	$1\frac{2}{3}$	$3\frac{5}{6}$

2-11. 1. $\frac{1}{4}$; 2. $\frac{7}{24}$; 3. $\frac{1}{12}$; 4. $\frac{1}{4}$; 5. $\frac{1}{6}$; 6. $\frac{1}{24}$; 7. $\frac{1}{8}$; 8. $\frac{1}{24}$; 9. $\frac{1}{12}$;

10. $\frac{1}{6}$

2-12. Answers will vary.

2-13. 2. 11 pack; 3. $1\frac{7}{10}$ knot; 4. $2\frac{1}{2}$ gang; 5. $25\frac{1}{2}$ school; 6. $3\frac{1}{2}$ hive;

7. $4\frac{2}{3}$ pride; 8. $9\frac{1}{6}$ pod; 9. 27 gaggle; 10. $3\frac{1}{8}$ host; 11. $2\frac{2}{15}$ army; 12. $8\frac{1}{2}$ band;

13. $6\frac{1}{8}$ muster; 14. $5\frac{1}{2}$ clutch; 15. 9 troop; 16. $9\frac{5}{8}$ bed; 17. $19\frac{1}{2}$ brace;

18. $6\frac{1}{4}$ tribe; 19. $16\frac{1}{2}$ bevy; 20. 12 herd

2-14. P. $\frac{7}{10}$; L. $\frac{8}{9}$; O. $1\frac{1}{3}$; E. $1\frac{1}{2}$; T. 4; R. $1\frac{4}{5}$; C. $\frac{6}{13}$; D. $1\frac{1}{8}$; O. $\frac{1}{49}$;

H. $1\frac{23}{40}$; S. $2\frac{6}{25}$; F. $1\frac{5}{9}$; I. $\frac{7}{32}$; V. $1\frac{3}{5}$; A. $\frac{27}{32}$; R. $\frac{5}{6}$; O. $\frac{1}{24}$; I. $3\frac{1}{5}$;

E. $\frac{5}{12}$; R. $3\frac{1}{9}$; C. $7\frac{4}{5}$; I. $\frac{3}{8}$

To divide fractions, you must multiply by the RECIPROCAL OF THE DIVISOR.

2-15. 2. $7\frac{1}{2}$ colt; 3. 10 eyas; 4. 12 baby; 5. $1\frac{4}{21}$ eaglet; 6. 25 spat; 7. $\frac{4}{5}$ poult;

8. $3\frac{2}{3}$ nestling; 9. $1\frac{5}{6}$ cygnet; 10. $\frac{15}{22}$ kit; 11. $1\frac{13}{17}$ calf; 12. $1\frac{1}{9}$ gosling;

13. $2\frac{1}{4}$ cub; 14. $1\frac{17}{28}$ elver; 15. $\frac{2}{3}$ fry

2-16. $1\frac{3}{4} \div 2\frac{5}{6} = \frac{21}{34}$ $1\frac{8}{9} \div 2\frac{3}{7} = \frac{7}{9}$ $9\frac{7}{8} \div 2\frac{3}{5} = 3\frac{83}{104}$

2-17.

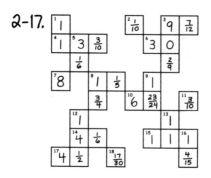

2-18. Simon Stevin; Flanders

2-19. **2.** millionths L; **3.** thousandths A; **4.** hundredths T; **5.** millionths I; **6.** ones N;
7. tenths T; **8.** hundredths E; **9.** hundred-thousandths R; **10.** millionths M; **11.** tenths T;
12. hundredths H; **13.** thousandths A; **14.** ten-thousandths T; **15.** millionths M;
16. tenths E; **17.** ten-thousandths A; **18.** hundredths N; **19.** thousandths S; **20.** tenths T;
21. hundredths E; **22.** hundred-thousandths N
The word *decimal* is derived from "decem," A LATIN TERM THAT MEANS TEN.

2-20. **1.** <; **2.** <; **3.** >; **4.** <; **5.** =; **6.** <; **7.** >; **8.** >; **9.** <; **10.** <; **11.** >; **12.** >;
13. >; **14.** =; **15.** <; **16.** <; **17.** >; **18.** =; **19.** <; **20.** >; **21.** <; **22.** <; **23.** =; **24.** >
To compare decimals you must UNDERSTAND PLACE VALUE.

2-21. Correct order: 0.00600; 0.00620; 0.023; 0.034; 0.04; 0.0401; 0.045;
0.06020; 0.080; 0.09; 0.1; 0.10124; 0.15; 0.230; 0.306; 0.753; 0.7539; 0.754;
0.76; 0.8; 0.805; 1.007 3.0; 10.01
Understanding place value is necessary TO ARRANGE DECIMALS IN ORDER.

2-22. **1.** 0.5; **2.** 7.05; **3.** 1; **4.** 3.56; **5.** 0.710; **6.** 0.8069; **7.** 217.62; **8.** 2.94; **9.** 31;
10. 0.7 **11.** 50.07; **12.** 0.4839; **13.** 0.202; **14.** 10.40398 **15.** 0.50; **16.** 48.3695; **17.** 40;
18. 11.88 **19.** 254.75; **20.** 1

2-23.

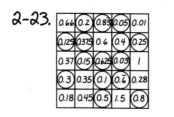

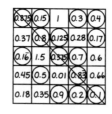

Card C wins.

2-24. **1.** $\frac{63}{100}$ C; **2.** $1\frac{3}{10}$ H; **3.** $\frac{11}{20}$ R; **4.** $\frac{3}{4}$ I; **5.** $\frac{1}{200}$ S; **6.** $\frac{3}{5}$ T; **7.** $\frac{9}{40}$ O; **8.** $5\frac{16}{25}$ P;
9. $\frac{1}{2}$ H; **10.** $\frac{7}{8}$ E; **11.** $1\frac{3}{100}$ R; **12.** $\frac{57}{100}$ C; **13.** $5\frac{9}{20}$ L; **14.** $5\frac{2}{5}$ A; **15.** $\frac{87}{1000}$ V;

16. $\frac{1}{5}$ I;   **17.** $\frac{1}{25}$ U;   **18.** $\frac{3}{25}$ S

In 1593, CHRISTOPHER CLAVIUS, a German mathematician, was the first European to use a decimal point for decimal fractions.

2-25.   To add and subtract decimals, the DECIMAL POINTS MUST BE ALIGNED.

2-26.

3.2	0.4	2.4
1.2	2	2.8
1.6	3.6	0.8

0.8	11.2	5.6	9.6
12	3.2	7.2	4.8
8	4	12.8	2.4
6.4	8.8	1.6	10.4

10.2	14.4	0.6	4.8	9
13.8	3	4.2	8.4	9.6
2.4	3.6	7.8	12	13.2
6	7.2	11.4	12.6	1.8
6.6	10.8	15	1.2	5.4

2-27.   **2.** 1 $5 dollar bill, 2 dimes, 1 penny;   **3.** 1 $5 bill, 3 $1 bills, 3 quarters (or 1 half dollar and 1 quarter), 2 pennies;   **4.** 1 $1 bill, 1 quarter, 1 dime, 1 penny;   **5.** 1 quarter, 1 dime, 1 nickel, 3 pennies;   **6.** 4 $1 bills, 3 quarters (or 1 half dollar and 1 quarter), 1 dime, 1 nickel, 3 pennies;   **7.** 1 $10 bill, 2 $1 bills, 2 quarters (or 1 half dollar), 2 dimes, 1 penny;   **8.** 1 $10 bill, 1 $5 bill, 1 quarter, 1 nickel, 3 pennies;   **9.** 1 $5 bill, 2 $1 bills, 3 quarters (or 1 half dollar and 1 quarter), 2 pennies;   **10.** 1 $5 bill, 3 $1 bills, 1; quarter, 1 dime;   **11.** 1 $10 bill, 1 $5 bill, 1 $1 bill, 1 quarter, 1 dime, 1 nickel, 3 pennies;   **12.** 3 $1 bills, 1 nickel, 4 pennies;   **13.** 1 $10 bill, 2 quarters (or 1 half dollar), 1 dime, 1 penny;   **14.** 1 $10 bill, 1 $5 bill, 3 $1 bills, 1 quarter, 1 nickel, 3 pennies;   **15.** 1 $10 bill, 1 $1 bill, 2 quarters (or 1 half dollar), 2 dimes, 1 penny

2-28.   When multiplying decimals, you must position THE DECIMAL POINT CORRECTLY.

2-29.   When dividing decimals, you must multiply the divisor by a power OF TEN TO MAKE IT A WHOLE NUMBER.

2-30.

$$\begin{array}{r} \boxed{4}\boxed{2} \\ +\ \boxed{3}\boxed{1} \\ \hline 73 \end{array} \qquad \begin{array}{r} \boxed{4}\boxed{3} \\ -\ \boxed{.1}\boxed{2} \\ \hline 42.88 \end{array} \qquad \begin{array}{r} \boxed{4}\boxed{1} \\ \times\ \boxed{3}\boxed{2} \\ \hline 1312 \end{array} \qquad \boxed{.1}\boxed{2}\overline{\smash{)}\boxed{4}\boxed{3}}\ \ 358.\overline{3}$$

$$\begin{array}{r} \boxed{.1}\boxed{4} \\ +\ \boxed{.2}\boxed{3} \\ \hline 0.37 \end{array} \qquad \begin{array}{r} \boxed{.4}\boxed{1} \\ -\ \boxed{.3}\boxed{2} \\ \hline 0.09 \end{array} \qquad \begin{array}{r} \boxed{.1}\boxed{3} \\ \times\ \boxed{.2}\boxed{4} \\ \hline .0312 \end{array} \qquad \boxed{4}\boxed{3}\overline{\smash{)}\boxed{.1}\boxed{2}}\ \ \overset{about}{0.00279}$$

2-31.   **1.** 45.30;   **2.** 32.74;   **3.** 50.43;   **4.** 9.78;   **5.** 1.99

2-32.   Accept any reasonable answers.

2-33.

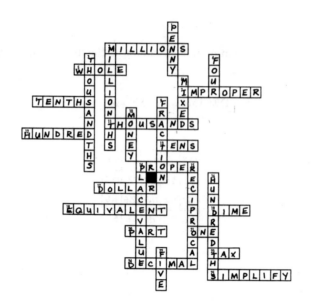

2-34. 1. $\frac{1}{16}$, $\frac{1}{32}$, $\frac{1}{64}$; 2. 0.0001, 0.00001, 0.000001; 3. $\frac{4}{5}$, $\frac{5}{6}$, $\frac{6}{7}$, ;

4. $0.1\overline{6}$, $0.\overline{14285}$, 0.125; 5. 2.1, 3.4, 5.5; 6. $\frac{1}{27}$, $\frac{1}{16}$, $\frac{1}{81}$; 7. 0.625, 0.75, 0.875;

8. $\frac{1}{36}$, $\frac{1}{49}$, $\frac{1}{64}$; 9. 1.2, 1.4, 1.6; 10. $\frac{1}{13}$, $\frac{1}{17}$, $\frac{1}{19}$

2-35. 1. 12,000 square miles; 2. 0.62 miles; 3. 0.06 inch; 4. 5 people; 5. 30,000 cells;

6. $\frac{620}{47}$; 7. $\frac{28}{65}$; 8. $\frac{200}{1}$; 9. $\frac{323}{468}$; 10. $\frac{3}{7,055}$

2-36.

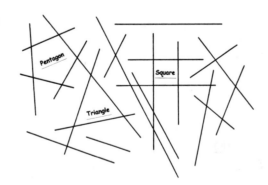

2-37. 1. 23% C, 0.283 A, $\frac{3}{4}$ N, 1 B, 2.83 E; 2. 0.176 W, $\frac{1}{4}$ R, $\frac{6}{20}$ I, 85% T, 1.75 T; 3.

14.5% E, 0.148N, 0.27 I, $\frac{2}{5}$ N, $\frac{7}{10}$ T; 4. $\frac{8}{20}$ E, $\frac{3}{7}$ R, 0.60 M, 62% S, $\frac{20}{25}$ O; 5. 1.30% F, 0.4 E,

50% A, $\frac{130}{250}$ C, $\frac{2}{3}$ H; 6. 11.20% O, 0.148 T, $\frac{2}{9}$ H, $1\frac{1}{4}$ E, $\frac{3}{2}$ R

Every fraction, decimal, and percent CAN BE WRITTEN IN TERMS OF EACH OTHER.

2-38. Your EFFORT WAS ONE HUNDRED PERCENT.

2-39. **1.** 5; **2.** 12; **3.** 3; **4.** 12; **5.** 20; **6.** 6; **7.** 15; **8.** 20; **9.** 100; **10.** 10; **11.** 40;
12. 18; **13.** 7; **14.** 10; **15.** 12; **16.** 15; **17.** 1; **18.** 7; **19.** 10; **20.** 25

2-40. **1.** 70; **2.** 61; **3.** 50; **4.** 48; **5.** 45; **6.** 43; **7.** 42; **8.** 40; **9.** 35; **10.** 32;
11. 30; **12.** 28; **13.** 25; **14.** 15; **15.** 12; **16.** 11; **17.** 9; **18.** 0.17; **19.** 0.15; **20.** 0.03

2-41. **1.** 45; **2.** 22%; **3.** 450; **4.** 15%; **5.** 216; **6.** 20; **7.** $33.\overline{3}\%$; **8.** 24; **9.** 900; **10.**
135; **11.** 99; **12.** 160; **13.** 37.5%; **14.** 25%; **15.** 56
15% of 160 = 24; $33.\overline{3}\%$ of 135 = 45;   25% of 900 = 216 (false);   37.5% of 56 = 20 (false);
22% of 450 = 99

2-42. **1.** 900%; **2.** 97%; **3.** 94%; **4.** 54,999,900% **5.** 392%; **6.** 610%; **7.** 286%;
8. 1,000%; **9.** 18% **10.** 92%

2-43. **1.** $5.99, $13.96; **2.** $32.50, $97.49; **3.** $9.48, $9.47; **4.** $58.42, $331.07; **5.** $9.80,
$18.19; **6.** $13.96, $55.83; **7.** $4.79, $91.10; **8.** $15.00, $84.98; **9.** $6.89, $12.80;
10. $257.49, $772.46
$1,486 − $414 = $1,072;   percent is 28%

2-44. **1.** $3.90, $68.89; **2.** $3.00, $62.99; **3.** $4.20, $74.19; **4.** $1.60, $41.55; **5.** $4.25,
$89.24; **6.** $1.78, $41.27; **7.** $7.70, $147.65; **8.** $5.25, $155.15 **9.** $7.20, $167.15;
10. $7.22, $172.21

2-45. **1.** 65%; **2.** Good Buys, $35; **3.** 80%; **4.** $40; **5.** $48.75, Computer Center;
6. $13.63; **7.** 40%; **8.** $45; **9.** Discount Dave, $11.91; **10.** 60%

Section 3
Measurement

3-1. **1.** 2 inches; **2.** $2\frac{1}{2}$ inches; **3.** $1\frac{1}{4}$ inches; **4.** 3 inches; **5.** $2\frac{3}{16}$ inches;

6. $\frac{7}{16}$ inch; **7.** $3\frac{1}{2}$ inches; **8.** $3\frac{9}{16}$ inches; **9.** $\frac{3}{4}$ inch; **10.** $1\frac{1}{2}$ inches;

11. 4; 1, All four segments have the same measure. Explanations may vary, but should note that
the segments stretching to the sides give the illusion that the center segments are of different
lengths. **12.** Segment AE. All of the segments have the same length. Explanations may vary,
but should include that the position of the segments distorts the true lengths.

3-2. **2.** $\frac{1}{2}$ E; **3.** $16\frac{1}{2}$ N; **4.** 4G; **5.** 15,840 T; **6.** $\frac{5}{11}$ H; **7.** 72 O; **8.** 33 F;

9. $\frac{2}{3}$ T;   **10.** 7,040 H;   **11.** 2 R;   **12.** $\frac{1}{2}$ E;   **13.** 440 E;   **14.** $52\frac{1}{2}$ B;   **15.** 66 A;   **16.** 320 R;

17. $\frac{1}{3}$ L;   **18.** 3,960 E;   **19.** 1,584 Y;   **20.** 3 C;   **21.** 660 O;   **22.** 6 R;   **23.** 6,336 N;

24. 1,980 S

The length of an inch was established during the reign of King Edward II of England. Edward declared that the inch was equal to the LENGTH OF THREE BARLEY CORNS.

3-3.   **2.** 96 H;   **3.** 318.4 E; **4.** 10 A;   **5.** $\frac{3}{4}$ V;   **6.** 256 O;   **7.** $\frac{1}{10}$ I;   **8.** R;   **9.** 30,000 D;

10. 9 U;   **11.** 32 P;   **12.** 3,494.0 O;   **13.** 88 I;   **14.** $\frac{1}{4}$ S;   **15.** $\frac{1}{16}$ S;   **16.** $\frac{1}{2}$ Y;   **17.** $\frac{3}{10}$ S;

18. 1,600 T;   **19.** 128 E;   **20.** $\frac{1}{5}$ M

THE AVOIRDUPOIS SYSTEM includes weights and measures based on a pound containing 16 ounces.

3-4.   **2.** 8 A;   **3.** $1\frac{1}{2}$ L;   **4.** $1\frac{1}{2}$ L;   **5.** $3\frac{1}{2}$ O;   **6.** 16 N;   **7.** 3 S;   **8.** $\frac{1}{4}$ E;   **9.** $\frac{3}{4}$ Q;

10. $\frac{1}{8}$ U;   **11.** 8 A;   **12.** $1\frac{1}{2}$ L;   **13.** $\frac{1}{4}$ E;   **14.** 6 D;   **15.** $3\frac{1}{2}$ O;   **16.** 16 N;   **17.** $\frac{1}{4}$ E;

18. 4 H;   **19.** $3\frac{1}{2}$ O;   **20.** 1 G;   **21.** 3 S;   **22.** 4 H;   **23.** $\frac{1}{4}$ E;   **24.** 8 A;   **25.** 6 D

Just as language changes over time, so do the units we use for measurement. Once most people knew that 63 GALLONS EQUALED ONE HOGSHEAD.

3-5.   **1.** F, 2 pints = $\frac{1}{4}$ gallon;   **2.** T;   **3.** F, $\frac{2}{3}$ foot = $\frac{2}{9}$ yard;   **4.** F, 4 quarts = 128 fluid ounces;   **5.** F, 2 tablespoons = $\frac{1}{8}$ cup;   **6.** T;   **7.** T;   **8.** F, 1 rod = 198 inches;   **9.** F, $\frac{1}{2}$ league = 7,920 feet;   **10.** F, 1 acre = 43,560 square feet

3-6.   **2.** 10 N;   **3.** 4 T;   **4.** 32,000 E;   **5.** 3,200 R;   **6.** 10 N;   **7.** 0.89 A;   **8.** 4 T;   **9.** 1 I;   **10.** 40 O;   **11.** 10 N;   **12.** 0.89 A;   **13.** 400 L;   **14.** 8.9 S;   **15.** 320 Y;   **16.** 8.9 S;   **17.** 4 T;   **18.** 32,000 E;   **19.** 100 M;   **20.** 40 O;   **21.** 89 F;   **22.** 32 U;   **23.** 10 N;   **24.** 1 I;   **25.** 4 T;   **26.** 8.9 S

The official name of the Metric System of Measurement is the INTERNATIONAL SYSTEM OF UNITS.

3-7.   Explanations for the answers may vary; common explanations are included.   **1.** F, 1 meter = 100 centimeters;   **2.** F, 2 liters = 0.02 hectoliters;   **3.** T;   **4.** T;   **5.** F, 35 centigrams = 350 milligrams;   **6.** T;   **7.** F, 58 centiliters = 0.58 liters;   **8.** F; 1.2 dekagrams = 0.12 hectograms;   **9.** F, 5.5 kilograms = 5,500 grams;   **10.** F, 15 deciliters = 1,500 milliliters;   **11.** F, 1,200 centimeters = 1.2 meters;   **12.** F, 2 kilograms = 20 hectograms = 200,000 centigrams;   **13.** T;   **14.** T;   **15.** F, 550 centimeters = 5.5 meters = 0.55 dekameters = 0.055 hectometers = 0.0055 kilometers

3-8.   **1.** 1 = 1;   **2.** 3 = 1 + 2;   **3.** 3 = 3;   **4.** 3 + 1 = 4;   **5.** 9 = 1 + 3 + 5;   **6.** 9 = 3 + 6;
7. 9 + 1 = 3 + 7;   **8.** 9 = 1 + 8;   **9.** 9 = 9;   **10.** 9 + 1 = 10;   **11.** 9 + 3 = 1 + 11;   **12.** 9 + 3 = 12;
13. 9 + 3 + 1 = 13;   **14.** 27 = 1 + 3 + 9 + 14;   **15.** 27 = 3 + 9 + 15;   **16.** 27 + 1 = 3 + 9 + 16;
17. 27 = 1 + 9 + 17;   **18.** 27 = 9 + 18;   **19.** 27 + 1 = 9 + 19;   **20.** 27 + 3 = 1 + 9 + 20;
21. 27 + 3 = 9 + 21;   **22.** 27 + 3 + 1 = 9 + 22;   **23.** 27 = 1 + 3 + 23;   **24.** 27 = 3 + 24;
25. 27 + 1 = 3 + 25;   **26.** 27 = 1 + 26;   **27.** 27 = 27;   **28.** 27 + 1 = 28;   **29.** 27 + 3 = 1 + 29;
30. 27 + 3 = 30;   **31.** 27 + 3 + 1 = 31;   **32.** 27 + 9 = 1 + 3 + 32;   **33.** 27 + 9 = 3 + 33;
34. 27 + 9 + 1 = 1 + 3 + 34;   **35.** 27 + 9 = 1 + 35;   **36.** 27 + 9 = 36;   **37.** 27 + 9 + 1 = 37;
38. 27 + 9 + 3 = 1 + 38;   **39.** 27 + 9 + 3 = 39;   **40.** 27 + 9 + 3 + 1 = 40

3-9.   **1.** 2 yards 1 foot 4 inches;   **2.** 2 gallons 3 quarts;   **3.** 7 pounds 9 ounces;   **4.** 2 gallons
1 quart;   **5.** 12 centimeters 3 millimeters;   **6.** 5 pounds 14 ounces;   **7.** 10 yards 2 feet;
8. 5 yards 6 inches;   **9.** 6 liters 998 milliliters;   **10.** 3 yards 1 foot;   **11.** 1 kiloliter 1 hectoliter;
12. 7 pints 5 fluid ounces;   **13.** 19 pounds 8 ounces;   **14.** 4 pounds 5 ounces;   **15.** 1 cup 2 fluid
ounces;   **16.** 6 centimeters

3-10.   Answers may vary depending upon which conversions are used; common answers follow.   **1.** 147.4 pounds;   **2.** 2.73 meters, 155.25 kilograms;   **3.** 182 meters;   **4.** 6 kilometers;
5. 7.62 centimeters, 12.7 centimeters;   **6.** 1,612 meters;   **7.** 163.5 feet, 490.5 feet;   **8.** No; 55.9
miles per hour;   **9.** 18.7 miles per gallon;   **10.** 112.5 grams;   **11.** 2.375 liters;   **12.** 190 liters

3-11.   **2.** 30 N;   **3.** 21 L;   **4.** 90 A;   **5.** 360 T;   **6.** $\frac{2}{3}$ H;   **7.** 50 E;   **8.** 30 N;   **9.** $\frac{1}{2}$ I;

10. 360 T;   **11.** $\frac{1}{2}$ I;   **12.** $\frac{1}{4}$ S;   **13.** 30 N;   **14.** 24 O;   **15.** 24 O;   **16.** 30 N;   **17.** $\frac{1}{2}$ I;

18. 30 N;   **19.** 2 P;   **20.** 90 A

If it is 9 A.M. IN LA, THEN IT IS NOON IN PA.

3-12.   **1.** 8 hours 45 minutes; 7 hours 45 minutes; 8 hours; 10 hours; 9 hours 30 minutes; 44
hours; 4 hours; $345;   **2.** 7 hours; 4 hours 30 minutes; 5 hours 45 minutes; 4 hours 30 minutes;
10 hours; 31 hours 45 minutes; 0; $203.20;   **3.** 7 hours 30 minutes; 8 hours 30 minutes; 9 hours
15 minutes; 8 hours 15 minutes; 5 hours 45 minutes; 6 hours 15 minutes; 45 hours 30 minutes; 5
hours 30 minutes; $337.75
No, the amount earned also depends upon the number of hours worked. Examples will vary.

3-13.   **1.** 37°;   **2.** 0°;   **3.** 20°;   **4.** 70°;   **5.** –15°;   **6.** 35°;   **7.** 10°;   **8.** 80°;   **9.** –10°;   **10.**
100°;   **11.** 60°;   **12.** 25°

3-14.

Wind Chill Table

Actual Temperature °F	30°	20°	10°	0°
Wind Speed (miles per hour)	Wind Chill Temperature			
10	16°	3°	–9°	–22°
20	4°	–10°	–24°	–39°
30	–2°	–18°	–33°	–49°
40	–5°	–21°	–37°	–53°

1. –39° F;   **2.** 16° F;   **3.** Actual temperature of 0° F and a wind speed of 40 mph;   **4.** 20° F;
5. 30 mph

3-15.   **1.** 10-gallon hat;   **2.** 99-pound weakling;   **3.** ton;   **4.** "60 Minutes";   **5.** *2001, A
Space Oddysey;*   **6.** cup;   **7.** *Yard,* also *Day;*   **8.** *451;*   **9.** *20,000;*   **10.** mile;   **11.** 9;
12. 24 hours or 24/7;   **13.** inch, mile;   **14.** ounce, pound;   **15.** dollar;   **16.** minute;
17. $0.50, dollar;   **18.** dozen;   **19.** day's;   **20.** 10 feet

3-16.

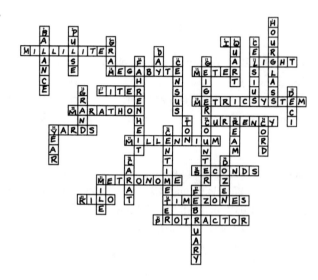

3-17.   **2.** 12 inches in a foot;   **3.** 10 years in a decade;   **4.** 500 sheets of paper in a ream;
5. 0 = the freezing point of water on the Celsius scale;   **6.** 16 fluid ounces in a pint;   **7.** 29 days
in February in a Leap Year;   **8.** 2,000 pounds in a ton;   **9.** 4 seasons in a year;   **10.** 4 time
zones in the 48 states;   **11.** 100 pennies in a dollar;   **12.** 3 strikes and you're out;   **13.** 98.6 is
the normal human body temperature;   **14.** 12 months in a year;   **15.** 60 minutes in an hour;
16. 100 centimeters in a meter;   **17.** 10 centuries in a millennium;   **18.** 3 digits in an area
code;   **19.** 16 ounces in a pound;   **20.** 9 innings of a baseball game

3-18.   **1.** Mercury, 0.39; Venus, 0.72; Mars, 1.53; Jupiter, 5.19; Saturn, 9.54; Uranus, 19.17;
Neptune, 30.04; Pluto, 39.42;   **2.** 5,870,000,000,000 (about 6 trillion miles);   **3.** Alpha Centauri,
1.32; Sirius, 2.67; Arcturus, 12.27; Capella, 13.80; Betelgeuse 159.51;   **4.** 6.310; 15.851; 39.818;
100.023

3-19
1. SPEEDOMETER
2. STOPWATCH
3. TIRE GAUGE
4. CLOCK
5. RAIN GAUGE
6. BAROMETER
7. CALENDAR
8. AUDIOMETER
9. METRONOME
10. SEISMOGRAPH
11. PROTRACTOR

12 WATE[R] ME[T]ER
13   R[U]LER
14 ODO[M]ETER
15 TH[E]RMOMETER
16   A[N]EMOMETER
17 AL[T]IMETER
18   [S]CALE

Accurate measurement depends upon using SPECIAL INSTRUMENTS.

3-20. **1.** Richter Scale; **2.** Gabriel Fahrenheit, Anders Celsius; **3.** absolute zero;
4. Daylight Savings Time; **5.** megabyte, gigabyte; **6.** Beaufort Scale; **7.** jeweler's stick;
8. fathoms, 6; **9.** carats; **10.** acre; **11.** nautical mile, 6,076; **12.** cord

Section 4
Geometry

4-1.

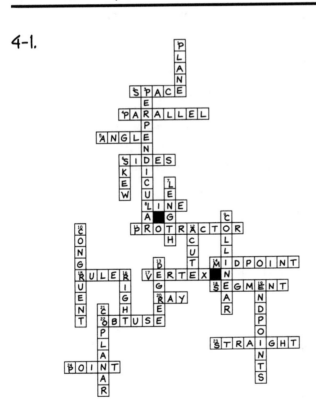

4-2. The word *acute* is taken from the Latin word ACUTUS MEANING SHARP. The word
obtuse is taken from the Latin word OBTUSUS WHICH MEANS BLUNT.

4-3. Fact: YOU ARE A PRO WITH A PROTRACTOR.

4-4. Message: THE SYMBOL FOR DEGREES WAS INTRODUCED BY CLAUDIUS PTOLEMY IN HIS WORK *ALMAGEST.*

4-5. The word *congruent* is taken from the Latin word *congruens,* which means "to meet together." Congruent angles are identical and will meet together IF PLACED ONE ATOP THE OTHER.

4-6. *Parallel Lines:* $\overleftrightarrow{AB} \parallel \overleftrightarrow{CD}, \overleftrightarrow{KL} \parallel \overleftrightarrow{MN}$; *Perpendicular Lines:* $\overleftrightarrow{GH} \perp \overleftrightarrow{OP}, \overleftrightarrow{IJ} \perp \overleftrightarrow{EF}$. Examples of parallel and perpendicular lines will vary.

4-7. *Parallel Lines:* $\overleftrightarrow{LE} \parallel \overleftrightarrow{KF}, \overleftrightarrow{CO} \parallel \overleftrightarrow{BI}$; *Perpendicular Lines:* $\overleftrightarrow{DJ} \perp \overleftrightarrow{AG}, \overleftrightarrow{LE} \perp \overleftrightarrow{CH}$, $\overleftrightarrow{CH} \perp \overleftrightarrow{KF}, \overleftrightarrow{KF} \perp \overleftrightarrow{BI}, \overleftrightarrow{LN} \perp \overleftrightarrow{BI}$; *Right Angles:* ∠BME, ∠NMP, ∠LMP, ∠BML, ∠CNM, ∠CNE, ∠ENO, ∠MNO, ∠NOF, ∠FOH, ∠HOP, ∠NOP, ∠MPO, ∠OPI, ∠IPK, ∠KPM, ∠NQO, ∠OQP, ∠PQM, ∠MQN; *Acute Angles:* ∠CND, ∠DNE, ∠FOG, ∠GOH, ∠IPJ, ∠JPK, ∠LMA, ∠AMB, ∠QMM, ∠QNM, ∠QNO, ∠QON, ∠QOP, ∠QPO, ∠QPM, ∠QMP; *Obtuse Angles:* ∠AMN, ∠DNM, ∠DNO, ∠GON, ∠GOP, ∠JPO, ∠JPM, ∠AMP, ∠BMO, ∠LMO, ∠CNP, ∠ENP, ∠FOM, ∠HOM, ∠IPN, ∠KPN

4-8. *Corresponding Angles:* ∠4 and ∠8, ∠1 and ∠5, ∠2 and ∠10, ∠5 and ∠13, ∠9 and ∠13; *Vertical Angles:* ∠1 and ∠4, ∠6 and ∠7, ∠10 and ∠11, ∠13 and ∠16, ∠14 and ∠15; *Alternate Interior Angles:* ∠4 and ∠5, ∠4 and ∠9, ∠8 and ∠13, ∠12 and ∠13, ∠3 and ∠6; *Same Side Interior Angles:* ∠2 and ∠9, ∠3 and ∠5, ∠4 and ∠11, ∠6 and ∠13, ∠12 and ∠14; *Alternate Exterior Angles:* ∠1 and ∠8, ∠1 and ∠12, ∠2 and ∠7, ∠5 and ∠16, ∠7 and ∠14; *Same Side Exterior Angles:* ∠2 and ∠8, ∠5 and ∠14, ∠7 and ∠16, ∠9 and ∠15, ∠1 and ∠10; *Linear Pairs:* ∠2 and ∠4, ∠3 and ∠4, ∠6 and ∠8, ∠9 and ∠10, ∠11 and ∠12

4-9. POLYGON IS TAKEN FROM THE GREEK TERM POLYGONOS MEANING MANY ANGLES.

4-10. 360° is the sum of THE MEASURES OF THE EXTERIOR ANGLES OF ANY POLYGON.

4-11.

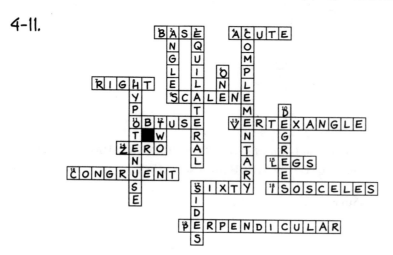

4-12.   *Acute:* ΔCHB, ΔAGC;   *Obtuse:* ΔECA, ΔECF, ΔGHB, ΔFHC, ΔEIC, ΔAFB, ΔGEC, ΔHFG, ΔGFB, ΔHFC;   *Right:* ΔABG, ΔACF, ΔIDC, ΔEDC, ΔAED, ΔBFC, ΔGBC

4-13.   **1.** D, which is the only right triangle. All of the others are acute.   **2.** A, which is the only scalene triangle. All of the others are isosceles triangles.   **3.** C, which is the only scalene triangle. All of the others are isosceles triangles.   **4.** D, which is the only scalene triangle. All of the others are isosceles triangles.   **5.** C, which is the only equilateral triangle. All of the others are scalene triangles.   **6.** B, which is the only isosceles triangle. All of the others are scalene triangles.   **7.** C, which is the only obtuse triangle. All of the others are acute triangles.   **8.** D, which is the only isosceles triangle that is not equilateral. All of the others are equilateral triangles.   **9.** D, which is the only scalene triangle. All of the others are isosceles triangles.   **10.** B, which is the only scalene triangle. All of the others are isosceles triangles.

4-14.   Drawings may vary.

4-15.   All of THE TRIANGLES ARE SCALENE.

4-16.   **1.** 46°;   **2.** 46°;   **3.** 64°;   **4.** 92°;   **5.** 35°;   **6.** 55°;   **7.** 90°;   **8.** 55°;   **9.** 24°;   **10.** 23°;   **11.** 90°;   **12.** 101°;   **13.** 67°;   **14.** 113°

4-17.   **1.** 56°;   **2.** 48°;   **3.** 98°;   **4.** 8°;   **5.** 90°;   **6.** 34°;   **7.** 76°;   **8.** 18°;   **9.** 137°;   **10.** 82°;   **11.** 34°;   **12.** 98°;   **13.** 82°;   **14.** 73°;   **15.** 107°;   **16.** 30°;   **17.** 100°;   **18.** 64°;   **19.** 70°;   **20.** 37°;   **21.** 58°;   **22.** 25°;   **23.** 31°;   **24.** 66°;   **25.** 83°;   **26.** 36°;   **27.** 62°;   **28.** 40°;   **29.** 65°;   **30.** 137°

4-18.   A pedal triangle is formed by joining the FEET OF THE ALTITUDES.

4-19.   The word *hypotenuse* is taken from the Greek words *hypo* and *teinein,* meaning to "stretch under." It was used by Pythagoras to describe the relationship of the legs of a right TRIANGLE TO THE LONGEST SIDE.

4-20.   **1.** obtuse;   **2.** acute;   **3.** right;   **4.** obtuse;   **5.** right;   **6.** right;   **7.** acute;   **8.** obtuse;   **9.** obtuse;   **10.** acute;   **11.** right;   **12.** obtuse
3,9; 4,16; 5,25; 9 + 16 = 25

4-21.   All RIGHT TRIANGLES ARE ISOSCELES OR SCALENE.

4-22.   ΔABC ≅ ΔTSU *or* ΔABC ≅ ΔUST; ΔJKL ≅ ΔQRP ≅ ΔVWX; ΔDEF ≅ ΔOMN ≅ ΔIHG

4-23.   **1.** B and C; SAS or ASA;   **2.** A and C; SSS;   **3.** A and C; HL or AAS;   **4.** A and C; SSS, ASA, SAS, or AAS;   **5.** B and C; SAS;   **6.** A and C; SAS;   **7.** A and C; SAS or AAS;   **8.** A and B; SAS;   **9.** A and B; HL, SSS, or SAS;   **10.** A and B; SAS or SSS

4-24.   **2.** ∠A ≅ ∠E;   **3.** $\overline{BC} ≅ \overline{DF}$;   **4.** $\overline{BC} ≅ \overline{DC}$;   **5.** $\overline{AD} ≅ \overline{BC}$;   **6.** $\overline{AD} ≅ \overline{DC}$;   **7.** ∠B ≅ ∠D;   **8.** $\overline{AC} ≅ \overline{EC}$;   **9.** $\overline{AC} ≅ \overline{ED}$;   **10.** ∠B ≅ ∠E

4-25.   *Parallelogram:* 1, 6, 7;   *Rectangle:* 1, 4, 6, 7, 8;   *Square:* 1, 4, 5, 6, 7, 8, 9, 10;
Rhombus: 1, 5, 6, 7, 8;   *Trapezoid:* 2;   *Isosceles Trapezoid:* 2, 3
Sum = 124; $124 \times 3 = 372$; $372 - 12 = 360$

4-26.   *Parallelogram:* F, G, I, J, K;   *Rectangle:* D, F, G, I, J, K, L;   *Square:* D, F, G, I, J, K,
L, M, N, O;   *Rhombus:* F, G, I J, K, M, N, O;   *Trapezoid:* A, H;   *Isosceles Trapezoid:* A, B, C, D,
E, H

4-27.   *Rectangles:* AFVS, ACTS, CFNK, EFNM, CFVT;   *Squares:* CEMK, KNVT, LRUQ;
Rhombus: BIJH   *Parallelogram:* OGKS;   *Trapezoids:* ACGO, ACKS, OGTS, GDEK, EFNK,
EFRP, ODES, EFVS, NRPM, KNVS

4-28.   **1.** 8;   **2.** 12;   **3.** 13.5;   **4.** 5;   **5.** 13.5;   **6.** 50;   **7.** 80;   **8.** 130;   **9.** 100;   **10.** 140;
11. 125;   **12.** 55;   **13.** 40;   **14.** 90;   **15.** 45;   **16.** 100

4-29.   **1.** 75;   **2.** 105;   **3.** 105;   **4.** 105;   **5.** 75;   **6.** 90;   **7.** 90;   **8.** 75;   **9.** 15;   **10.** 60;
11. 45;   **12.** 110;   **13.** 70;   **14.** 40;   **15.** 50;   **16.** 55

4-30.

4	1	4	2	1
3	3	5	4	5
5	2	1	3	2
2	3	5	1	5
4	1	2	3	4

1	2	1	2	4
5	3	2	4	5
2	4	5	3	3
1	3	4	5	1
1	3	5	4	2

4-31.   The two properties are CONGRUENCE AND SIMILARITY.

4-32.   **1.** 42;   **2.** 72;   **3.** 18;   **4.** 66;   **5.** 46;   **6.** 68;   **7.** 98;   **8.** 90;   **9.** 57;   **10.** 90;
11. 57;   **12.** 45;   **13.** 90;   **14.** 65;   **15.** 80;   **16.** 133;   **17.** 43;   **18.** 45;   **19.** 33;   **20.** 75;
21. 90;   **22.** 80;   **23.** 102;   **24.** 58;   **25.** 72

4-33.   **1.** 90;   **2.** 40;   **3.** 46;   **4.** 30;   **5.** 24;   **6.** 18;   **7.** 136;   **8.** 106;   **9.** 138;
10. 7;   **11.** 14;   **12.** 180;   **13.** 22;   **14.** 88;   **15.** 180;   **16.** 10;   **17.** 18;   **18.** 48;   **19.** 54;
20. 50;   **21.** 14;   **22.** 16.12;   **23.** 7.5;   **24.** 6.5;   **25.** 3.63;   **26.** 3.97

4-34.

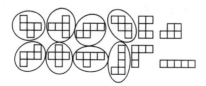

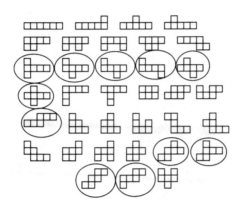

4-35. *Squares:* AHCN, 8, 4;   AETM, 16, 16;   KLUY, 2, $\frac{1}{4}$;   GLRX 5, $1\frac{9}{16}$;   ALQP, 12, 9;

NCSM, 8, 4;   *Rectangles:* HETS, 12, 8;   HLQD, 8, 3;   NCDP, 6, 2;   PDSM, 6, 2;   AHSM, 12,

8;   AHDP, 10, 6

4-36.   **1.** 10, 1;   **2.** 3, 2;   **3.** 6, 5;   **4.** 7, 2;   **5.** 4, 3;   **6.** 15, 10;   **7.** 18, 10;   **8.** 20, 12

4-37.   Quadrilaterals that have the same area MAY NOT ALWAYS HAVE THE SAME PERIMETER.

4-38.   **1.** $5\frac{3}{4}$, $1\frac{17}{32}$;   **2.** 9, $2\frac{21}{32}$;   **3.** $10\frac{3}{4}$, $4\frac{27}{32}$;   **4.** $7\frac{3}{4}$, $2\frac{1}{32}$;   **5.** 15, 7;

6. $11\frac{1}{4}$, $4\frac{3}{16}$;   **7.** $13\frac{3}{4}$, $7\frac{1}{2}$;   **8.** $16\frac{1}{4}$, $9\frac{1}{32}$

4-39.   **1.** 6;   **3.** 20.25;   **4.** 43.96;   **5.** 78.5;   **6.** 31.4;   **7.** 94. 2;   **8.** 56.25;   **9.** 9.5;   **10.** 81;
11. 75.36;   **12.** 18;   **13.** 196;   **14.** 25
Pi = 3.1415926535897

4-40.   **1.** 56.52, 254.34;   **2.** 37.68, 113.04;   **3.** 25.12, 50.24;   **4.** 12.56, 12.56;   **5.** 50.24,
200.96;   **6.** 18.84, 28.26;   **7.** 37.68, 113.04;   **8.** 62.8, 314;   **9.** 69.08, 379.94;   **10.** 31.4, 78.5

4-41.   **1.** 72 sq. units;   **2.** 13 sq. units;   **3.** 20 sq. units;   **4.** 5 sq. units;   **5.** 32 sq. units;
6. 16 sq. units;   **7.** 31 sq. units;   **8.** 15 sq. units;   **9.** 20 sq. units;   **10.** 52 sq. units;   **11.** 15 sq.
units;   **12.** 52 sq. units

4-42.   Every rectangular prism is THREE DIMENSIONAL.

4-43.   Volume and surface area are measured in cubic units and square units RESPEC-
TIVELY.

4-44.   **2.** 8 sides on a stop sign;   **3.** 90 degrees of a right angle;   **4.** 180 degrees in a triangle;   **5.** 6 sides of a hexagon;   **6.** 2 semicircles of a circle;   **7.** 1 wheel on a unicycle;   **8.** 540
degrees in a pentagon;   **9.** 9 squares on a tic-tac-toe board;   **10.** 360 degrees in a circle;   **11.** 5

sides of a pentagon;   **12.** 9 planets in the solar system;   **13.** 2 hemispheres of a sphere;
14. 4 angles in a quadrilateral;   **15.** 4 right angles in a rectangle;   **16.** 360 degrees in a quadrilateral;   **17.** 3 sides of a triangle   **18.** 5 circles on the Olympic flag;   **19.** 3 dimensions of a
cube;   **20.** 8 sides of an octagon

4-45.   **1.** line;   **2.** pentagon;   **3.** straight angle;   **4.** rhombus;   **5.** diameter;
6. right triangle;   **7.** hexagon;   **8.** triangle;   **9.** point;   **10.** ray;   **11.** vertical angles;   **12.** pi;
13. angle;   **14.** right angle;   **15.** heptagon;   **16.** compass;   **17.** octagon;   **18.** acute angle;
19. circle;   **20.** central angle;   **21.** acute triangle;   **22.** face;   **23.** square;   **24.** rectangle;
25. center;   **26.** hypotenuse;   **27.** cylinder;   **28.** parallel;   **29.** cone;   **30.** base;   **31.** segment;
32. cube;   **33.** plane;   **34.** radius;   **35.** polygon;   **36.** equilateral triangle;   **37.** obtuse triangle;   **38.** perpendicular;   **39.** prism;   **40.** trapezoid;   **41.** chord;   **42.** complementary angles;
43. isosceles triangle;   **44.** decagon;   **45.** obtuse angle;   **46.** congruent;   **47.** vertex;
48. supplementary angles;   **49.** quadrilateral;   **50.** pyramid

Section 5
Algebra

5-1.   **F.** 13;   **G.** 16;   **R.** 25;   **N.** 28;   **O.** 38;   **H.** 21   **K.** 0   **I.** 7;   **E.** 4;   **L.** 39;   **A.** 24;
T. 40;   **B.** 3;   **W.** 6;   **S.** 8
In 1557 Robert Recorde first used the = symbol in *The Whetstone of Witte,* THE FIRST ALGE-
BRA BOOK WRITTEN IN ENGLISH.

5-2.   **1.** 618, big;   **2.** 7,738, bell;   **3.** 514, his   **4.** 34, he;   **5.** 663, egg;   **6.** 7,334, heel;
7. 5,317, lies;   **8.** 345, she;   **9.** 3,807, lobe;   **10.** 338, bee;   **11.** 51, is;   **12.** 3,704, hole;
13. 733, eel;   **14.** 7,718, bill;   **15.** 3,045, shoe;   **16.** 7,735, sell;   **17.** 5,507, loss;   **18.** 771, ill;
19. 637, leg;   **20.** 706,006, googol

5-3.

```
A R C H I M E D E S
1 2 3 4 5 6 7 8 9 10

I S A A C   N E W T O N
11 12 13 14 15   16 17 18 19 20 21

C A R L   F R I E D R I C H   G A U S S
22 23 24 25   26 27 28 29 30 31 32 33 34   35 36 37 38 39
```

5-4.   **1.** T;   **2.** H;   **3.** E;   **4.** D;   **5.** E;   **6.** N;   **7.** S;   **8.** I;   **9.** T;   **10.** Y;   **11.** P;   **12.** R;
13. O;   **14.** P;   **15.** E;   **16.** R;   **17.** T;   **18.** Y
Between any two real numbers there is another real number. This is called THE DENSITY
PROPERTY.

5-5.   **1.** 3, –6, S, I;   **2.** 10, –2, R, W;   **3.** –6, 2, I, L;   **4.** 2, –6, L, I;   **5.** 5, –5, A, M;   **6.** 10, –1,
R, O;   **7.** 4, 5, N, A;   **8.** 4, –3, 5, N, H, A;   **9.** –5, –6, 2, M, I, L;   **10.** 1, –1, 4, T, O, N
In 1845 the word *vector* was first used by an Irish mathematician named SIR WILLIAM
RONAN HAMILTON.

5-6. **1.** −32, D; **2.** 14, E; **3.** −19, P; **4.** 14, E; **5.** −68, N; **6.** −32, D; **7.** −34, S; **8.** 68, O; **9.** −68, N; **10.** −9, T; **11.** 31, H; **12.** 14, E; **13.** −8, I; **14.** −68, N; **15.** −9, T; **16.** 14, E; **17.** 52, G; **18.** 14, E; **19.** 36, R; **20.** −34, S

If you add positive and negative integers, the sum may be positive, negative, or zero. It DEPENDS ON THE INTEGERS.

5-7. **1.** 6, F; **2.** −30, O; **3.** −58, R; **4.** −17, A; **5.** −27, D; **6.** −27, D; **7.** −7, I; **8.** −25, N; **9.** 30, G; **10.** −25, N; **11.** 25, U; **12.** 41, M; **13.** 57, B; **14.** 13, E; **15.** −58, R; **16.** −93, S; **17.** −17, A; **18.** −58, R; **19.** 13, E; **20.** 25, U; **21.** −93, S; **22.** 13, E; **23.** −27, D

Any subtraction problem can be written as an addition problem. The same rules FOR ADDING NUMBERS ARE USED.

5-8.

					Sum = 10
−6 × −3 18	−23 × −2 46	−46 × 1 −46	36 ÷ −2 −18	120 ÷ 12 10	Sum = 10
−6 × −7 42	120 ÷ −4 −30	−242 ÷ 11 −22	−90 ÷ −15 6	−168 ÷ −12 14	Sum = 10
−170 ÷ 5 −34	−390 ÷ 15 −26	98 ÷ 49 2	−15 × −2 30	−19 × −2 38	Sum = 10
−5 × 2 −10	76 ÷ −38 −2	208 ÷ 8 26	−17 × −2 34	190 ÷ −5 −38	Sum = 10
72 ÷ −12 −6	2 × 11 22	200 ÷ 4 50	7 × −6 −42	252 ÷ −18 −14	Sum = 10
Sum = 10	Sum = 10	Sum = 10	Sum = 10	Sum = 10	Sum = 10

5-9. **L.** −7; **R.** 12; **S.** 48; **Y.** 576; **X.** 127; **H.** −64; **W.** 116 **I.** −17; **F.** −76; **B.** −204; **E.** −171; **U.** 104; **N.** −2; **T.** 101; **O.** 3; **M.** −6; **G.** −72; **P.** 5

Use the following strategy for operations with integers: Simplify all EXPRESSIONS WITHIN GROUPING SYMBOLS FIRST.

5-10. Answers may vary; possible answers include: **1.** −4 + −3 + −2 + −1 = −10; **2.** (−3 + −4) − (−2)(−1) = −9; **3.** −4 + −2 + −3 − −1 = −8; **4.** (−4 + −3)(−1 − −2) = −7; **5.** −4 − −2 + −3 + −1 = −6; **6.** −4 + −3 + (−2 × −1) = −5; **7.** −4 + −2 − (−3 − −1) = −4; **8.** −4 + −2 + (−3 × −1) = −3; **9.** −4 + −2 − (−3 + −1) = −2; **10.** −2 + −3 + (−4 × −1) = −1; **11.** −4 + −1 − (−3 + −2) = 0; **12.** −4 + −1 + (−3 × −2) = 1; **13.** −4 − −2 − (−3 + −1) = 2; **14.** −(−4 + −2) − (−3 × −1) = 3; **15.** −4 × −2 + −3 + −1 = 4; **16.** (−1 + −4) ÷ (−3 − −2) = 5; **17.** −3 × −4 ÷ −2 × −1 = 6; **18.** (−3 + −4)(−2 − −1) = 7; **19.** −1 − −2 − (−4 + −3) = 8; **20.** −4 × −3 + −2 + −1 = 9; **21.** −4 × −3 − −2 × −1 = 10

5-11. **E.** 15; **T.** 6; **O.** −18; **Y.** −16; **H.** −10; **A.** −59; **O.** −60; **M.** 20; **E.** 9; **T.** −9; **E.** 2; **N.** −32; **T.** 8; **S.** −8; **S.** −54 **L.** −72; **E.** 36 **I.** −31; **E.** 625 **N.** 324; **T.** −108; **E.** 144; **B.** −137; **P.** 243

Rene Descartes was the first man to use a raised number for powers. However, he continued to write x^2 as xx, because the expression occupied the same amount of space as xx and it allowed the TYPE TO BE SET ON THE SAME LINE.

5-12. **P.** 3; **T.** –1; **M.** 6; **W.** –46; **U.** –7; **L.** 7 **I.** 8; **G.** 14; **S.** 1; **R.** 2; **N.** 5; **H.** 9; **E.** 24; **O.** 4; **B.** 40; **F.** 21; **A.** 46; **V.** –9; **Y.** –48

Since any distance is ALWAYS POSITIVE, THE NUMBER IS FREE OF A SIGN.

5-13. **1.** 10; **2.** –7; **3.** –12; **4.** –3; **5.** 3, –15; **6.** 4, –1; **7.** 8, 1; **8.** –13, –8, –4; **9.** 7, –5; **10.** –10, –14; **11.** –9, 9; **12.** 5, –11; **13.** 2, –6; **14.** –2, 6

5-14. **1.** E, 8; **2.** X, 100; **3.** P, 20; **4.** R, 6; **5.** E, 8; **6.** S, 12; **7.** S, 12; **8.** I, 20; **9.** O, 400; **10.** N, 5; **11.** I, 20; **12.** F, –8; **13.** N, 5; **14.** E, 8; **15.** Q, 24; **16.** U, 0.2; **17.** A, 20; **18.** L, 30; **19.** S, 12; **20.** T, 200; **21.** E, 8; **22.** N, 5

Evaluate each EXPRESSION IF N EQUALS TEN.

5-15. **A.** 19; **B.** 7.2; **E.** –32; **G.** 9; **H.** 5 **I.** –45; **L.** 8; **M.** 11; **N.** 5.2; **O.** 12.7; **P.** 3.6; **R.** –49; **S.** –13; **T.** –2; **U.** –24; **Y.** 16

THE PYTHAGOREANS: "ALL THINGS ARE NUMBERS."

5-16.

$3e - e - 2 = 0$ e = __1__	$4m - 7m = -24$ m = __8__	$-2 = -15 + p$ p = __13__	$-\frac{1}{2}r = -6$ r = __12__
$a + 4 + 2 = 20$ a = __14__	$c - 30 = -19$ c = __11__	$t - 3 = -1$ t = __2__	$14 = -7 + 3h$ h = __7__
$7(y-1) - 2y = 13$ y = __4__	$7 - (1-q) = 11$ q = __5__	$(x-3) + 17 = 30$ x = __16__	$d - 24 = -15$ d = __9__
$8(f-7) = 64$ f = __15__	$2 = -10 + y + 2$ y = __10__	$-27w = -81$ w = __3__	$-2 + (1+z) = 5$ z = __6__

Magic Number is 34.

5-17. **A.** 14; **R.** 31; **D.** –12 **I.** 6; **T.** 4; **E.** 113; **M.** –1; **Y.** 7.5; **O.** –0.25; **B.** 8; **S.** 0.25; **H.** –3 **U.** 17; **N.** –2; **Z.** 76

To make an equivalent equation you must add or subtract the same number from both sides of the equation and multiply or divide BOTH SIDES BY THE SAME NONZERO NUMBER.

5-18. **1.** 1; **2.** –4; **3.** 6; **4.** 10; **5.** –3; **6.** 0; **7.** –2; **8.** –6; **9.** –1; **10.** 5; **11.** 7.5; **12.** –7; **13.** 2; **14.** 4; **15.** 22; **16.** –1.25; **17.** –1.3; **18.** 3

"I HAVE THE RESULT, BUT I DO NOT YET KNOW HOW TO GET IT."

5-19. **W.** 120; **N.** 40; **L.** $1.\overline{3}$; **E.** 10.99; **H.** 8; **O.** 24; **A.** 240; **V.** 6; **T.** 1.75; **P.** 16; **B.** 1; **U.** 3.25; **S.** 96.25 **K.** 4; **R.** 1.5; **F.** 5

Francois Viete was the first mathematician to use letters of the ALPHABET FOR UNKNOWN VALUES.

5-20. **1.** D; **2.** U; **3.** H; **4.** S; **5.** R; **6.** N; **7.** G; **8.** I; **9.** E; **10.** Q; **11.** C; **12.** L; **13.** B; **14.** A; **15.** F; **16.** Y; **17.** M; **18.** O; **19.** T

If you multiply or divide both sides of an inequality by a negative number, you must CHANGE THE DIRECTION OF THE INEQUALITY SYMBOL.

5-21.   **1.** R;   **2.** H;   **3.** N;   **4.** E;   **5.** I;   **6.** T;   **7.** M;   **8.** Q;   **9.** A;   **10.** O;   **11.** U;   **12.** L;   **13.** S;   **14.** V

MOST INEQUALITIES HAVE MORE THAN ONE SOLUTION.

5-22.   **1.** W, $9a^2$;   **2.** I, $5a$;   **3.** L, $3a^3$;   **4.** L, $4a$;   **5.** I, $2a^2$;   **6.** A, $4a^4$;   **7.** M, $15a^3$;   **8.** O, $2a$;   **9.** U, $4a^7$;   **10.** G, $4a^3$;   **11.** H, $8a$;   **12.** T, $2a^8$;   **13.** R, $3a^9$;   **14.** E, $6a^4$;   **15.** D, $3a^5$

In 1631, WILLIAM OUGHTRED was the first mathematician to use "x" as a symbol for multiplication.

5-23.   **1.** $3x^3$, $2x^2$, $-7x$, 2;   **2.** $5x^3$, $4x^2$, $5x$, 9;   **3.** $6x^3$, $7x^2$, $6x$, 3;   **4.** $11x^2$, $9x$, -4;   **5.** $8x^3$, $5x^2$, $-13x$;   **6.** $2x^3$, $8x^2$, $-9x$, 1;   **7.** $4x^3$, $-x^2$, $4x$, -12;   **8.** x^3, 7;   **9.** $-2x^3$, $3x^2$, -17;   **10.** $-4x^3$;   **11.** $10x^2$, 18;   **12.** $-2x^2$, -10

Polynomial comes from two Greek words: POLUS AND NOMOS WHICH MEAN "MANY PARTS."

5-24.   **1.** 48;   **2.** 30, 25;   **3.** x;   **4.** 18;   **5.** 12, xy^2;   **6.** x^2;   **7.** -3, -40;   **8.** 19, 20;   **9.** -9;   **10.** 3, 8;   **11.** 21;   **12.** 41;   **13.** -16, -12, 10;   **14.** 38;   **15.** xy, 2;   **16.** 1;   **17.** 16;   **18.** 4

To multiply a binomial by a monomial use the Distributive Property. To multiply two binomials use FOIL or use the Distributive Property TWICE AND COMBINE SIMILAR TERMS.

5-25.   **1.** $(x - 9)(x + 3)$;   **2.** $3x(x - 3)$;   **3.** $(x + 2)(x - 2)$;   **4.** $(x - 5)(x - 9)$;   **5.** $(x - 3)(x + 6)$;   **6.** $(2x - 1)(x + 2)$;   **7.** $(x - 8)(x + 5)$;   **8.** $(2x + 3)(x + 1)$;   **9.** $(x - 1)(x - 5)$;   **10.** $4x(x + 11)$;   **11.** $(3x - 1)(x - 2)$;   **12.** $(2x + 1)(x + 4)$;   **13.** $(x - 1)(x + 3)$;   **14.** $(x + 6)(x + 5)$;   **15.** $3x(x + 10)$;   **16.** $(x - 8)(x - 3)$;   **17.** $2x(x + 4)$;   **18.** $(x - 7)(x + 7)$;   **19.** $6x^4(x - 4)$;   **20.** $(2x + 3)(4x - 1)$;   **21.** $x(x - 10)$;   **22.** $(x + 1)(x - 11)$;   **23.** $(x + 9)(x - 7)$;   **24.** $(x - 4)(x + 8)$;   **25.** $(4x - 1)(x + 13)$;   **26.** $(2x + 1)(x - 10)$;   **27.** $(x - 11)(x + 8)$;   **28.** $2x(x + 13)$;   **29.** $x(x + 9)$;   **30.** $(3x - 1)(2x - 1)$;   **31.** $(x + 7)(x + 11)$;   **32.** $4x(x + 10)$;   **33.** $6x^4(x - 3)$

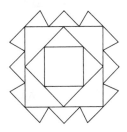

5-26.   **1.** $(x - 6)(x + 3)$;   **2.** $(x + 8)(x - 5)$;   **3.** $(x + 5)(x + 2)$;   **4.** $(x - 5)(x - 4)$;   **5.** $(x + 7)(x - 6)$;   **6.** $(x - 6)(x - 4)$;   **7.** $(x - 20)(x - 1)$;   **8.** $(x + 4)(x + 2)$;   **9.** $(x - 3)(x - 1)$;   **10.** $(x - 8)(x + 3)$;   **11.** $(x + 7)(x + 8)$;   **12.** $(x + 3)(x + 4)$;   **13.** $(x - 6)(x - 2)$;   **14.** $(x + 5)(x + 3)$;   **15.** $(x + 8)(x - 4)$;   **16.** $(x - 20)(x + 2)$;   **17.** $(x + 9)(x - 6)$

EACH OF THESE TRINOMIALS CAN

BE FACTORED

5-27.   **1.** 0, 3;   **2.** –3, –7;   **3.** –4, 5;   **4.** 0, 5;   **5.** –1, 1;   **6.** –7, –1;   **7.** –8, 2;   **8.** 10, –6;   **9.** 6, 4;   **10.** 6, –6;   **11.** 8, –5;   **12.** –4, 3;   **13.** –2, –3;   **14.** –9, 7

✕ ☐ 𝖤 ◲

Rebus is X SQUARED.

5-28.   **1.** D, $x - 2$;   **2.** E, $\frac{1}{2}$;   **3.** N, $\frac{3}{x+2}$;   **4.** O, $\frac{1}{7}$;   **5.** M, $\frac{x+4}{x+9}$;   **6.** I, $\frac{3}{2x+6}$;

7. N, $\frac{3}{x+2}$;   **8.** A, $\frac{2}{5}$;   **9.** T, $\frac{x+5}{3}$;   **10.** O, $\frac{1}{7}$;   **11.** R, $\frac{1}{x-2}$;   **12.** C, $\frac{x+2}{x-3}$;   **13.** A, $\frac{2}{5}$;

14. N, $\frac{3}{x+2}$;   **15.** N, $\frac{3}{x+2}$;   **16.** O, $\frac{1}{7}$;   **17.** T, $\frac{x+5}{3}$;   **18.** E, $\frac{1}{2}$;   **19.** Q, $\frac{3}{2x-10}$;

20. U, $\frac{6x^2}{x+5}$;   **21.** A, $\frac{2}{5}$;   **22.** L, $\frac{x+9}{x+2}$;   **23.** Z, $\frac{4}{x-1}$;   **24.** E, $\frac{1}{2}$;   **25.** R, $\frac{1}{x-2}$;

26. O, $\frac{1}{7}$

Since division by zero is undefined, the DENOMINATOR CAN NOT EQUAL ZERO.

5-29.   **1.** S, $\frac{2}{x^2}$;   **2.** Y, $4x^2y^2$;   **3.** M, 1;   **4.** B, $\frac{1}{2}$;   **5.** O, $x^2 + 2x$;   **6.** L, $x + 7$;   **7.** A, 2;

8. N, $x^2 + 2xy + y^2$;   **9.** D, $\frac{8}{x^2}$;   **10.** M, 1;   **11.** U, $\frac{3}{2}$;   **12.** L, $x + 7$;   **13.** T, $\frac{1}{x+3}$;   **14.** I, –1;

15. P, $\frac{x-4}{x+4}$;   **16.** L, $x + 7$;   **17.** Y, $4x^2y^2$

Multiplication and division are inverse operations. To divide rational expressions you must find the reciprocal of the expression to the right of the division SYMBOL AND MULTIPLY.

5-30.   **1.** $\frac{2}{x}$;   **2.** $\frac{-3}{4x}$;   **3.** $\frac{1}{2x}$;   **4.** $\frac{11x}{x-4}$;   **5.** $\frac{4x+4}{x+2}$;   **6.** $\frac{-x-3}{5}$;   **7.** $\frac{-x+1}{4}$;

8. $\frac{1}{x-3}$;   **9.** $\frac{5x+2}{x^2}$;   **10.** $\frac{8x-1}{6x^2}$;   **11.** $\frac{7x}{18}$;   **12.** $\frac{2x+1}{x^2+x}$;   **13.** $\frac{3}{4}$;   **14.** $\frac{2}{x+1}$

5-31.   **1.** 17;   **2.** 18, $\frac{7}{x}$;   **3.** $\frac{2}{x}$;   **4.** $\frac{1}{x}$;   **5.** 5;   **6.** 1;   **7.** 4;   **8.** $\frac{52}{x-3}$;   **9.** $\frac{32}{x-3}$;

10. $\frac{6}{2x-3}$;   **11.** $\frac{1}{x-3}$ **12.** 14

The division symbol was first used in 1659 by SWISS MATHEMATICIAN JOHANN RAHN.

5-32. **O.** –5; **H.** $\frac{9}{28}$; **A.** $\frac{4}{35}$; **U.** ∅; **E.** 7; **S.** 6; **B.** $\frac{2}{5}$; **T.** $-\frac{1}{3}$; **P.** $\frac{1}{2}$; **N.** 5;

L. –1; **R.** –14 **I.** $-2\frac{1}{2}$; **M.** –3, 2; **V.** 1, 4; **X.** 6, $-\frac{2}{3}$

Some PROBLEMS HAVE EXTRANEOUS SOLUTIONS.

5-33. **1.** L, I; **2.** N, E; **3.** I, S; **4.** T, A; **5.** K, E; **6.** N, F; **7.** R, O; **8.** M, T; **9.** H, E;
10. L, A; **11.** T, I; **12.** N, T; **13.** E, R; **14.** M, L; **15.** I, N; **16.** U, M; **17.** M, E; **18.** A,
N; **19.** I, N; **20.** G, F **21.** L, A; **22.** X, E; **23.** N, C; **24.** H, O; **25.** R, D
The word LINE IS TAKEN FROM THE LATIN TERM "LINUM" MEANING FLAXEN CHORD.

5-34. **1.** C; **2.** A; **3.** R; **4.** T; **5.** E; **6.** S; **7.** I; **8.** A; **9.** N; **10.** C; **11.** O;
12. O; **13.** R; **14.** D; **15.** I; **16.** N; **17.** A; **18.** T; **19.** E; **20.** S; **21.** Y **22.** S; **23.** T;
24. E; **25.** M
The CARTESIAN COORDINATE SYSTEM.

5-35. **1.** U, –2; **2.** S, 2; **3.** E, 3; **4.** D, 4; **5.** B, 5; **6.** Y, 6; **7.** L, 17; **8.** E, 3;
9. O, 10; **10.** N, –3; **11.** H, –4; **12.** A, 37; **13.** R, –7; **14.** D, 4; **15.** E, 3; **16.** U, 19;
17. L, 17; **18.** E, 3; **19.** R, –7
The expression f(x) to represent a function was first USED BY LEONHARD EULER.

5-36. **1.** 5, 3; **2.** 3, –3; **3.** 2, 0; **4.** 5, –2; **5.** 2, 10; **6.** –2, –1; **7.** –4, –9; **8.** 4, 0;
9. 0, –3; **10.** –2, 10; **11.** –1, 1; **12.** 4, 10; **13.** 8, 6; **14.** –3, 1

5-37. **1.** 4, 3; **2.** 2, 14; **3.** 7; **4.** 5, 3; **5.** 1; **6.** 5, 10; **7.** 3; **8.** 9; **9.** 3, 15; **10.** 5, 2;
11. 3, 2, 18; **12.** 2, 13; **13.** 11; **14.** 8, 6; **15.** 12; **16.** 2, 17; **17.** 3, 19; **18.** 16, 4;
19. 6, 2; **20.** 9, 3
RENE DESCARTES FIRST USED THE RADICAL SYMBOL THAT WE STILL USE TODAY.

5-38.
1. $3\sqrt{15}$; **2.** 5; **3.** $5\sqrt{3}$; **4.** $2\sqrt{2}$; **5.** $5\sqrt{3}$; **6.** 5; **7.** $3\sqrt{3}$; **8.** $\sqrt{6}$; **9.** $3\sqrt{15}$;
10. $3\sqrt{15}$; **11.** $\sqrt{6}$; **12.** $5\sqrt{3}$; **13.** $8\sqrt{10}$; **14.** 7; **15.** $3\sqrt{3}$; **16.** 5; **17.** 7; **18.** $2\sqrt{2}$;
19. $8\sqrt{10}$; **20.** $2\sqrt{2}$

5-39. **L.** 49; **N.** 0.25; **T.** 18; **A.** 0.8; **D.** 20; **C.** 11; **R.** 9; **V.** 4; **H.** ∅ **I.** 6.25;
S. 25; **E.** 2.25; **B.** 7
A radical equation is an equation with VARIABLES IN THE RADICAND.

5-40. **1.** 0 M, 3 A;   **2.** –10 Y, 10 H;   **3.** 3 A, 6 V;   **4.** –3 E, 3 A;   **5.** –7 D, –5 O;
6. $-2 - \sqrt{6}$ U, $-2 + \sqrt{6}$ B;   **7.** –9 L, –3 E;   **8.** –6 R, –5 O;   **9.** –5 O, 5 T

Some quadratic equations have two real roots, some may have two conjugate imaginary roots, and some MAY HAVE A DOUBLE ROOT.

Section 6
Data Analysis

6-1.

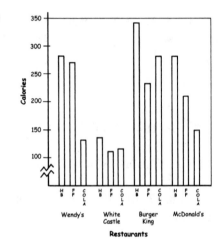

6-2.

Movie	Ticket Sales (in millions)
E.T.	⬭⬭⬭⬭
Forrest Gump	⬭⬭⬭◖
Independence Day	⬭⬭⬭◖
Home Alone	⬭⬭⬭
Star Wars	⬭⬭⬭⬭⬭
Star Wars: The Phantom Menace	⬭⬭⬭⬭◖
Return of the Jedi	⬭⬭⬭◖
The Empire Strikes Back	⬭⬭⬭
Titanic	⬭⬭⬭⬭⬭⬭
Jurassic Park	⬭⬭⬭⬭

6-3.

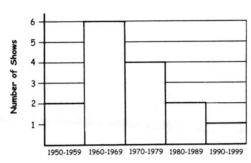

6-4.   **1.** increasing, then decreasing;   **2.** 36° F

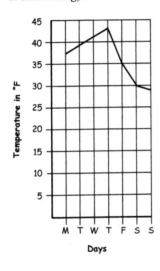

6-5.   3 ounces ≈ 80 grams;   600 grams ≈ 20 ounces;   4 ounces ≈ 110 grams;
250 grams ≈ 8.8 ounces

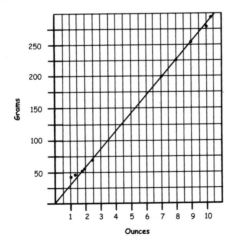

6-6.   **1.** Washington, D.C.;   **2.** January;   **3.** July and August;   **4.** Caribou;   **5.** Miami

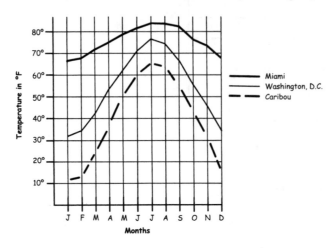

6-7.   **1.** Asia and Africa;   **2.** 22%;   **3.** 28%

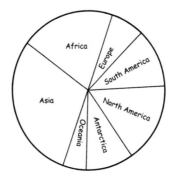

6-8.   Eating: 1 hr., 20 min.;   Attending Classes: 5 hrs., 45 min.;   Traveling: 40 min.;
Playing Soccer: 2 hrs.;   Doing Homework: 2 hrs., 30 min.;   Watching TV: 2 hrs., 30 min.;
Sleeping 7 hrs., 30 min.;   Miscellaneous Activities: 1 hr., 45 min.

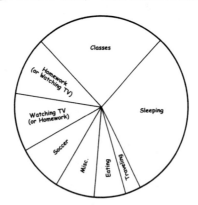

6-9. Age of U.S. Presidents at Their Inauguration

4	2 3 6 6 7 8 9 9
5	0 1 1 1 1 2 2 4 4 4 4 4 5 5 5 5 6 6 6 7 7 7 7 8
6	0 1 1 1 2 4 4 5 8 9

Range: 27
Mean: 54.837209 ... or about 55
Median: 55
Modes: 51 and 54

6-10.

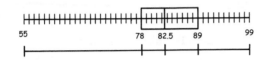

6-11.   **1.** F = 11,   S = 70,   E = 68,   H = 71,   **2.** W = 14,   U = 84,   I = 85,   **3.** R = 22, T = 87,   N = 90,   A = 83,   O = 93,   **4.** Y = 88,   M = 6
Sixty-two and two-sevenths IS THE MEAN OF YOUR ANSWERS.

6-12.   The means are 93, 83, 85, and 90. Student One is Joe. Student Two is John. Student Three is Sally. Student Four is Maria.

Section 7
Potpourri

7-1.   Answers will vary according to the student's birthday. False statements are numbers 3, 5, 6, 8, 10, 12, 16, and 18. The final answer should return students to their birthday.

7-2.   **2.** X, $\frac{36}{3}$;   **3.** P, 5(2 + 3);   **4.** R, $3\frac{4}{5}$;   **5.** E, 2 out of 5;   **6.** S, 3 quarters;   **7.** S, $\frac{3}{5}$;
8. E, $\frac{12}{27}$;   **9.** D, 45 × 9.2;   **10.** I, 81 ÷ 9;   **11.** N, 192 ÷ 3;   **12.** D, 258/3;   **13.** I, $\frac{18}{18}$;   **14.** F, 27;
15. F, 4;   **16.** E, 150%;   **17.** R, 24 ÷ $\frac{1}{2}$;   **18.** E, 256;   **19.** N, 39 × $\frac{2}{2}$;   **20.** T, 16;   **21.** W,
38%;   **22.** A, 32;   **23.** Y, 40 to 50;   **24.** S, $4^1 - 2^2$

Numbers can be EXPRESSED IN DIFFERENT WAYS.

7-3.   **1.** addition;   **2.** factor;   **3.** perpendicular;   **4.** quadrilateral;   **5.** ratio;   **6.** equivalent;
7. geometry;   **8.** infinite;   **9.** kilowatt;   **10.** fraction;   **11.** probability;   **12.** sphere;
13. equiangular;   **14.** percent;   **15.** polygon;   **16.** parallel;   **17.** symmetry;   **18.** degrees;
19. calculator;   **20.** subtraction

7-4.   **1.** 36;   **2.** 20;   **3.** 72;   **4.** 19;   **5.** 68;   **6.** 70;   **7.** 27;   **8.** 183;   **9.** 192;   **10.** 100

7-5.   **2.** 3,143, symmetry;   **3.** 2356.4, algebra;   **4.** 44, geometry;   **5.** 192, geometry;

6. 977.27, permutations, combinations;   **7.** $3\frac{3}{4}$, geometry, trigonometry;   **8.** 40, polyhedra,

functions;   **9.** 15.9, circles, fractions;   **10.** $4\frac{1}{4}$, algebra;   **11.** 1,503, pi;   **12.** 9.558, pi;

13. 0.2592, geometry;   **14.** 8, decimals, logarithms;   **15.** 20.96, number theory, geometry;

16. 20, coordinates, pi;   **17.** $10\frac{1}{8}$, trigonometry, algebra;   **18.** 90.61, calculus, functions,

infinity;   **19.** 16.26, sequences, series,;   **20.** 1.632, algebra

7-6.   **1.** true;   **2.** false;   **3.** true;   **4.** false;   **5.** false;   **6.** true;   **7.** false;   **8.** true;
9. true;   **10.** false;   **11.** false;   **12.** false;   **13.** true;   **14.** false;   **15.** false

7-7.   **1.** 38.2;   **2.** prime;   **3.** 2,350;   **4.** less than;   **5.** same;   **6.** 99.36;   **7.** 103;
8. 100 pennies;   **9.** 8;   **10.** multiple of 8;   **11.** factor of 25;   **12.** 7 is a factor;   **13.** one half
After reversing the letters, the answer should be: YOU HAVE FOLLOWED DIRECTIONS.

7-8.   Answers will vary.

7-9.   Answers will vary.

7-10.   There may be more than one answer for some problems. Possible answers include the
following.   **2.** multiply by 3, add 3;   **3.** multiply by 3, add 3;   **4.** add 2, multiply by 3;
5. multiply by 2, add 6;   **6.** divide by 2, subtract 1;   **7.** divide by 2, subtract 1;   **8.** add 8, divide
by 2;   **9.** divide by 4, subtract 1;   **10.** divide by 2, add 1.5;   **11.** multiply by 2.5, add 1;
12. subtract 2, multiply by 1.5

7-11.   **1.** Sixth sense;   **2.** Going in circles;   **3.** Simple as one, two, three;   **4.** One in a
million;   **5.** Forty winks;   **6.** Behind the eight ball;   **7.** Back to square one;   **8.** Play second
fiddle;   **9.** Seventh heaven;   **10.** A picture is worth a thousand words;   **11.** Two heads are
better than one;   **12.** Put two and two together;   **13.** Half a loaf is better than none;
14. A bird in hand is worth two in the bush;   **15.** Two is company but three is a crowd

7-12.   **a** = 2, **b** = 9, **c** = 3, **d** = 7, **e** = 12;   **1.** 30;   **2.** 909;   **3.** 63;   **4.** 50;   **5.** 198;   **6.** 81;
7. 47;   **8.** 270;   **9.** 500;   **10.** 9;   **11.** 3,888;   **12.** 423;   **13.** 80;   **14.** 355;   **15.** 423

7-13.   **2.** O, 1888;   **3.** S, 105;   **4.** Y, 1892;   **5.** M, 1800;   **6.** B, 1876;   **7.** O, 1714;   **8.** L,
1947;   **9.** F, 1250;   **10.** O, 1709;   **11.** R, 1903;   **12.** Z, 1911;   **13.** E, 1942;   **14.** R, 1972;
15. O, 1608
In Roman numerals, there is NO SYMBOL FOR ZERO.

7-14. $1 Washington; $2 Jefferson; $5 Lincoln; $10 Hamilton; $20 Jackson;
$50 Grant; $100 Franklin
24–34   22–35–14   53–15   45–43–51–44–45